# Hegel's Theory Recognition

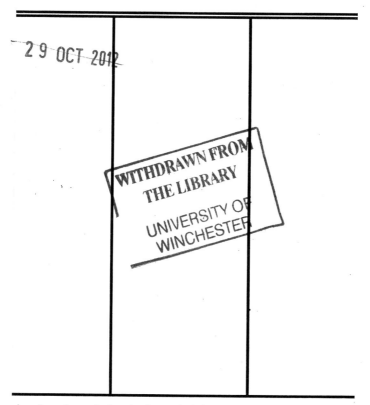

**Continuum Studies in Philosophy**
Series Editor: James Fieser, University of Tennessee at Martin, USA

*Continuum Studies in Philosophy* is a major monograph series from Continuum. The series features first-class scholarly research monographs across the whole field of philosophy. Each work makes a major contribution to the field of philosophical research.

# Hegel's Theory of Recognition

## From Oppression to Ethical Liberal Modernity

Sybol Cook Anderson

continuum

**Continuum International Publishing Group**

The Tower Building
11 York Road
London SE1 7NX

80 Maiden Lane
Suite 704
New York, NY 10038

www.continuumbooks.com

Extracts from *Hegel: Elements of the Philosophy of Right* (1991), ed. Allen W. Wood, trans. H.B. Nisbet © Cambridge University Press 1991, reproduced with permission.

**British Library Cataloguing-in-Publication Data**
A catalogue record for this book is available from the British Library.

ISBN-13: PB:978-1-4411-5293-0

**Library of Congress Cataloging-in-Publication Data**
Anderson, Sybol Cook.
Hegel's theory of recognition: from oppression to ethical liberal modernity/Sybol Cook Anderson.
    p. cm.
  Includes bibliographical references and index.
ISBN-13: 978-1-4411-5293-0 (PB)

  1. Hegel, Georg Wilhelm Friedrich, 1770–1831. 2. Recognition (Philosophy) 3. Ethics, Modern—19th century. I. Title.

B2948.A485 2009
323.101—dc22                                                              2008046611

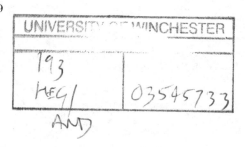

Typeset by Newgen Imaging Systems Pvt Ltd, Chennai, India
Printed and bound in Great Britain by the MPG Books Group

# Contents

# Acknowledgments

I am grateful for this opportunity to acknowledge the wonderful people and institutions that have supported my work on this book.

My research for this book began at Johns Hopkins University, with tremendous intellectual and moral support from colleagues and friends in the Departments of Philosophy and Political Science. My deepest heartfelt thanks to my adviser and friend, Dean Moyar. Special thanks also to Eckart Förster, Hilary Bok, Jennifer Culbert, and Richard Flathman for their encouragement and helpful comments on the early manuscript. The Ford Foundation provided both financial support and the camaraderie of its staff and network of Ford Fellows.

My colleagues and students at St. Mary's College of Maryland have been with this project from the beginning. Their support has been, in a word, *amazing*. It has run the gamut from gracious invitations to present my work publicly to modest offers simply to pore over pages with me and share ideas. I am especially grateful to Iris Ford, Terell Lasane, Kate Norlock, Angela Johnson, Alan Paskow, Katharina von Kellenbach, Celia Rabinowitz, Brad Park, Linda Coughlin, and Diane Wimberly for their careful reading, stimulating conversations, moral support, and friendship. Special thanks to President Maggie O'Brien and the Maryland Higher Education Commission for the Henry C. Welcome Fellowship, which provided invaluable research support.

Other colleagues in the profession have also been wonderful to me. There are not words to express my gratitude to Robert Bernasconi and Ellen Feder for their influence upon my life, thinking, and professional development. Sincere thanks also to the Collegium of Black Women Philosophers and to the philosophy departments at American University, the University of Memphis, Morgan State University, Towson University, and Bowie State University for inviting me to share my work with them and for their stimulating responses to it. I am deeply grateful to Ludwig Siep for his comments on an early version of the manuscript. Very special thanks to Sarah Campbell, Tom Crick, and Jim Fieser for their kind support throughout the publication process.

My family and friends have sustained me through this most exhilarating journey. I extend my deepest gratitude to my best friend and favorite interlocutor, Lane Anderson. I dedicate this work to the loving memory of my parents, Giles and Ella Mae Cook, and my sisters, America and Sarah.

# Abbreviations

## Works by Hegel

FPS    *First Philosophy of Spirit*, in H. S. Harris and T. M. Knox (eds and trans.), *System of Ethical Life and First Philosophy of Spirit*. Albany, NY: SUNY Press, 1979.

HHS    *Hegel and the Human Spirit*, a translation with commentary of Hegel's *Jena Philosophie des Geistes 1805/06*, by Leo Rauch. Detroit: Wayne State University Press, 1983.

LHP    *Lectures on the History of Philosophy*, 3 volumes, trans. Elizabeth Haldane and Frances H. Simson. New York: Humanities Press, 1968.

LNR    *Lectures on Natural Right and Political Science*, trans. J. M. Stewart and P. C. Hodgson. Berkeley: University of California Press, 1995.

LPR    *Lectures on the Philosophy of Religion*, volume 3, ed. and trans. R. F. Brown, P. C. Hodgson, and J. M. Stewart. Berkeley: University of California Press, 1985.

NL    *Natural Law*, trans. T. M. Knox. Philadelphia: University of Pennsylvania Press, 1975.

PH    *The Philosophy of History*, trans. J. Sibree. New York: Dover Books, 1956.

PhG    *Phänomenologie des Geistes*, ed. Eva Moldenhauer and Karl Markus Michel. Frankfurt am Main: Suhrkamp, 1986.

PhS    *Phenomenology of Spirit*, trans. A. V. Miller. New York: Oxford University Press, 1977.

PR    *Elements of the Philosophy of Right*, ed. Allen Wood, trans. H. B. Nisbet. New York: Cambridge University Press, 2000.

PWH    *Lectures on the Philosophy of World History*, trans. H. B. Nisbet. New York: Cambridge University Press, 1975.

SEL    *System of Ethical Life*, in H. S. Harris and T. M. Knox (eds and trans.), *System of Ethical Life and First Philosophy of Spirit*. Albany, NY: SUNY Press, 1979.

SS    *Philosophy of Subject Spirit*, 3 volumes, ed. and trans. M. J. Petry. Boston: D. Reidel Publishing Company, 1978.

VPR     *Vorlesungen über Rechtsphilosophie*, 1818–1831, 4 volumes, hrsg. Karl-Heinz Ilting. Stuttgart-Bad Cannstatt: Frommann-Holzboog Verlag, 1974.

VPR 17  *Vorlesungen über Natturecht und Staatswissenschaft* (1817 Heidelberg), hrsg. Staff of the Hegel Archive. Hamburg: Felix Meiner, 1983.

VPR 19  *Philosophie des Rechts* (1819), ed. Dieter Henrich. Frankurt am Main: Suhrkamp, 1983.

W       *Werke*, 20 volumes, ed. E. Moldenhauer and K. Michel. Frankfurt am Main: Suhrkamp, 1970–1971.

All texts are cited by page number except *PhS*, cited by paragraph number; *PR* and *VPR17*, by section number; and *LHP*, *PWH*, *SS*, *VPR*, and *W*, by volume and page number. In *PR*, 'R' indicates a remark by Hegel and 'A' an addition from student notes.

## Works by Other Authors

CHT     Taylor, Charles. 'Comparison, history, truth,' in *Philosophical Arguments*. Cambridge, MA: Harvard University Press, 1995.

GR      Honneth, Axel. 'Grounding recognition: a rejoinder to critical questions,' *Inquiry*, 2002, 45, 499–520.

HER     Williams, Robert R. *Hegel's Ethics of Recognition*. Berkeley: University of California Press, 1997.

JPD     Young, Iris Marion. *Justice and the Politics of Difference*. Princeton: Princeton University Press, 1990.

MC      Kymlicka, Will. *Multicultural Citizenship*. New York: Oxford University Press, 1995.

PL      Rawls, John. *Political Liberalism*. New York: Columbia University Press, 1996.

PoR     Taylor, Charles. 'The politics of recognition,' in Amy Gutmann (ed.), *Multiculturalism: Examining the Politics of Recognition*. Princeton: Princeton University Press, 1994.

RMO     Honneth, Axel. 'Recognition and moral obligation,' *Social Research*, Spring 1997, 64 (1), 16–35.

SR      Honneth, Axel. *The Struggle for Recognition: The Moral Grammar of Social Conflicts*, trans. Joel Anderson. Cambridge, MA: MIT Press, 1996.

TCL     Berlin, Isaiah. 'Two Concepts of Liberty,' in Henry Hardy (ed.), *Liberty*. New York: Oxford University Press, 2002.

Introduction

# Redeeming Recognition

*We, you and I, each of us, we are the descendants of a proud tradition of people asserting our dignity.*

(Urvashi Vaid)*

Since the 1960s 'New Left' emancipatory movements have claimed that women, ethnic minorities, gays and lesbians, and other social groups are oppressed. Awareness of this fact has given rise to 'the politics of difference,' arguments for redressing injustices endured by some citizens because of their collective identity differences. Some theorists argue the appropriate corrective is the public acknowledgment of differences.[1]

On the face of it, these latter arguments run in tension with the classical liberal thesis that equality requires treating all the same in public *regardless* of our differences. Still, the question of the meaning and possibility of a *liberal* politics of difference has occupied liberal theorists for more than three decades—at least as early as John Rawls's 1971 publication of *A Theory of Justice*. For Rawls and others, achieving social justice for citizens treated unjustly because of their differences is a crucial step in promoting democratic equality (Rawls 1999: 52ff.; *PL* lviiff.). Ultimately, for some liberals, this is justified by the doctrine of toleration and the principle of neutrality. Compensations, for instance, by way of distributive justice or group-differentiated rights, are necessary to promote equal dignity and ensure all citizens equal chances for autonomy.[2]

However, treating issues related to difference ultimately as matters of toleration fails to obviate the tension, which emancipatory movements are at pains to underscore, between liberalism's advocacy of *de jure* equality and the persistence in liberal democracies of *de facto* inequality. Although liberal theorists have identified essential components of a viable response to emancipatory claims (provisions for rights and distributive justice), they rarely address sufficiently the underlying presuppositions, attitudes, and self-understandings that ultimately determine the *efficacy* of such provisions—those understandings that determine whether or not citizens, in their everyday interactions, will actually treat one another in a manner consistent with liberal justice. That is, liberal proponents of difference, in attending primarily to *political* questions, have insufficiently addressed the broader *social* issues crucially implicated in the politics of difference.

To state the problem differently, most liberal theorizing fails to take adequate account of emancipatory claims of oppression. Of course, emancipatory movements seek rights and economic justice; however, equally importantly, as Axel Honneth famously argued, they protest the moral injustice of their violated *social relationship* expectations: their reasonable belief that in a liberal democracy they will be treated as equal moral persons (*SR* 2). Accordingly, they demand the abolition of social and institutional practices of misrecognition that ignore or denigrate their identities. I would add that they strive to impress upon majorities that they, too, make important contributions to collective life and do so not *in spite of* their different and disfavored identities, but partly *in virtue of* them—through agency informed by those identities. Liberal theory proclaims that differences do not matter in the public sphere (a dubious ideal), but they turn out to matter very much. We require a liberal social theory that acknowledges that in societies in which differences are disfavored, *political* provisions for special rights and redistribution are quickly undermined by *social* attitudes. We require a social theoretical response to a social problem.

In this book I argue, following Hegel, that political acts can only secure *de facto* equality for all citizens when, indeed, crucial *social* conditions have been met: most notably the widespread achievement of relationships of mutual recognition. Required for this achievement is the cultivation of a distinctive social and self-understanding that Hegel elucidates in the *Phenomenology of Spirit:* recognitive understanding. This form of understanding grounds individuals' affirmation simultaneously of their interdependence as social members and independence as authoritative agents. It is a necessary condition of concrete freedom and *de facto* equality.

However, the subject of recognition has recently become contentious. Some scholars argue, for instance, that because recognition essentially means 'assimilating the other to the same,' or ultimately belies a desire for sovereignty, its proponents merely substitute one mode of domination for another (Markell 2003: 11; Oliver 2001: 23ff.). These concerns stem partly from our apparent lack of an adequate concept of recognition. Many theorists assume and do not explicitly define its sense,[3] so we are far from anything like a consensus as to its meaning. For care ethicists, it may designate relationships of love and concern, whereas for discourse ethicists it may mean acknowledgment of the 'particularity and equality' of discourse participants (*RMO* 18). Some theorists suggest a strong sense of recognition as acknowledgment of the equal value of all cultures,[4] whereas others argue for a weaker 'symbolic recognition' of the acceptance of different identities in public (Galeotti 2002: 10ff.).

Determining whether recognition can be adequate to the task of overcoming oppression requires that we first arrive at a clear conception of it. I aim both to clarify the meaning of recognition and to argue its efficacy for overcoming oppression. I do so by reconstructing and defending Hegel's conception of recognition, elaborated in the *Phenomenology of Spirit* and later applied to his theory of liberal institutions in the *Philosophy of Right*. Revealing recognitive understanding to be a necessary condition of mutual recognition and liberal freedom, Hegel lays the groundwork for a liberal social theory that can support a viable liberal politics of difference.

I begin by taking the crucial question of the contemporary debate concerning the politics of difference, and thus the central question of this book, to be the following: *Given the commitment of liberal democracies to the principles of equality, freedom and justice, are we obligated to ensure the positive public recognition of the identities of diverse individuals and groups?* Scholars of various stripes have argued that recognition *is* required for freedom. Some cite as justification Hegel's ontological thesis that practical identity, or the self realized through agency, is both initially formed and subsequently actualized—freely developed and expressed in concrete actions—only in the context of relationships of mutual recognition.[5] I review these arguments in Chapter 4, but I prepare now for that discussion by distinguishing two notions of identity that, being both integrally related and the objects of emancipatory demands for recognition, are of central importance in this book.

First is the notion of *collective identity*, which every individual possesses simply by virtue of having been born with certain biological traits (e.g., sex, skin color, disability) or belonging to defined collectivities (e.g., a nation, ethnic group, or socio-economic class). The important point is that individuals frequently come to share certain forms of life—certain understandings, values, and practices—with others so defined. Thus, when I speak of myself as female, American, African-American, black, working-class, heterosexual, and so on, and refer to these as my collective identity characteristics, I claim not only that they are certain of my biological and social traits, but also that my sharing these traits with other individuals has significance for my way of being in the world. For one thing, inasmuch as I was raised within a particular family and specific cultures, my practical identity—my sense of my own agency—was first constituted in the context of definite forms of life that influenced my judgments, values, and choices. These forms of life have informed my understanding and agency, even if over time I have revised my judgments and values. Most significantly, *every-one* is associated with a number of collective identities simply by virtue of having shown up in the world, whether or not we identify with them or consider them salient.

However, second, every person can also be described in terms of his or her *unique* way of being in the world: his or her *individual identity*. Individual identity is informed to some degree by collective identities, whether one affirms that association oneself, or it is ascribed to one by others. For instance, I may not identify strongly with my gender or define myself in terms of it. However, this may have little effect upon how others define and treat me. This identity therefore has some bearing upon my experiences and agency. Nevertheless, individual identity is not entirely determined by the collective identities that inform it. In liberal democracies individuals are free to choose the degree to which they identify with their collective identities; they are to that extent free to conceive and construct their indi-vidual identities—to invent themselves and to be *self*-actualizing.[6]

Collective identities and the forms of life they represent are nevertheless important constituents of individual identity, not only because they form the background horizon of an individual's identity formation, but also because they continue to influence individuals' processes of self-actualization. This is true in both the positive sense that collective identities may continue to function as significant horizons of judgment and value for individuals, and in the negative sense that they may serve as the basis of discrimina-tion that limits individuals' chances for self-actualization. For this reason I stress, along with Hegel and Axel Honneth, that not only does recogni-tion play the crucial role of forging practical identity and facilitating indi-viduals' self-actualization, but *failures* of recognition are a significant form of moral injury (*SR* 2). In fact, the harm to individual agency wrought by forms of misrecognition means, as Charles Taylor explains, that 'due recognition is not just a courtesy we owe people . . . [but] a vital human need' (*PoR* 26). It is therefore a primary good to be safeguarded by liberal democracies.

But the attempt to reconcile the recognition of identity differences with liberalism poses challenges. Some liberals argue that public neutrality—our commitment to treating all citizens equally *regardless* of their differences—is the very thing required to secure our most basic freedoms. Others cau-tion, moreover, that acknowledging differences can be a two-edged sword, for in the very attempt to recognize ethnic, gender, religious, and other differences publicly, collective identities can be essentialized in ways that frustrate rather than encourage self-actualization—and self-actualization can be compromised just as effectively by positive stereotypes as by negative ones.

Meanwhile, many critical, postmodern, and communitarian theorists criticize liberal theory as too universalistic, atomistic, and indifferent to social issues to address the concerns of emancipatory movements. They see liberalism's commitment to neutrality as wrongly presuming that our status as merely 'abstract persons'—members of a society in which our differences are considered irrelevant to our essential identity as rational humans—constitutes us as free and equal. These critics are quick to point out that the very fact that countless numbers of us suffer oppression within a socio-political structure that is purportedly 'difference-blind' gives evidence that what liberalism has effectively secured for many is merely a corresponding 'abstract freedom,' a liberty that is, in a sense, 'liquidated' like all objects of abstraction, such that it becomes essentially an *idea* (see, for example, Horkheimer and Adorno 2000: 13). Some claim explicitly that liberal principles and norms are by nature culturally hegemonic, hence inherently prone *not* to guarantee *everyone equally* the 'concrete' freedom to which we all reasonably aspire (I. Young 1999: 416). Unfortunately, none of these critics seems to have succeeded any more than liberal theorists have in recommending a viable, constructive, and practicable program for the recognition of difference. I therefore turn to Hegel.

My over-arching reason for attempting to re-actualize Hegel's social theory is that it is grounded in a conception of recognition that is both responsive to emancipatory demands and consistent with liberal principles. But there are four specific reasons I appropriate Hegel. First, he offers a precise conception of recognition as 'spiritual *unity* in its doubling [*Verdopplung*]' (*PhS* ¶178; *PhG* 145).[7] While this formulation is far from immediately transparent, Hegel's elaboration of it, occupying three chapters of the *Phenomenology*, makes possible a perspicuous reformulation. Most importantly, Hegel's *Phenomenology* account of recognition in terms of the experience of human consciousness both corroborates the claims of emancipatory movements that their oppression is attributable to violations of their social relationship expectations and indicates intrinsically how oppression may be overcome. He shows recognition to entail mutuality and to depend upon the cultivation of recognitive understanding.

My second reason for looking to Hegel's theory of recognition is that it not only indicates *that* mutual recognition is a necessary condition of freedom, but also makes clear *how* and *why* this is so. Ultimately, it is because

freedom is socially mediated. In Hegel's view, freedom is not to be conceived in purely individualistic terms as either the liberty 'to do or forbear doing' what we will, as Locke suggested (1994: 167–168), or the ability
to choose not to act on the basis of one's inclinations, as Kant argued
(1996: 53). Rather, Hegel contends that freedom is the ability to *determine*
one's will. That is, it is not merely the ability either to *follow* or to *override*
one's inclinations, in which case one is in truth determined by *them*; rather,
the free will makes 'reference to itself' (*PR* §7).[8] However, we only experience ourselves as determining our own wills through relationships with
other subjects. Hegel illustrates by citing the example of 'friendship and
love,' in which

> we are not one-sidedly within ourselves but willingly limit ourselves with
> reference to an other, even while knowing ourselves in this limitation as
> ourselves. In this determinacy, the human being should not feel deter-
> mined; on the contrary, he attains his self-awareness only by regarding
> the other as other . . . Freedom is to will something determinate, yet to
> be with oneself [*bei sich*] in this determinacy. (*PR* §7A)

When we act in relation to 'ordinary' objects [including people who have
no significant influence upon our 'feeling' (*PR* §7A)], we may indeed deliberate in accordance with a Lockean or Kantian view of freedom: we may
either act in accordance with our inclinations or choose to override our
inclinations and determine the 'right' course of action. However, circumstances are different when others come to *count* for us. In this case, we allow
them to influence our inclinations and actions, that is, to *limit* us—but they
only limit us insofar as they are *different* from us: insofar as we agree, there
is no limitation of our own will. But when we are called upon to limit ourselves, we come to *experience* our individual wills as *free*, as the products of
our own choices.[9]

Accordingly, Hegel's conviction that others are implicated in our freedom leads him not to reject so much as to synthesize and refine the
traditional views to make explicit that freedom is necessarily socially mediated. I am free when I experience myself as both *determining* what I desire
to do or forbear doing, *and determining*, not to *override* my inclination and
desires, but rather which ones it is rational to *fulfill*. Both are processes
of self-determination conditioned by my relationships with significant
others.

Hegel's conception of freedom therefore posits individual freedom as
dependent upon the freedom of others. His analysis of recognition is part

of the basis of this thesis—for freedom is also conditioned by others inasmuch as their recognition is a necessary condition of one's practical identity formation and actualization. Here we may recall his well-known claim that '[s]elf-consciousness exists in and for itself when, and by the fact that, it so exists for another; that is, it exists only in being acknowledged' (*PhS* ¶178; *PhG* 145). However, in order to *experience* oneself as recognized by another, one must also recognize the cognitive authority of that other. Thus in order to experience oneself as free, one must interact with significant others whom one regards as free.

But Hegel argues further, in the *Philosophy of Right*, that recognition is not only significant in private relationships of friendship and love but also in public life. To experience full freedom, individuals must determine their own wills in the public sphere as much as in private life. They must therefore allow others in public life to count for them. Indeed, Hegel stresses that to experience themselves as free, individuals must cultivate *ethical* bonds with others in public life that mirror the 'immediate ethical life,' grounded in friendship and love, they enjoy as family members. This is the basis of an ethical life in which individuals find themselves 'at home' in the world (*VPR* 4:102).

That said, a third reason to appropriate Hegel's theory of recognition is that his conception involves, specifically, the recognition of *difference*—in his terms, the 'right of particularity' (*PR* §154). I have just cited his conviction that individuals only come to awareness of themselves as free when they allow significant others to limit them, which those others can only do *qua* other. The force of this claim becomes clear in the *Phenomenology* through Hegel's account of the achievement of mutual recognition, which he proclaims preserves the 'absolute' difference between subjects who, having attained recognitive understanding, come to acknowledge and affirm their particularity (*PhS* ¶671; *PhG* 493). As a result, they release each other for free agency; they let each other 'go free' (*PhS* ¶181; *PhG* 146). Accordingly, in the *PR* Hegel vigorously defends the 'right of particularity' as a condition of ethical life and freedom.

Hegel's application of his concept of recognition to his speculative analysis of liberal institutions in the *PR* is my fourth reason for appropriating his theory. There, Hegel not only makes clear *why* public recognition is necessary for freedom, but also *how* it may be carried out consistently with liberal principles. With regard to why public recognition is required for freedom, again, Hegel suggests that it is because of a kind of continuity between *private* experiences of recognition, which make us aware of our distinctiveness and capacity for self-actualization, and *public* recognition, which mirrors the private forms and secures our opportunities for self-actualization. This translates into the insight that freedom depends upon our ability to actualize a public ethical life [*Sittlichkeit*], the concept of which we grasp through our experiences of mutually recognitive relationships in private, family life (*PR* §166).

As for how public forms of recognition may be instantiated, Hegel recommends a particular arrangement of social and political institutions, each of which facilitates a distinctive pattern of mutual recognition among social members: civil society is the domain in which individuals and groups are recognized in their particularity, whereas the state recognizes their universal humanity via its procedural commitment to liberal neutrality. The implication is that beyond securing *de jure* equality for citizens *politically* through rights and distributive justice, a liberal society must affirm distinctively *social* institutions through which we establish relationships of mutual recognition and secure *de facto* equality.

Hegel's theory of recognition therefore supplies us with valuable critical tools with which to analyze and evaluate our contemporary problem of social oppression and work our way beyond our current theoretical impasses in our efforts to redress it. His theory captures the salient feature of emancipatory claims for recognition largely overlooked by liberal theory, and without which it is impossible to construct a viable liberal politics of difference: that they are fundamentally claims about violated social relationship expectations.

Some will question the propriety of looking to Hegel for insight into the contemporary problem of difference. There are, first of all, the well-known problems of Hegel's disdain for democratic government and his reputation as a theorist who submerges all individuality into the absolute unity of the state. What can the 'great totalizer' say to *us* about individual freedom and overcoming oppression? Second, we must surely reject Hegel's disparaging comments about women and non-European cultures, and, it would seem, his theory of recognition with them. For what can a sexist and racist say to *us* about recognizing differences?

First, I argue that while it is in some sense true that Hegel's is a totalizing scheme—since in the *Phenomenology* he resolves all shapes of spirit into 'absolute spirit,' and in the *Philosophy of Right* he celebrates the unity of the state—nevertheless, in both cases he posits a *differentiated* totality, a unity constituted of diversity in which individual freedom and authority are secured. Accordingly, while Hegel is a proponent of constitutional monarchy and an opponent of democracy, he nevertheless strongly advocates for *representative* government. As for his thoughts on gender and race, these pose perhaps the greatest challenges to my attempt to appropriate his theory. However, I argue that they are not insurmountable challenges, for it is possible to overcome them by appeal to other crucial elements of his theory. It is possible to use Hegel to correct Hegel.

In what follows, I advance two connected arguments: one *diagnostic* and the other *interpretive*. The diagnostic argument occupies Chapters 1 through 4 and establishes in what sense the positive public recognition of differences is indicated as a solution to the problem of oppression. My method here is primarily critical theoretical, in two senses. First, I diagnose and address the problem of recognition and difference within a specific historical and social context—the contemporary demands of historically oppressed groups in the US—through normative reflection upon our specific social, historical, and political circumstances.[10] Second, I take as my starting point the empirical claims of emancipatory movements concerning the 'fact' of contemporary social oppression and seek to explain that fact as the first step toward resolving the question of whether we are obligated to recognize differences.

In Chapters 1 and 2, I assess whether, from a liberal perspective, social and institutional practices involving the misrecognition of differences are legitimately categorized as modes of oppression. I do so by constructing a liberal conception of oppression, but one that brings both liberal and critical theoretical perspectives to bear on the problem of working out what *counts* as oppression. Specifically, I appeal to both liberal notions of freedom, drawing upon Isaiah Berlin's famous analysis in 'Two Concepts of Liberty,' and recent theories of oppression advanced by critical theorists, especially Iris Marion Young, Marilyn Frye, Ann Cudd, Jean Harvey, T. L. Zutlevics, and Sandra Bartky.[11] The resulting conception indicates, in response to the central question of the book, that our liberal commitment to equality, freedom, and justice entails that we are obligated to desist from social and institutional practices of misrecognition.

However, it is a separate question whether we are obligated to recognize differences publicly. In Chapter 3, I begin exploring this question by examining recent attempts by John Rawls and Will Kymlicka to address the problem of difference by appeal to the principle of toleration. Both advance remarkable proposals that adhere to the doctrines of individual rights and liberal neutrality, but each interprets neutrality differently. In *Political Liberalism*, Rawls ultimately treats neutrality in the traditional sense as indifference to differences. Through his device of an overlapping consensus, he accommodates the 'fact of pluralism' by foregrounding the *shared* elements of different comprehensive views (*PL* xix). The result is a program of uniform basic rights supplemented by provisions for distributive justice. These provisions do not stipulate benefits for disadvantaged citizens, but rather requirements for arranging the basic structure so that inequalities are fair. By contrast, in *Multicultural Citizenship* Kymlicka suggests that neutrality requires the differential treatment of differences in order to bring them into parity. He argues the legitimacy of extending special group-differentiated rights in a few well-reasoned cases.

Both Rawls and Kymlicka identify vital components of a liberal politics of difference, but I contend that their proposals nevertheless obscure the manner in which social disadvantages still accrue to bearers of disfavored identities in ways that perpetuate social oppression. This suggests that a form of positive public recognition may be needed to supplement provisions for special rights and distributive justice.

Still, the question remains of what exactly public recognition should entail and on what grounds we may legitimately claim that it is required to overcome oppression. I derive valuable insight from Axel Honneth and Charles Taylor, perhaps the most prominent contemporary theorists of recognition. Both are proponents of Hegel's social freedom thesis. In Chapter 4, I highlight their suggestion that freedom requires a *continuity* of private and public recognition mainly because the self-understanding and capacity for agency we acquire in primary relationships motivate and inform our interactions with others in the public realm. My analyses of Honneth's arguments in *The Struggle for Recognition* and other writings, and of Taylor's landmark essay 'The Politics of Recognition' enable me to formulate a provisional conception of recognition as an act that acknowledges the legitimacy of different ways of life. Moreover, Taylor's writings on intercultural dialogue illuminate the processes through which diverse individuals and groups might reasonably come to recognize each other in precisely this sense. However, two difficulties in Honneth's and Taylor's arguments compel me to look beyond them for a still more adequate conception of recognition.

I therefore turn to Hegel's theory of recognition, which occupies Chapters 5 through 7. My interpretive argument elucidates Hegel's conception of recognition in order to give a clear sense to 'public recognition' and illuminate how Hegel's theory answers the emancipatory demand in a manner consistent with liberalism. Chapter 5 is devoted to the *Phenomenology*. Reading that text as centrally concerned with the problem of knowledge, I offer an interpretation that illuminates three crucial features of Hegel's theory of recognition. First, recognition, as an act that affirms a specific form of *cognition* plays a central role in the dialectic of spirit, and its achievement is, in one sense, the dialectic's penultimate moment.[12] Second, contrary to

many critical theoretical and postmodern interpretations, Hegel deliberately portrays mastery and slavery as a failure of recognition, not as his considered theory.[13] I argue that the struggle to the death ensues, not because
the protagonists desire to dominate each other, but because they reason
erroneously that they must stake their bodily existence in order to realize their ostensibly 'true' nature as 'pure self-consciousness' (*PhS* ¶189;
*PhG* 150). The struggle is the *necessary* consequence of their faulty self-
understanding. Third, the shape of knowledge that is adequate to successful recognition, and is in fact the condition of its possibility, is recognitive
understanding. Hegel portrays two shapes of moral spirit—conscience and
the beautiful soul—as actualizing their essential natures as authoritative
agents through a speech act in which they mutually acknowledge their universality and particularity. Most importantly, the experience of conscience
and the beautiful soul reveals how recognitive understanding culminates
in social relations characterized by equality and reciprocity, even if these
relationships are always in some sense agonistic by virtue of their dialogical character—and even though, as Hegel says, the absolute difference
between subjects is preserved in their unity (*PhS* ¶671; *PhG* 493).

After reconstructing Hegel's definition of recognition, I turn to his application of the conception to his theory of liberal institutions in the *Philosophy
of Right*. Chapters 6 and 7 examine Hegel's portrait of liberal ethical life,
which, I argue, presupposes the attainment of recognitive understanding
by at least some of its citizens, who are agents of conscience. Here Hegel
argues that individuals' pursuit of self-interest in liberal modernity, unmediated by a regard for the interests and good of the social whole, leads to
such a degree of social corruption and socio-economic instability that its
promise of freedom is severely undermined. To enjoy genuine freedom,
social members must acknowledge their *inter*subjectivity and interdependence: they must cultivate recognitive understanding, through which their
agency can be recognized as conscientious, and hence as legitimate. If they
do, they win the 'right of particularity,' their liberty to express their differences 'in all directions' (*PR* §184). They exercise this right through agency
within ethical corporations, where their differences are not merely tolerated but welcomed. Thus, ethical life presupposes social members who
endorse the social freedom thesis, understand the public recognition of
differences to be a necessary condition of liberal freedom and affirm social
as well as political institutions that facilitate relationships of mutual recognition. Liberal modernity becomes distinctively *ethical*.

In both the *Phenomenology* and the *Philosophy of Right*, Hegel elucidates the
meaning of recognition and reveals how patterns of mutual recognition

can be realized in everyday social interactions in ways that undermine oppression. Thus he recommends a model of public recognition that lays the groundwork for a viable liberal politics of difference. My hope is that we will redeem Hegel's theory, for Hegel reveals how recognition enables us to redeem the promises of freedom, equality, and social justice for which so many have struggled for so long.

# Chapter 1

# Oppression Reconsidered

*We need to think clearly about oppression, and there is much that mitigates against this . . . We need this word, this concept, and we need it to be sharp and sure.*

*(Marilyn Frye)\**

A man works full time at the world's richest university but must work a second job and borrow against his retirement to make ends meet. He listens as his president responds to student demands for a living wage policy: 'I cannot give in, and if the university is at such a point where people say it's so badly off that we must give in, I'll resign before we give in' (Rudenstine 2005). A student is denied his high school diploma because he wore a bolo tie to graduation, in violation of the dress code stipulating that boys must wear ties. When the student explains that a bolo tie is formal attire in his culture, a school official responds: 'The First Amendment protects religion, and we do everything possible to honor that. There is nothing that requires us to follow everyone's different cultures' (Manning 2005). An obstetrician arrives at the hospital and asks a staff member why his patient is not being prepped for delivery. 'She's black,' comes the reply. 'I assumed she was on welfare' (Christopher 2005: 134). An immigrant is questioned by police officers searching for a rape suspect. The man reaches for identification, and the police open fire, shooting at him 41 times and spraying him with 19 bullets (*Washington Post*).

Many Americans would readily acknowledge that in each of these scenarios one set of individuals, deliberately or unwittingly, fails to acknowledge appropriately the dignity or legitimacy of another. Many would also agree that the resulting behaviors are wrongs done: in some cases, reprehensible social injustices. However, some critical theorists argue further that they are manifestations of *oppression*: severe injustices some suffer because of their social group membership.[1] These theorists agree with social activists that oppression remains a fact of life in post–civil rights America: ethnic minorities, women, homosexuals, and the poor number among the victims of contemporary American oppression.

One might concede that such failures of acknowledgment are unjust but hesitate to call them oppressive. We typically think of oppression as severe and deliberate abuses of groups of people, their unjust imprisonment, torture and impoverishment at the hands of tyrannical regimes—what happens to unfortunate people in *other* countries. In the US, it belongs to the distant past: the expulsion of Native Americans, the enslavement and segregation of African Americans, and the internment of Japanese Americans were cases of oppression, and such cases no longer occur within our borders (many would claim). However, recent theorists of oppression urge us to broaden our thinking to see that sometimes oppression involves 'the disadvantage and injustice some people suffer not because a tyrannical power coerces them, but because of the everyday practices of a well-intentioned liberal society' (*JPD* 41). Here, Iris Marion Young emphasizes the prevalence today of *structural* oppression, 'the vast and deep injustices some groups suffer as a consequence of often *unconscious* assumptions and reactions of well-meaning people in ordinary interactions, media and cultural stereotypes, and structural features of bureaucratic hierarchies and market mechanisms—in short, in the normal processes of everyday life' (*JPD* 41). Jean Harvey agrees: 'In Western industrialized societies the most common forms of oppression are all . . . *civilized oppression* (where neither physical force nor the use of law is the main mechanism)' (2000: 177). These analyses corroborate Young's and Axel Honneth's observations that emancipatory movements' claims of oppression are directed fundamentally toward the 'righting' of 'wronged' social relationships (*JPD* 15–16; *SR* 2). Emancipatory struggles are, at bottom, moral demands for recognition of the equal dignity of persons *in* their differences and for the cessation of oppressive misrecognition *of* those differences. My opening cases may be paradigm cases of oppression after all.

For those who remain skeptical, part of what mitigates such assurance is the relative dearth of conceptual analyses of oppression. Despite the abundance of liberal theorizing about freedom, there has until recently been nothing close to a comprehensive *liberal* theory of oppression. Ann Cudd's excellent study, *Analyzing Oppression*, is the exception; her 'comprehensive, general theory of oppression' begins with a genealogy of the concept that traces its origin to early modern liberalism and engages liberal theory at several points of analysis (2006: 21). Cudd defines oppression as 'an institutionally structured, unjust harm perpetrated on groups by other groups through direct and indirect material and psychological forces,' adding that the harms can be understood more specifically in terms of 'unequal and unjust institutional constraints' (28, 52).

Cudd's analysis and definition are extremely useful, but in this chapter I follow a different path to a distinctively liberal definition of oppression that names the harm of oppression even more sharply and surely. At the same time, I establish from a liberal perspective the justification for applying the term 'oppression' to practices of misrecognition, such as those I opened with. This is my first step toward answering the central question of this book: *Given the commitment of liberal democracies to equality, freedom, and justice, are we obligated to ensure the positive public recognition of the identities of diverse individuals and groups?* For clearly oppression is incompatible with freedom, equality, and justice. If social and institutional practices of misrecognition are legitimately labeled modes of oppression, then we ought to resist and abolish them. Of course, the requirement to resist and abolish practices of misrecognition does not entail a requirement to recognize differences positively and publicly. That public recognition is required to overcome oppression is the second step of my argument and the subject of Chapters 3 and 4.

This chapter has three parts. First, after specifying the criteria of an adequate conception of oppression, I examine liberal conceptions of freedom. These form foundations of my liberal concept of oppression since oppression is generally conceived of as the negation of freedom. Second, I construct a provisional liberal definition of oppression based on something of a liberal consensus on the nature of freedom. I then enrich that definition by appeal to critical theories of oppression in order to dispel worries that a liberal conception of oppression must necessarily be too individualistic, atomistic, and abstract. Finally, I offer a liberal conception of oppression.

## Foundations of a Liberal Conception of Oppression

### Criteria of an adequate conception

I begin by specifying three criteria of an adequate liberal conception of oppression:

$CO_1$:  An adequate conception of oppression must reconcile our ordinary sense of 'oppression' as 'severe, unjust hardships,' with the claims of emancipatory movements that certain everyday practices of misrecognition are oppressive.

$CO_2$:  It must enable us to distinguish *severe* unjust hardships from non-severe ones.

$CO_3$:  It must adequately reflect liberal principles.

On the face of it, $CO_1$ is daunting. We are to reconcile one sense that oppression is extraordinary with the idea that it is ordinary, happening all the time. A reasonable starting point is the common characterization of oppression by both perspectives as *unjust constraints upon freedom*. This is evident when we consider the kinds of acts generally recognized as paradigm cases of oppression: enslavement, prolonged and unjust imprisonment, torture, and so on. A successful liberal conception of oppression will capture and further elucidate the sense of oppression as unjust constraints upon freedom.

However, not all unjust constraints upon freedom are oppressive; they do not all entail *severe* hardships. Therefore the resulting conception must, second, permit us to distinguish clearly between severe unjust constraints upon freedom and non-severe ones ($CO_2$). To illuminate the difference: imagine you apply for a more advanced position in your firm and are not considered only because you are an introvert, and your prospective supervisor happens not to like introverts. In such a case, you can reasonably claim that you have been treated unjustly (that your liberty has in some sense been unjustly constrained) but it does not seem you can say, on that basis, that you are oppressed. After all, you possess the requisite qualifications for advancement, and another opportunity is bound to come along through which you may advance your career.[2] The situation may be different, however, if you are, say, a double amputee. Despite your being highly qualified, the likelihood that prospective employers are unprepared to accommodate your disability (lacking adequate understanding as well as facilities to accommodate it, ADA legislation notwithstanding), suggests that your chances of advancing your career—even of finding employment in the first place—may be seriously, unjustly constrained. An adequate conception of oppression will provide a standard for distinguishing injustices such as this that culminate in *severe* hardship.

Insofar as I appeal to liberal theory for such a standard, the resulting conception must, third, adequately reflect a liberal perspective ($CO_3$). One way to approach this is to examine the ways liberals have used the concept. However, in the absence of a comprehensive liberal theory, this approach only suggests how *some* liberals have understood oppression: primarily as enslavement and domination (e.g., Hobbes and Rousseau) and as arbitrary and unjust rule culminating in the abrogation of citizens' rights (e.g., Locke) (see also Cudd 2006: 3–7). I seek a more comprehensive concept grounded in our understanding of liberalism's supreme political value, freedom. This task is not as straightforward as it may seem, for liberals disagree about the meaning of freedom and about the range and scope of legitimate impositions on freedom. Among the leading views, proponents of negative liberty can be distinguished from adherents of positive liberty.[3] The former, conceiving of freedom as the absence of coercion within a certain range of individual activity, are concerned primarily (although not exclusively) with protecting the sphere of inalienable rights: that is, with the question of *what* can be publicly governed and what remains the individual's private, 'interference-free' domain. By contrast, proponents of positive liberty think of freedom as 'self-mastery,' or autonomy and self-actualization, and are mainly interested in the source of authority: in the question of *who* governs and how best to maximize citizens' opportunities for rational autonomy. Although at first glance these two ways of conceptualizing freedom are very different, I argue that underlying them is a single idea of freedom—a consensus on what freedom surely is, whatever else it might be. It is therefore possible to construct, on the basis of a liberal 'consensus' on the nature of freedom, a liberal conception of oppression, understood generally as the negation of freedom.

## Liberal conceptions of freedom

### Negative liberty

One of the most articulate discussions of negative liberty appears in Isaiah Berlin's essay 'Two Concepts of Liberty.' According to the negative conception, he writes,

> I am normally said to be free to the degree to which no man or body of men interferes with my activity. Political liberty in this sense is simply the area within which a man can act unobstructed by others. If I am prevented by others from doing what I could otherwise do, I am to that degree unfree; and if this area is contracted by other men beyond a certain minimum, I can be described as being coerced, or, it may be, enslaved. (*TCL* 169)

Here we have a clear statement of the core sense of negative liberty as a kind of 'contraction' of freedom in order to carve out a 'coercion-free zone' for citizens; hence the well-known formulations of negative liberty as the '*absence* of coercion by others' or 'freedom *from*' kinds of interference. This conception of freedom is most often associated with the classical English political philosophers, especially Hobbes, Locke, and Mill. It is captured, for instance, in Hobbes' claim that 'a free-man *is he that . . . is not hindred to doe [sic] as he has a will to do*' (1968: 262).

Proponents of negative liberty emphasize that the specification of an inviolable sphere of individual freedom is necessary to guarantee an individual's ability to pursue his or her own conception of the good at all, that is, to be self-determining to any degree. In Berlin's words,

> there ought to exist a certain minimum area of personal freedom which must on no account be violated; for if it is overstepped, the individual will find himself in an area too narrow for even that minimum development of his natural faculties which alone makes it possible to pursue, and even to conceive, the various ends which men hold good or right or sacred. (*TCL* 171)

The general idea is that there is a range of crucial functions an individual must always be able to perform without interference by others in order always to be able to meet, at the very least, her basic survival needs. Thus, in the US we protect the rights of free speech and conscience to ensure that citizens are always able to voice opinions about matters of government; this empowers us to work toward the realization of social conditions required for the fulfillment of our ends. If speech were restricted, possibilities for the realization of certain of our ends might be effectively thwarted. Primarily for this reason adherents of negative liberty argue that a line must be drawn between, on the one hand, a sacrosanct area of individuals' 'private' lives, where no other persons can interfere and over which the individual alone is sovereign, and, on the other hand, the sphere of life that is subject to public regulation.

However, we also see the necessity of demarcating the sphere of individual freedom when we consider that the very notion of securing the fullest measure of freedom for citizens entails a limitation upon our agency with respect to others. If freedom were unlimited, every individual would be at liberty to interfere with every other—but then no one's freedom would be, in truth, unlimited. Each individual would find his ability to meet basic needs or develop his capacities seriously jeopardized because it would always be threatened by the ungoverned free agency of others. This threat would result from the simple fact that human interests often conflict, even when persons desire to cooperate peacefully.

The proponents of negative liberty agree, then, that a line of demarcation *must* be drawn between private and public authority. However, Berlin also cites the belief that an inviolable sphere of freedom is necessary for realizing individuals' capacities for conceiving and pursuing their good, for developing their 'natural *faculties*,' an idea stressed by adherents of negative freedom, from Mill to Rawls. Mill, for instance, suggests that if an individual is not permitted to be sovereign over 'the part [of his conduct] which merely concerns himself,' then

> there will be no scope for spontaneity, originality, genius, for mental energy, for moral courage . . . Whatever is rich and diversified will be crushed by the weight of custom, by men's constant tendency to conformity, which breeds only 'withered' capacities, 'pinched and hidebound,' 'cramped and dwarfed' human beings. (*TCL* 174, citing Mill 1978)

In Benjamin Constant's words, we must preserve an inviolable sphere of individual liberty, for if we do not, we 'degrade or deny our nature.'[4] Thus the negative conception emphasizes self-actualization, a concern not often credited to it but, rather, to the positive conception.

### Positive liberty

Whereas negative liberty is often conceived loosely as *freedom from* coercion by others, positive liberty is often characterized as the *freedom to* realize one's own ends, to be self-actualizing. The concern with a positive conception of liberty, Berlin says, is a consequence of 'the wish on the part of the individual to be his own master' (*TCL* 178). That is, the concern stems not from a desire to mark off one area of life over which one is sovereign, but rather to experience oneself as ultimately having authority over the whole of one's experience. Berlin explains:

> I wish my life and decisions to depend on myself, not on external forces of whatever kind. I wish to be the instrument of my own, not other men's, acts of will. I wish to be a subject, not an object; to be moved by reasons, by conscious purposes, which are my own, not by causes which affect me, as it were, from outside . . . This is at least part of what I mean when I say that I am rational . . . I wish, above all, to be conscious of myself as a thinking, willing, active being, bearing responsibility for my choices and able to explain them by reference to my own ideas and purposes. I feel free to the degree that I believe this to be true, and enslaved to the degree that I am made to realize that it is not. (*TCL* 178)

Kant's autonomous rational legislator springs quickly to mind, but then so does the image of the rugged American individualist—self-determined and self-determining. In fact, from Berlin's formulation we can see that positive liberty bears some resemblance to negative liberty. Both are concerned fundamentally with securing the freedom of individuals to be self-actualizing, to pursue their conceptions of the good.

However, there is (at least) one important distinction to be made between the positive and negative conceptions. Whereas negative liberty focuses primarily upon the scope and range of the *sphere* of freedom, that is, with *what* is governed, positive liberty emphasizes the *source* of authority, that is, *who* governs. The positive sense is concerned with the question 'What, or who, is the source of control or interference that can determine someone to do, or be, this rather than that?' (*TCL* 169). The ideal answer from the perspective of positive liberty is 'Oneself.' Its defenders are interested in maximizing individuals' opportunities to live *autonomously*.

By 'autonomy' is usually meant 'self-mastery,' but this can be understood in at least two ways: either as *political self-rule*—as governing ('mastering') oneself through democratic or representative government—or as something like Kantian *rational self-legislation*, in which one allows one's 'higher' rational powers to master one's 'lower' bodily and affective nature.[5] Proponents of positive liberty address both kinds of autonomy, but many especially emphasize the latter: freedom as willing in accordance with one's own 'authentic,' rational nature. Although this idea has some connection to the idea of realizing one's individual identity, the claim here is stronger. Individuals are free not merely when they are at liberty to actualize their identities but, more specifically, *only* when their identities are rationally self-defined, and they subject their drives and passions (one component of identity) to the mastery and control of their reason (another component).

The general idea, then, is that each person is a 'divided' self with an 'authentic' nature, interest, and will (specifically, that determined by reason) that is to be distinguished from the 'lower' nature guided by the passions. We act freely when we realize the authentic, rational self. Accordingly, adherents of rational autonomy stress that while one may think, 'I am my own master' and 'slave to no man,' one may nevertheless be enslaved to one's ' "unbridled" passions' (*TCL* 179), a form of bondage as deleterious as enslavement to another person. We need only think of individuals who suffer from alcoholism or drug addiction to know this is true. Accordingly, while T. H. Green grants that freedom must be understood to some extent in the negative sense—'It always implies . . . some exemption from compulsion by others' (1917: 3)—he stresses that even if one is free in that sense, one is in another sense unfree if enslaved by one's impulses and passions. In such a case one is essentially 'in the condition of a bondsman who is carrying out the will of another, not his own' (2).

According to some versions of rational autonomy, a person is autonomous when she is able to live her life according to a *plan* shaped by reasons and motives that stem from her own rational nature and not from manipulative or distorting forces, whether these be internal (her passions and inclinations) or external (Zutlevics 2002: 85). The concern here is with living a self-determined 'whole life,' fulfilling a life plan that expresses one's own will and, moreover, is to a significant degree invulnerable to determination by external forces. Here, a life plan is conceived not as 'some inflexible or unchanging set of goals,' but rather as 'whatever it is that a person *broadly wants to do* in and with his or her life,' the *general* scheme she sets for her life, which is always subject to revision (R. Young 1986: 8).

Of course, these autonomy theorists also ascribe a central role to rationality in the devising of life plans. However, in their view, the rationality of plans is not necessarily indexed to abstract universal criteria of rationality, but rather to the ability of individuals to determine rational ends on the basis of both knowledge and interest. Accordingly, these theorists stress the importance of the concrete conditions enabling individuals to determine rational ends. In order to guarantee their ability to actualize their 'authentic' selves, individuals must not only be morally self-legislating but also politically self-governing.

Rousseau is perhaps the best-known adherent of this conception.[6] According to him, individuals bind themselves together in society in the first place to guarantee their survival and freedom. It is well known that Rousseau generally prefers the natural state of humanity to the actualized civilization of eighteenth-century France, although he acknowledges that individuals' livelihood and happiness are better secured in society. For this reason alone individuals relinquish their natural independence and, via a social contract, submit to laws expressing the general will, the common *rational* interest of the people. Their submission not only protects them from 'personal dependence' upon the arbitrary wills of others, but also guarantees that they are *self*-legislating, since the general will expresses their own rational will (1967: 22). Now the citizen can *recognize* the law and is genuinely autonomous, for submission to the general will is manifestly submission to her own self.[7] Hence, Rousseau's famous summation: 'In short, each giving himself to all, gives himself to nobody' (1987: 18).

In general, proponents of positive liberty seem to agree that the best way to secure freedom is to create conditions in which individuals may lead genuinely autonomous, self-determined lives—that is, lives governed by

plans of their own design that are determined by reason. Such individuals
might stress the following claim of Berlin:

> I wish to be somebody, not nobody; a doer—deciding, not being decided
> for, self-directed and not acted upon by external nature or other men as
> if I were a thing, or an animal, or a slave incapable of playing a human
> role, that is, *of conceiving goals and policies of my own and realizing them.*
> (*TCL* 178; My emphasis)

On the positive conception, only such a person is called *free*.

### Summation: a liberal 'consensus' on freedom

The negative and positive conceptions of liberty are primarily concerned
with two distinct questions—'How much government should there be?'
versus 'Who should govern?' In Berlin's words, 'The former want to curb
authority as such. The latter want it placed in their own hands' (*TCL*
212). Berlin concludes that the two positions are ultimately incommensurable, and the endeavor to reconcile them into a single view of liberty
misguided, the vestige of an outdated rationalist, monistic metaphysics
(*TCL* 42). However, I have argued that the two conceptions share a common ground: both are ultimately concerned with securing individuals'
opportunities for self-actualization. The questions posed are, 'How much
government should there be *if we are to secure individuals' opportunities
for self-actualization?*' and 'Who should govern *if we are to secure individuals' opportunities for self-actualization?*' The two conceptions, then, do not
involve incommensurable ideas of freedom itself, but rather different perspectives on the best way to *secure* freedom, that is, on the *conditions of*
freedom. The defenders of both negative and positive conceptions of freedom agree that freedom *itself* is *unimpeded opportunities for self-actualization,*
even if they disagree about the best way to secure freedom so conceived.
This shared conception of freedom will ground the liberal definition of
oppression I will construct.

## Toward a Liberal Conception of Oppression

### A provisional definition

Earlier I put forward some standard meanings of 'oppression' as severe,
unjust hardship and the negation of freedom. I then argued that, for liberals,

freedom is unimpeded opportunities for self-actualization. Combining these ideas, I reach a provisional liberal definition of oppression:

$O_p$: *Oppression is that condition in which impediments to (constraints upon) individuals' opportunities for self-actualization constitute severe, unjust hardships for those individuals.*

Defenders of negative and positive liberty may still have different notions of what specific practices count as oppressive. However, these differences may turn on differences in weight given to specific terms in the provisional definition: proponents of negative liberty might think of oppression first and foremost in terms of *constraints upon* freedom, whereas adherents of positive liberty might fix upon impeded *opportunities for self-actualization*. Indeed, Berlin, expounding the negative conception, writes: 'Coercion implies the deliberate interference of other human beings within the area in which I could otherwise act' (*TCL* 169). By contrast, Rousseau conceives of oppression as the violation of the people's sovereign will, actualized as their constitution:

> As the particular will acts incessantly against the general will, so the government makes a continual effort against the sovereignty. The more this effort is increased, the more the constitution is altered; and as there is here no other corporate will which, by resisting that of the Prince, may produce equilibrium with it, it must happen sooner or later that the Prince at length oppresses the sovereign and violates the social treaty. (1967: 89)

Differences in emphasis notwithstanding, negative and positive conceptions of oppression may converge on a single, more fundamental liberal conception captured by $O_p$. For both negative and positive libertarians, oppression involves severe, unjust constraints upon individuals' opportunities for self-actualization.

Thus $O_p$ meets the third criterion of adequacy ($CO_3$): it adequately reflects a liberal perspective. I will now enrich that provisional definition by incorporating insights from critical theory.

### Critical theories of oppression

When we compare $O_p$ to definitions advanced by critical theorists, the affinities are evident. For critical theorists, too, 'oppression' designates the imposition of unjust social and institutional constraints upon individuals' chances for self-actualization (Bartky 1990; Cudd 2006; Frye 1983; Harvey 2000; Young 1990; and Zutlevics 2002). I now draw upon their analyses in order to clarify three essential features of oppression that will enrich $O_p$:

1. The constraints imposed are *systemic*, which partly accounts for the severity of oppression.
2. The individuals in question are targeted because of their *social group membership*.
3. The constraints imposed result from *unintentional* as well as deliberate actions and beliefs.

### Oppression as a system

While injustice is a defining characteristic of oppression, it is the *severity* of the injustices involved that distinguish oppression. Again, while all oppression is unjust, not all injustice is oppressive. Stated differently, while unjustly suffering constraints upon one's opportunities for self-actualization is a necessary condition of oppression, it is not a sufficient one. Recall the example of being overlooked for a promotion because you are an introvert. This is unjust but not oppressive, because you undoubtedly have other opportunities to advance your career. By contrast, if you are impeded from advancing because your disability (or sex, ethnicity, sexual orientation, age, etc.) is not accommodated or accepted by sufficiently many employers, the hardships you suffer may be severe, both in terms of your compromised ability to sustain your livelihood and the cost to your dignity.

Obviously, different people will have different notions of what counts as severe, unjust hardship. With regard to employment discrimination, for instance, some might add the further distinction that it only results in severe hardship if it completely thwarts one's ability to sustain oneself. If one can still acquire food, clothing, and shelter, through public assistance or other means, one may be unjustly disadvantaged but not oppressed. For others, however, being repeatedly denied employment by virtue of one's collective identity characteristics will count as severe hardship, even if one is able to secure one's sustenance, because of the cost to one's self-respect of being rendered incapable of exercising one's capabilities in a way that contributes to the well-being of one's family and the good of society.

Rather than haggle over such differences concerning specific, determinate outcomes of unjust behavior, I propose that we think of the severity condition in terms suggested by Marilyn Frye, as involving a *system* of constraints:

> The experience of oppressed people is that the living of one's life is confined and shaped by forces and barriers which are not accidental or occasional and hence avoidable, but are systematically related to each other in such a way as to catch one between and among them and restrict or penalize motion in any direction. *It is the experience of being caged in*: all avenues, in every direction, are blocked or booby trapped. (1983: 4; My emphasis)

Frye conceives the severity of oppression not in terms of the gravity of single determinate consequences, but rather in terms of something pervasive about the overall *experience* of the oppressed: 'the experience of being caged in.'

To make her point, Frye asks us to imagine a bird confined in a cage. If we fix our attention on a single wire of the cage, we may be unaware of the other wires and wonder why the bird does not escape. It is easy enough to go around a single wire. Moreover, even if we become aware of additional wires one at a time, so long as we myopically conceive of them as isolated wires we may still not grasp why the bird does not make its way around them. 'There is no physical property of any one wire,' Frye writes, '*nothing* that the closest scrutiny could discover, that will reveal how a bird could be inhibited or harmed by it except in the most accidental way' (4–5). However, when we step back and acquire a 'macroscopic view,' we see the whole cage and grasp 'in a moment' why the bird does not escape. 'It is perfectly *obvious* that the bird is surrounded by a network of systematically related barriers, no one of which would be the least hindrance to its flight, but which, by their relations to each other, are as confining as the solid walls of a dungeon' (5).

Similarly, the severity of oppression consists partly in the fact that its victims are completely constrained and veritably immobilized by a *system* of unjust social and institutional practices: in Frye's words, 'by networks of forces and barriers that expose [them] to penalty' (3). Under slavery, for instance—an uncontroversial case of oppression—African Americans were subject to an entire system of laws, customs, and other formal and informal social practices that, *taken together*, maintained their absolute subordination and servitude. Legislation was supplemented not only by socially accepted violence against slaves, but also by scientific and philosophical ideologies expounding the natural inferiority of Africans, and so on. Thus

victims of oppression—unlike non-oppressed people—are subject to mul-
tifarious injustices that combine to 'press,' 'reduce,' and 'immobilize' them
in conditions of complete subordination.

I have just described the system of oppression during slavery as comprised
of laws, customs, and ideologies. But no Americans are enslaved today. What
kind of system do *we* confront? As perhaps in all ages, today's oppression
involves political, social, and economic institutions—in Cudd's terms, a
system of both material and psychological forces (2006: 22). Violence and
economic deprivation are the main material forces of oppression, whereas stereotypes and schemas, through which oppressors and oppressed alike assert
and reinforce the 'exceptionality' of the oppressed, are its primary psychological forces (74ff.). These correspond explicitly to three of Young's 'five faces
of oppression': violence, exploitation, and cultural imperialism (although
marginalization and disempowerment are easily recognized as co-implicated)
(*JPD* 9, 39). What is clear is that oppression is carried out through a pervasive
system of social, political, and economic beliefs, practices, and institutions—
again the 'often unconscious assumptions and reactions of well-meaning people in ordinary interactions, media and cultural stereotypes, and structural
features of bureaucratic hierarchies and market mechanisms' (41).

The systemic character of contemporary oppression is in this way
intimately connected to what T. L. Zutlevics highlights as its distinguishing characteristic: that it compromises individuals' chances for *resilient*
autonomy (2002: 85ff.). By 'resilient autonomy,' Zutlevics means an individual's reasonable confidence that he can live a whole life according to
a rational plan of his own choosing. In her words: 'The idea of resilience
captures . . . the reasonable projectability of one's substantive desires and
values into the future.' Crucial, then, to the notion of resilient autonomy
is the '*non-vulnerability*' of an individual's life plan for his experience of
concrete freedom (87–88).

Zutlevics distinguishes resilient autonomy from dispositional autonomy,
in which individuals enjoy control over determinate spheres of their lives
for undetermined durations. She observes that non-oppressed people not
only enjoy dispositional autonomy, but are confident that, barring major
external impediments, *they always will*—for they largely determine their
own futures. By contrast, persons who are oppressed may enjoy some kinds
of dispositional autonomy, but they lack the confidence that they will
*always* be able to fulfill their own life plans. For example, a small number
of American slaves with benevolent masters made some decisions central
to their own life plans: whether or not to marry, have children, *keep* their
children, and so on. However, this happy condition was entirely contingent

upon the will of the master, even upon his financial stability or very life, for circumstances changed dramatically upon the master's financial or ultimate demise. Therefore, even if slaves enjoyed some dispositional autonomy, they lacked resilient autonomy (87–90).

In highlighting the distinction between resilient and dispositional autonomy, Zutlevics touches a crucial element of contemporary demands for recognition: the desire of the oppressed, not merely for validation of their cultures or for the just distribution of goods and wealth, but for *resilient autonomy*. Emancipatory movements call attention to the fact that our toleration of pervasive impediments to their agency constitutes their oppression. They certainly expect to confront obstacles to the fulfillment of their ends, but not to lack what members of majority groups enjoy: *sustained* confidence in their ability to realize their life plans, notwithstanding occasional impediments.

I appropriate Zutlevics' notion of resilient autonomy for the liberal definition of oppression that I am constructing, but with the following modification: following Hegel, I replace the traditional, thicker idea of autonomy as the freedom to choose a plan of life, with a thinner conception of it as 'self-conscious self-determination,' or one's willingness and ability to be *self*-limiting in response to the claims of others. Hegel's conception can be illuminated by appeal to Rainer Forst's idea of autonomy as 'a basic right to justification' that constitutes individuals as 'morally independent addressees and authors of intersubjective claims' (1997: 65). For Forst, an individual is autonomous if she can require that others supply adequate reasons for the claims they make upon her and if she can similarly supply reasons for her own actions.

I advance a thinner notion of autonomy because thicker conceptions are not uncontroversial. Questions arise about the appropriateness of invoking traditional liberal conceptions of autonomy in arguments addressing pluralistic and multicultural societies. I propose a thin conception of autonomy that may be acceptable to both nonliberals and liberals. For example, the adherents of a nonliberal religion might grant the reasonableness of acknowledging members' rights to be offered reasons for their fealty— even if the reasons ultimately reduce to 'because the sacred doctrine says so.'[8] The notion of autonomy I am recommending denotes an individual's resilient ability to be ultimately *self*-limiting in response to others' claims and to act on the basis of reasons they themselves find acceptable.

## Oppression and social groups

A hallmark of oppression, according to critical theorists, is that it is perpetrated against social groups (Cudd 2006: 23; *JPD* 9). Accordingly, social

groups are the primary subjects in critical theories of oppression. A hallmark of liberalism is its propensity to privilege individuals over groups.
Liberals might accordingly worry about critical theories of oppression. For
methodological individualists, in particular, since the individual is prior
to the group, and all groups are reducible to the individuals that comprise
them, social and political explanations ought to refer, not to groups, but to
individuals and their actions.

I do not deny that there is a sense in which we can speak meaningfully of
the oppression of individuals *qua* individuals. For instance, we can speak
sensibly of a young man oppressed by a controlling, abusive father, in
which case our account need only refer to the two individuals involved.
However, in the present discussion we are concerned with social and political oppression, which is targeted against individuals not *qua* individuals
but as members of social groups. In the Declaration of Independence, the
American colonists claimed they were oppressed, not as individuals, but
as a social group—as 'these Colonies'—which the Crown had constrained
unjustly and severely. The concept of social group is essential to explanations of the social and political oppression of individuals.

Cudd defines a social group as a collective 'formed by or maintained
by some social fact or action, either intentionally or as an unintended
consequence of some social fact or action' (2006: 35). Groups formed
intentionally are called associations, or voluntary social groups. They are
distinguished from non-voluntary social groups, which are formed unin-
tentionally, again, as a result of some social fact or action. Thus individuals
choose association membership (e.g., in a corporation, club, or a particular church, mosque or synagogue), but they typically *find* themselves as
members of non-voluntary social groups (e.g., of a gender, ethnicity, or
age group). In both cases, social group members share at least one socially
salient 'interest.' For associations it is usually a shared set of chosen values
or projects. For non-voluntary social groups the 'interest' typically follows
from the shared burdens or benefits that accrue to their group (41)

Of course, social groups are ontologically reducible to individuals, but
it is a mistake to conclude from this that the concept of a social group is
meaningless. As Cudd suggests, this is akin to claiming that the concept
'gross national product' is meaningless because it can be reduced to the
buying and selling behavior of individuals (33, 46). In fact, the concept of a
social group is indispensable for describing some social phenomena involving non-voluntary groupings. She offers a clear example:

> [H]ow do we explain the door opening ritual, as it is called by feminists,
> in a case where a small man with packages rushes to open the door for a

large able-bodied woman (Frye 1983: 5)? It does not make sense unless we include in the explanans reference to default assumptions about social groups, namely the stereotype about women being weak and small. For the man cannot infer that the woman actually needs help here, or that he is in a good position to offer it, unless he draws that inference based on social groupings of persons rather than on the visible individual traits in the actual situation. If one objects that it is custom or habit that explains why the man always opens doors for women, then one must explain the origin of the custom or habit, and this explanation will rely on references to social groups. Furthermore, this example involves social groupings that the persons did not voluntarily enter, so that one cannot reduce the group to . . . intentional states. (46–47)

Methodological individualism may be appropriate for explaining associations. In Young's words, 'Individuals constitute associations, they come together as already formed persons and set them up, establishing rules, positions, and offices' (*JPD* 44–45). But the defining of non-voluntary social groups from, as it were, both inside and outside makes the concept of a social group rather more complex, clearly more than just a collection of individuals. Sometimes a social group is plainly constituted partly of socially constructed meanings not reducible to the intentional states of group members and involving reference to collective identities. A social group is therefore ontologically real, not only as a collection of individuals, but also as a *relation* among individuals within and without the group (44).

Oppressed individuals are constrained severely and unjustly precisely because of socially constructed relations and meanings that supervene on their mere ontological aggregation. The concept of a social group is therefore essential to the concept of oppression. Those who still worry that a reference to groups is contrary to liberal thinking might recall the reason why liberals privilege individuals over groups: to protect individuals from the abrogation of their rights by groups (e.g., their religion, culture, or nation-state) (see, e.g., *MC* 7). It is entirely consistent with liberalism to protect individuals from oppression by majority groups if they are oppressed because of their social group membership. Thus it is not a betrayal of liberalism but an expression of its chief concern to make reference to social groups when conceptualizing oppression.

### Unintentional acts of oppression

I proceed to a third feature of oppression: that because of its systemic character, the constraints imposed upon social groups result from *unintentional*

as well as deliberate actions and beliefs. Considering the derivation of the
term 'oppression,' Marilyn Frye writes:

> The root of the word 'oppression' is the element 'press' . . . Presses are
> used to mold things or flatten them or reduce them in bulk, sometimes
> to reduce them by squeezing out the gasses or liquids in them. Something
> pressed is caught between or among forces and barriers which are so
> related to each other that jointly they restrain, restrict or prevent the
> thing's motion or mobility. (1983: 2)

The imagery of pressing may suggest a deliberate activity: one may think
of an agent pressing an object *in order to* mold or restrain it. Accordingly,
one might characterize oppression as deliberately imposed upon victims,
as indeed it often is.[9] But it is not always the result of intentional actions.
I have noted Iris Young's claim that some individuals suffer structural
oppression as a result of 'often *unconscious* assumptions and reactions of
well-meaning people' (*JPD* 41). Similarly, Berlin notes that according to
negative libertarians, '[t]he criterion of oppression is the part I believe to
be played by other human beings, directly or indirectly, with or without the
intention of doing so, in frustrating my wishes' (*TCL* 170).[10] Thus, just as an
object may be pressed between two other objects 'accidentally,' oppressive
practices may be unintentional acts of harm.

Other theorists highlight two ways in which the seemingly benign practices and understandings of well-intentioned agents can be modes of
oppression: by entrenching social hierarchies and by reinforcing implicit
assumptions of inferiority, both of which sustain *de facto* inequality. The
former is analyzed by Jean Harvey in her account of '*civilized* oppression'
grounded in relationships of 'moral subordination' (2000: 177). Sandra
Bartky addresses the latter phenomenon in her analysis of psychological
oppression.

In 'Social Privilege and Moral Subordination,' Harvey sets out to undermine 'one of the great myths about oppression': that it always involves overt
and highly visible acts of aggression (177). She stresses that not only is
oppression frequently invisible, but in contemporary Western societies it
takes on a 'civilized' character, inasmuch as it is fundamentally 'rooted
in distorted and morally inappropriate relationships, which underlie and
contribute harms of a more tangible kind (like poverty or unemployment)' (177). Harvey calls attention to the character of social relationships
as *moral* relationships obtaining among members of a 'moral community
[that] includes moral agents and moral patients: roughly, those capable

of being under moral obligation, and those to whom obligations can be owed' (178). Thus our social relationships can be analyzed and evaluated in terms of how we fulfill our obligations to one another.

Harvey highlights, in particular, the empirical fact that modern social relationships are typically hierarchical relationships that, moreover, frequently involve moral *subordination*: socially privileged persons enjoy a *de facto* moral status that exceeds their ostensible moral status as equal 'persons.' Their elevated moral status derives from their 'relationship power' over others who, *as a result of the relation*, have a *de facto* subordinated moral status, one lesser than their proper moral status (181). Harvey therefore stresses the need to critique our social relationships. She observes that there are two paths to the oppressive moral subordination of others: (1) through failing to recognize overtly their equal moral status and (2) through blocking their 'effective moral empowerment,' their ability to exercise basic rights, fulfill duties and obligations, and otherwise engage with other moral agents in properly balanced moral relationships (179). Harvey is most concerned with the latter, which is far less visible. She explains:

> Some well-intentioned agents, not themselves victims, have worked against oppression by trying to amend the overtly recognized moral status of the victims. But these reformers have sometimes found themselves baffled as to why such amendments, especially if turned into law, leave the same groups of people marginalized and still oppressed in some way. For nonvictims it is genuinely difficult to see the second route to moral subordination, that via the lack of moral empowerment. Sanctions that involve neither physical force nor the use of law mask what is happening, and this difficulty is increased if the agents responsible are without malicious intent, which is more common than not. (180)

Harvey maintains that our primary focus upon issues of legal equality, at the expense of attention to social relationships and practices that block individuals' effective moral empowerment, leave many baffled as to why minority groups continue to complain about oppression. In particular, because victims of civilized oppression are often educated, articulate, and self-possessed, non-victims have difficulty imagining such persons being disempowered by means other than overtly oppressive laws and brute force: 'Surely such qualities are just the ones needed to make an individual appropriately powerful, that is, non-oppressed? If the person's overtly recognized moral status is all that it should be, and he/she has the attributes above, what can go wrong?' (180).

What goes wrong is that many accepted and seemingly benign institutional structures and social practices ultimately effect the disempowerment of some individuals. Harvey focuses specifically upon the ways in which power and social privilege operate to create distorted moral relationships insofar as they inappropriately involve increasing transfers of power from the subordinated to the privileged. That is, it is not simply the case that the socially privileged enjoy more 'socially constructed assets,' such as higher salaries and more prestigious social positions, but the privileged actually increase their shares of these assets through the increased transfer to them of 'relationship power' (181).

Relationship power is the ability some agents possess to determine the agency and ends of others by virtue of their relative social positions. Harvey observes that the socially privileged enjoy more relationship power, not only vis-à-vis their employees, children, and (sometimes) spouses, but also often with respect to strangers. Consider, for instance, the preferential treatment accorded to attractive, expensively dressed men in most social settings. However, relationship power is not always direct; two forms of indirect power are (1) support power, which involves peer mediation of superiors' exercises of direct power, either by reinforcing or thwarting that power; and (2) consequential power, which involves outsider responses to exercised direct power.

For the sake of brevity, I will cite one example of support power, which speaks directly to the issue of how persons with 'powerful' attributes can nevertheless become morally disempowered. Harvey observes that

> [t]he black police officer, the woman priest or professor, the openly homosexual politician all have assigned powers because of their roles, but the first to move into such roles in some places may not be able to count on the support power that is taken for granted by their long-accepted colleagues, the white, male, physically able, heterosexual police officers, priests, professors, and politicians. When this phenomenon occurs, those concerned are doubted more often, ridiculed more often, supervised more closely, maneuvered into the least critical decision-making whenever possible, and when challenged in some outrageous rather than legitimate way by someone over whom they technically have direct power, find no minimal and fair-minded support from peers. (184)

Thus the direct power exercised by members of oppressed groups is sometimes undermined by the support power that mediates it. Even when the oppressed are professionally privileged, they may remain *morally* subordinated, hence effectively disempowered, by their professional peers and subordinates who remain morally more privileged, hence effectively more empowered.

Significantly, the continual transfer of relationship power from the socially subordinated to the socially privileged in distorted moral relationships is what often culminates in the disempowerment of members of minority groups. But social or professional inequality need not entail moral subordination and oppression. It is *non*-oppressive when the privileged display 'moral deference,' that is, *awareness* of their power and a willingness to 'explore what is involved, especially by listening to articulate people at the receiving end of such power' (187). Securing the effective moral empowerment of all social members is a mutual, democratic endeavor.

Harvey notes that the blocking of effective moral empowerment can sometimes be 'internal'; the attitudes and assumptions of the morally subordinated about their own capacities to exercise power can lead to self-undermining behavior (180). Sandra Bartky calls this phenomenon 'psychological oppression,' a condition in which members of subordinated groups internalize 'intimations' of their inferiority that compromise their authentic sense of self (1990: 22). Psychological oppression typically results from pressures to conform to the standards and ways of life of majority cultures, who assert their values and modes of expression as the 'norm,' or as 'universal,' and correspondingly designate the values and practices of minority cultures as 'different,' merely particular, and inferior. This means that some members of minority cultures, rather than being fully self-determined, are 'defined from the outside, positioned, placed, by a network of dominant meanings they experience as arising from elsewhere, from those with whom they do not identify and who do not identify with them' (*JPD* 59–60).

This internalization of the majority culture's standards and values can take two forms. In the most benign instances members of minority groups are simply forced to confront and comprehend the images well enough to respond to them. However, in the most severe cases, they actually identify with the images, accepting them as the truth. This 'breaking [of] the spirit of the dominated,' Bartky comments, 'make[s] the work of domination easier,' by obscuring the real causes of oppression. The privileged thereby 'maintain their ascendancy with more appearance of legitimacy' (1990: 23). Meanwhile, the subordinated are caught in the double bind of an existence within a society that proclaims their formal equality even as it 'bars [them] from the exercise of many of those typically human functions that bestow this status' (31). Living with this contradiction, the subordinated become divided selves, conforming to the majority identity while unable to realize fully their own authentic identities.

Just as individuals hardly intend to internalize a conception of themselves as inferior (yet they do), so, too, many people commit practices of misrecognition without intending to oppress others. Unfortunately, many of these practices just happen to have become institutionalized, part of our way of life: all the more reason for us to reflect critically upon our social and institutional relationships.

## Conclusion: A Liberal Conception of Oppression

Joining these critical theoretical perspectives to $O_p$, I arrive at the following liberal definition of oppression:

$O_f$: *Oppression is that condition in which, through deliberate or unintentional acts, a system of social and institutional constraints is imposed upon social groups that thwarts their members' resilient autonomy.*

$O_f$ retains the elements of $O_p$ as involving constraints upon individuals' opportunities for self-actualization that culminate in severe, unjust hardships for those persons. The notion of self-actualization is now captured by that of resilient autonomy. The crucial severity condition is now expressed in terms of both the *system* of constraints and the loss of *resilient* autonomy. Again, oppression is not necessarily indicated by isolated experiences of injustice, but rather by 'networks' of unjust social and institutional forces that thwart resilient autonomy. Therefore, $O_f$ satisfies the second criterion of adequacy ($CO_2$): it permits us to distinguish severe from non-severe constraints upon freedom.

# Chapter 2

# Misrecognition as Oppression

*Many people in the United States would not choose the term 'oppression' to name injustice in our society. For contemporary emancipatory movements, on the other hand . . . oppression is a central category of political discourse . . . A major political project for those of us who identify with at least one of these movements must thus be to persuade people that the discourse of oppression makes sense of much of our social experience.*

*(Iris Marion Young)\**

I opened Chapter 1 by citing four empirical cases of misrecognition exemplifying Young's 'five faces of oppression': exploitation, disempowerment, marginalization, cultural imperialism, and violence (*JPD* 9, 39). I then defined oppression, from a liberal and critical theoretical perspective, as a system of social and institutional constraints imposed upon social groups that thwarts individuals' resilient autonomy ($O_f$). In the present chapter I analyze the four cases in terms of $O_f$ in order to establish that the forms of misrecognition they represent are legitimately called modes of oppression. Thus $O_f$ meets the first criterion of adequacy (it reconciles our ordinary sense of 'oppression' with the claims of emancipatory movements that everyday practices of misrecognition are oppressive) and makes clear that we are obligated to resist and abolish practices of misrecognition.

I explore two cases—the first involving exploitation and disempowerment, and the other, cultural imperialism—in more detail than the cases of marginalization and violence. This enables me to probe more deeply the subtle injustices inherent in civilized oppression, of which exploitation, disempowerment, and cultural imperialism are poignant examples. Marginalization and violence each tends to wear its injustice on its face, so these cases can be handled more swiftly. Again, each case exemplifies a *mode* of oppression—one component of a system of practices through which oppression is carried out. A person is oppressed if she suffers enough instances of these injustices that she lacks resilient autonomy.

## Exploitation and Disempowerment

The first case, concerning the plight of the low-wage employee of a wealthy university, captures Young's ideas of exploitation and disempowerment. In her view, exploitation involves the systematic transfer of power from one individual or group to another in a way that augments the latter's power, status, and wealth (*JPD* 49). I claim that exploitation becomes *oppressive* when individuals sustain an enduring and inescapable substantial loss of power. For instance, the power some workers initially possess to negotiate the price of their labor and other conditions of employment diminishes in the transfer of power entailed by the structuring of their work to the point that they suffer a loss of control that is, for all practical purposes, inescapable. This condition, in which some workers lack even the power to make autonomous decisions about the performance of their tasks, is what Young calls powerlessness. She defines it in negative terms: 'the powerless lack the authority, status, and sense of self that professionals tend to have' (57). The status and privilege professionals possess, and that the powerless lack, come in three general forms: (1) opportunities for developing and expanding capacities and expertise, (2) everyday work autonomy that accords individuals greater social status, and (3) an entire mode of life that is characterized as 'respectable' (57).

In 2001, Frank Morley was a custodian at Harvard University and one of the institution's 971 service employees earning less than the living wage for the city of Cambridge ($10.68 per hour plus benefits). While Morley himself earned $10 per hour, most service employees earned only the state minimum wage of $6.50 without benefits. Morley's take-home pay was insufficient to cover his expenses, and he worried that continuing to borrow against his retirement to pay debts would leave him completely dependent upon Social Security when he finally did retire (Herbert 2001). However, Harvard president Neil Rudenstine (2005) refused to 'give in' to student pressure to secure a living wage for the university's struggling workers.

That pressure had been applied by students for nearly three years. In 1999, soon after the city of Cambridge passed the living wage law, Harvard's Progressive Students Labor Movement (PSLM) launched a campus campaign. In May 2000, an ad hoc review committee appointed by Rudenstine rejected the living wage but recommended an expanded benefits package that included partial health benefits, a literacy program, and free Harvard museum passes. One year later, the new benefits program still had not been implemented, despite the university's $120 million operating budget surplus that year (its largest ever).

Consequently, in April 2001 the PSLM staged a widely publicized three-week occupation of the president's office. Rudenstine indeed resigned but first appointed another review committee, this time comprised of workers, students, faculty, and administrators. In December his successor agreed to portions of the committee's minimal recommendations, which included raising the wages of some service workers to between $10.83 and $11.30 per hour.

The PSLM's victory would not likely have been achieved by the workers themselves, who were powerless to move the administration. 'Not too many folks pay attention to janitors,' Morley commented. 'Universities pay attention to students: It's their bread and butter' (Ferdinand 2001). However, student advocacy alone had been ineffective. Not until students were supported by faculty and administrators, high-ranking public officials, and Hollywood celebrities did Harvard finally negotiate.

Backlash followed victory, however, as the least powerful activists were made to pay. Four Harvard law students received official reprimands. Moreover, the PSLM reports that since 2001 'a disturbing pattern of continued management abuse of workers across the low wage sectors has become glaringly obvious,' including 'broken contract promises, intimidation of workers for union activity, discrimination and harassment of female, minority, and older workers, and covert outsourcing of unionized labor to exploitative and unaccountable subcontracting firms' (Harvard Progressive Students Labor Movement). For instance, when one night employee applied for a daytime position, she was told the job required 'man's work' and was only open to males—a violation of Federal law. Soon after the employee complained about her discriminatory treatment, she was fired (*ibid.*).

Of greatest concern to Young is the structural character of exploitation: that it perpetuates pre-capitalist slave and feudal power relations inimical to liberal modernity (*JPD* 48). In capitalist societies the presumption is that workers contract freely with employers on a basis of formal equality. However, in reality many workers are compelled by necessity (and inadequate education) to work for less than subsistence wages. Moreover, once they accept low-wage jobs, workers effectively transfer not only their labor power, but also their bargaining and decision-making power. In positions of definite subordination, such workers are expected to perform work as they are told to and not to question labor practices or work conditions. Arguably, many Americans expect this of the employee–employer relation, especially between nonprofessionals and the professionals who manage them. We tend not to reflect upon the extent to which these power

exchanges occur within coercive contexts—that is, as Young observes, that '[s]ocial rules about what work is, who does what for whom, how work is compensated, and the social process by which the results of work are appropriated, operate to enact relations of power and inequality' (50). A structure is erected that perpetually transfers power unidirectionally to managers and owners.

Not only is exploitation structural, but it also discriminates, facilitating a 'steady transfer' of the benefits of labor from 'one social group to . . . another' (49–50). Low-wage jobs typically involve menial labor, work that is 'servile, unskilled, low-paying work lacking in autonomy' (52). Most of these jobs—custodians, laborers, maids, and so on—are filled by persons of color and women, such that today just about anyone can have a colored or female servant. Young explains:

> [I]n the United States today there remains significant racial structuring of private household service. But . . . much service labor has gone public: anyone who goes to a good hotel or a good restaurant can have servants. Servants often attend the daily—and nightly—activities of business executives, government officials, and other high-status professionals. In our society there remains strong cultural pressure to fill servant jobs—bellhop, porter, chambermaid, busboy, and so on—with Black and Latino workers. These jobs entail a transfer of energies whereby the servers enhance the status of the served. (52)

The real difficulty is that racial structuring of servile labor occurs within a context in which high-level, prestigious positions are still predominantly occupied by persons from more privileged backgrounds. The result is that women and minorities in servile positions work primarily to enhance the status and power of the privileged.

Of course, not all relations involving power differentials and subordination are exploitative or disempowering. A graduate student is in a subordinate position relative to his professors, for example, and a CEO has greater power than an operations manager. As Zutlevics points out, 'Sometimes it is appropriate for people to engage their own talents and energies for the advancement of others, even when those others are socially advantaged,' as in the case of a speech writer who uses his skills in the service of a politician (2002: 93). Again, what distinguishes these cases from exploitation is that here the transfer of powers and energies does not result in a substantial net loss of power for subordinates. The graduate student's temporary subordination will lead to an advanced degree and greater employment potential.

The operations manager retains significant decision-making and bargaining power within the corporation. The speech writer derives a measure of respectability and satisfaction from his role in the political process.

Furthermore, not all exploitation is oppressive. Exploitation becomes oppressive when persons are disempowered to the point of lacking resilient autonomy. For instance, we might say that a software designer who earns $50,000 a year, unaware that he can command a higher salary, is exploited by an employer who underpays him but pays himself one million dollars per year. However, because such a person can leave the company and easily obtain a higher-paying position elsewhere, we cannot say that he is oppressed. By contrast, a custodian in the same firm who makes less than subsistence wages without benefits, accordingly lacks the means to further his education, and therefore can only 'escape' to other low-paying work, is vulnerable to oppression. The structure of the marketplace and employment practices impose a *system* of material constraints upon his agency.

Exploitation and disempowerment are, moreover, *imposed* constraints simply because conditions could be otherwise. Although society requires the performance of menial labor—we need custodians, laborers, and maids—these positions need not entail a net loss of bargaining and decision-making power. Furthermore, compensation for these positions need not be below subsistence level.

That exploitation and disempowerment are oppressive by liberal standards is corroborated by Berlin:

> What troubles the consciences of Western liberals is not . . . the belief that the freedom that men seek differs according to their social or economic conditions, but that *the minority who possess it have gained it by exploiting, or, at least, averting their gaze from, the vast majority who do not.* They believe, with good reason, that if individual liberty is an ultimate end for human beings, none should be deprived of it by others; least of all that some should enjoy it at the expense of others. Equality of liberty; not to treat others as I should not wish them to treat me; repayment of my debt to those who alone have made possible my liberty or prosperity or enlightenment; justice in its simplest and most universal sense—these are the foundations of liberal morality. (*TCL* 172; My emphasis)

If justice entails giving those who have made one's freedom and prosperity possible their due, then denying their fair share is certainly unjust. Doing so persistently, such that their own freedom and prosperity are effectively thwarted in the process is surely oppressive.

Exploitation and disempowerment are forms of misrecognition that can justly be called modes of oppression by liberal standards. First, they potentially constrain individuals' opportunities for resilient autonomy by virtue of both the loss of decision-making power and control experienced by the exploited and the material deprivation they suffer. Second, victims may be subject to social and economic structures that render them powerless to escape their condition. This latter is the severity condition by which we can distinguish oppressive from non-oppressive cases.

## Cultural Imperialism

The second case of misrecognition, involving a student denied his high school diploma because he wore a bolo tie to graduation, is an example of cultural imperialism: 'the universalization of a dominant group's experience and culture, and its establishment as the norm' (*JPD* 58–59). Such practices are a leading cause of psychological oppression.

Thomas Benya wore a bolo tie to graduation as a tribute to his Cherokee heritage. Although the bolo is recognized in Native American culture as formal attire, it was not so acknowledged by Benya's high school. He was denied his diploma for violating the graduation dress code and advised that to receive his diploma he must schedule a conference with school administrators.

The school insisted its position was justified because Benya had been warned that his bolo was not acceptable. Furthermore, the school had sent a letter to all parents and seniors, advising that 'adherence to the dress code is mandatory.' Boys were to wear 'dark dress pants with white dress shirts and ties.' A Muslim girl was permitted to wear a head scarf and long pants for religious reasons, in keeping with the school's commitment to abide by First Amendment protection of religion (Marimow 2005). However, school officials did not feel obligated to recognize other cultural differences. 'We have many students with many different cultural heritages, and there are many times to display that,' one official claimed. 'But graduation is a time when we have a formal, *uniform* celebration. If kids are going to participate, they need to respect the rules.' Another spokesperson added: 'We set the standard to make sure all our ceremonies are formal and respectful' (Marimow 2005).

Benya carried out his tribute nonetheless, not imagining that his diploma would be withheld as punishment: 'I did not feel that I should change my heritage for an hour and a half . . . to show respect when they aren't showing respect to me' (Marimow 2005). Citing the history of Native Americans being 'pushed around,' his mother added, 'If he had not stood up for himself, he would have been part of the problem of Native Americans being treated in this way' (Manning 2005).

To be subject to cultural imperialism is essentially to be pushed around in this manner. It is 'to experience how the dominant meanings of a society render the particular perspective of one's own group invisible at the same time as they stereotype one's group and mark it out as Other' (*JPD* 58–59). This paradoxical claim is illuminated by the fact that Benya's bolo tie was considered a *non*-tie—that is, not a Western necktie—even as it was deemed an 'other' kind of tie belonging to an 'other' cultural tradition. Where there is cultural imperialism, that which is not recognized as part of the majority culture is designated by the majority as 'other' or 'abnormal' and, hence, essentially ignored, treated as not worthy of notice. Consequently, Young adds, 'Often without noticing they do so, the dominant groups project their own experience as representative of humanity as such. Cultural products also express the dominant group's perspective on and interpretation of events and elements in the society, including other groups in the society, insofar as they attain cultural status at all' (59). When this happens, members of the dominant culture can fail to grasp that their perspective is just that—one perspective among other reasonable and valid perspectives.

What is worse, even in multicultural societies such as ours frequently when majority cultures do acknowledge 'other' cultures, they stereotype and marginalize them (60). Thus, beyond simply failing to acknowledge the legitimacy of other cultural norms and practices, members of majority cultures often actively denigrate them. What begins as a benign myopia deteriorates into injustice when majority groups assert the superiority of their form of life and pressure or coerce other groups into compliance with them. Subordinated groups are manipulated into assimilation lest they be marked as deviant or inferior. 'As remarkable, deviant beings,' Young comments, 'the culturally imperialized are stamped with an essence,' which becomes the basis of stereotyping (59). 'These stereotypes so permeate the society that they are not noticed as contestable. Just as everyone knows that the earth goes around the sun, so everyone knows that gay people are promiscuous, that Indians are alcoholics, and that women are good with children' (59). Of course such stereotypes are often debilitating, making it difficult for persons marked by them to express their individuality freely. Meanwhile, Young observes that because white males, for example, escape group marking, they are freer to *self*-actualize (59).

Of course, pressures to earn a living and acquire a social status render members of subordinated groups vulnerable to cultural imperialism. In some professions, women are expected to be 'aggressive, like men,' even though non-aggressive men are respected. In corporate and academic environments, African Americans are sometimes chided for letting traces of dialect slip, for 'talking too Black,' even while other dialects—for instance, Bostonian—are appreciated. These pressures to conform mean that some individuals, rather than being fully self-determining, are 'defined from the outside, positioned, placed, by a network of dominant meanings they experience as arising from elsewhere, from those with whom they do not identify and who do not identify with them.' (59–60). Eventually they may come to internalize the dominant culture's stereotypes and inferiorized images of them.

Young concludes that the injustice of cultural imperialism stems partly from the asymmetry of the demand for conformity: 'the oppressed group's own experience and interpretation of social life find little expression that touches the dominant culture, while that same culture imposes on the oppressed group its experience and interpretation of social life' (60). From a liberal perspective we may recognize cultural imperialism as potentially oppressive, first, insofar as it thereby constrains individuals' chances to be resiliently autonomous. When individuals are so pressured to internalize the norms of a majority culture that they cannot freely express and honor their own cultural identities, they cannot be *self*-actualizing.

Second, such constraints are imposed socially and institutionally insofar as the subordinated are coerced into conformity by means of social expectations and practices. Indeed, the imposition of external cultural expectations can interfere with persons' life chances in tangible ways. Benya's case is potentially oppressive inasmuch as his high school diploma is essential to his prospects for earning an above-subsistence income and for admission to college. Had the school board withheld it, his life would have been altered dramatically: until such time as he earned a GED, he would have been confined to menial labor and the limited opportunities typically available to non-degreed persons of color—a nearly inescapable cycle of poverty that would be cruel and unusual punishment for asserting a Native American notion of formality and respectability.

## Marginalization

The third case, of a woman who receives inadequate medical care because professionals assume she is on welfare, reveals the effects of marginalization. 'Marginals,' Young explains, 'are people the system of labor cannot or will not use' typically persons of color, the elderly, the disabled, and the poor (*JPD* 53). Ironically, the woman who reported the incident, Gail C. Christopher, is *not* on welfare but is vice president for Health, Women, and Families at the Joint Center for Politics and Economic Studies. She nevertheless experienced marginalization that, in her words, 'could have cost me and my child our lives' (Christopher 2005: 134).

Marginalization is an especially dangerous mode of oppression since exclusion from mainstream social life can render individuals vulnerable to serious material deprivation, 'even extermination' (*JPD* 53). As Christopher's case makes clear, such deprivation extends beyond the lack of essential commodities such as food and clothing to include severely limited access to vital basic services such as prompt and effective medical care. Moreover, marginalization ultimately costs some citizens their equal citizenship rights, such as the right to privacy, and seriously compromises their self-respect and efforts at self-determination through everyday decision-making.[1] For example, persons dependent upon social services are frequently subjected to 'patronizing, punitive, demeaning, and arbitrary treatment' by agents of the system set up to assist them (54). Young explains:

> Being a dependent in our society implies being legitimately subject to the often arbitrary and invasive authority of service providers and other public and private administrators, who enforce rules with which the marginal must comply, and otherwise exercise power over the conditions of their lives . . . Medical and social service professionals know what is good for those they serve, and the marginals and dependents themselves do not have the right to claim to know what is good for them . . . Dependency in our society thus implies, as it has in all illiberal societies, a sufficient warrant to suspend basic rights to privacy, respect, and individual choice. (54)

We have recently witnessed the potentially fatal effects of marginalization. We will not soon forget the images of the thousands of poor, elderly, and disabled citizens of New Orleans, Louisiana, who, unable to evacuate the city, were left behind to suffer the devastating blows and aftermath of Hurricane Katrina—who were found on rooftops, in sweltering attics, or dead in their wheelchairs because federal rescue efforts did not begin until five days after the storm. Some attribute this devastation to the invisibility of the marginalized in our society. Author Patricia Elam (2005) comments:

> The United States has become, in essence, one of the Third World countries we criticize smugly for being unable to care for its own. During Katrina, reporters and commentators echoed the same empty phrase: I never expected to see anything like this in America. That's because we've gotten used to seeing streams of dazed and downtrodden people of color in the Sudan, India or even Iraq. That's because in America, these are the invisible people . . . Usually, we can build our houses far from these invisible people, but this time, most of us were unable to turn away from the images as they literally fought to stay above water.

That marginalization severely constrains individuals' resilient autonomy should be clear. First, marginalized persons are denied access to meaningful work, the means of providing for their sustenance as well as of exercising their talents and capacities toward the fulfillment of life plans of their own design. Second, the resulting dependency of the marginalized upon the existing social welfare bureaucracy further thwarts their efforts to be self-determining insofar as agents of the system interfere in dependents' personal decisions in ways that undermine their self-respect. Ultimately, however, the *severity* of the injustice of marginalization—its oppressive character—derives from the potential threat to life and veritable inescapability of the deprivation and invisibility that result from it.

## Violence

Young describes oppressive violence as the knowledge of some persons 'that they must fear random, unprovoked attacks on their persons or property, which have no motive but to damage, humiliate, or destroy the person' (*JPD* 61). In the US African Americans, Arab Americans, Latin Americans, women, homosexuals, and transgendered persons are frequent victims of violent assault. In a well-known case, Amadou Diallo was brutally murdered by four New York City police officers searching for a rape suspect, despite the fact that he was unarmed. All four officers were acquitted. Many read the jury's decision as 'a clear signal that there is a state-sanctioned "open season" for police to kill unarmed blacks' (Sewell 2000).

But part of what makes violence against social groups oppressive is the degree to which it is tolerated by the larger society. In Young's words,

'What makes violence a face of oppression is less the particular acts themselves . . . than the social context surrounding them, which makes them possible and even acceptable' (*JPD* 61). It is true: cases such as Diallo's are neither isolated nor rare (Marable 2007: 183). The unfortunate result is that those who are not directly affected become somewhat de-sensitized to such practices, since they occur so frequently (*JPD* 62).

Quite the opposite is the case for members of groups living with the knowledge that they are always vulnerable to attack because of their identities (vulnerable even to police, who are supposed to protect them). The need for constant vigilance partly constitutes the oppressive character of violence. Consider, for instance, the estimate that one in four women in the US suffer at least one rape or physical assault in their lifetime (Tjaden and Thoennes 2000: iii). 'Just living under such a threat of attack on oneself or family or friends,' Young writes, 'deprives the oppressed of freedom and dignity, and needlessly expends their energy' (*JPD* 62).

From a liberal perspective, we can easily see how this is true. Individuals who must be continually vigilant against violent attack must perpetually arrange their lives so as to render themselves less vulnerable. Those who can hide their identity—homosexuals, for instance—are often compelled to do so for reasons of safety. However, those who must wear their identities 'on their faces' have to employ other strategies, such as meeting hostility and harassment with docility and avoiding certain environments altogether (Zutlevics 2002: 101). As in all cases of psychological oppression, when individuals are so compelled by the threat of violence to suppress their authentic identities and limit their self-expression, their resilient autonomy is effaced.

## Conclusion: Misrecognition as Oppression

The analysis of cases of misrecognition establishes that $O_f$ meets its first (and final) criterion of adequacy ($CO_1$): it is reconcilable with the claims of emancipatory movements that social and institutional practices of misrecognition are modes of oppression, since they comprise a system of social and institutional constraints imposed upon social groups that thwart individuals' chances for resilient autonomy. Today in the US, people all around us are oppressed.

Clearly we must desist from practices of misrecognition. The challenge is to determine *how* to do so. How do we reform institutions in order to desist from such practices, and what do we do to people who commit them?

Is new legislation required or, as Iris Young claims, significant restructuring of both public and private institutions (*JPD* 226ff.)? Must we develop deeper moral sensitivity and understanding? Answering all of these questions is beyond the scope of this book. However, as I elucidate the meaning of recognition, I do pursue an answer to the question of how *public recognition* might enable us to desist from practices of misrecognition.

This indicates the first criterion of a theory of recognition adequate to the task of overcoming contemporary oppression:

CR$_1$:  An adequate conception of recognition specifies the means by which acts of recognition undermine or reverse social and institutional modes of oppression; that is, whether through legislation, institutional reform, the cultivation of a different moral understanding that informs social relationships, or other means.

In Chapters 5 through 7, I develop such a conception by appeal to Hegel's theory of recognition. Before turning to Hegel, however, I take up another question: whether desisting from practices of *mis*recognition really does entail extending positive public recognition to social groups.

Chapter 3

# Overcoming Oppression: The Limits of Toleration[1]

*As it is presently interpreted, the established image of equality both masks and justifies the level of prevailing inequalities. It does this by singling out as important certain things—such as abstract political rights and economic opportunities—and by de-emphasizing other things as unimportant, such as the large discrepancies in material well-being that are to be found in contemporary society.*

(*Walter Feinberg*)[2]

A reasonable response by liberals to awareness that social and institutional practices of misrecognition are modes of oppression might be to reassert the principle of toleration. Toleration promises all citizens the freedom to express their religious, moral, and cultural ways of life privately, with the assurance that their differences will be treated impartially in the public sphere. The principle thus aims to sustain peacefully a plurality of ways of life in a political community while securing the legal status of all citizens as equal persons. But toleration turns out to be an inadequate solution to contemporary oppression. Recall, for instance, that in modern liberal democracies widely accepted relationships of moral subordination compromise the effective moral empowerment of socially disadvantaged minorities, undermining their *de facto* status as equal citizens. Differences are said not to matter in public, but we experience them as mattering very much.

The question of how to redress injustices related to problems of difference has occupied liberals for more than three decades. In this chapter, I highlight the influential work of John Rawls and Will Kymlicka. Both treat issues of difference ultimately by appeal to the principle of toleration (*PL* 3; see also Patrick 2000: 29), even though they recommend different approaches; Rawls is committed to proceduralism whereas Kymlicka embraces nonproceduralism. Their approaches are appeals to toleration insofar as they limit their concern to a circumscribed range of differences: religious, moral, philosophical, and cultural conceptions of the good. Both bracket collective identity differences such as race, gender, and sexuality, claiming these involve issues beyond the scope of their immediate concern to make specific advances in liberal theory.

Rawls aims to render 'an account of political and social justice that is more satisfactory' by deriving the basic principles of a truly just liberal society characterized by reasonable pluralism (*PL* xxx). Although he defers issues of gender and race, as well as 'the claims of democracy in the firm and the workplace' (*ibid.*), he is confident that the principles he derives can redress injustices related to these differences, just as '[t]he same equality of the Declaration of Independence which Lincoln invoked to condemn slavery can be invoked to condemn the inequality and oppression of women' (xxxi). To Rawls's mind resolving these issues is essentially 'a matter of understanding what earlier principles require under changed circumstances and of insisting that they now be honored in existing institutions' (*ibid.*).

Similarly, Kymlicka's core objective is to establish the legitimacy of extending special rights to minority cultures in order to secure their freedom to realize their conceptions of the good—especially colonized indigenous groups such as Native Americans and Puerto Ricans, for whom he thinks such justification is readily available. He acknowledges that other cultures—African Americans, women, homosexuals, the poor, the disabled, and refugees—constitute special, more complicated cases (*MC* 19).[3] This diversity of social groups entails that there be a wide-ranging analysis of minority claims to rights: 'Each raises its own distinctive issues, and must be examined on its own merits' (19). Understandably, Kymlicka does not take up in this single work the great diversity of special cases but focuses instead upon the more tractable claims through which he can at least establish the legitimacy of special rights.

I begin the following discussion with an overview of liberal treatments of difference primarily as differences in conceptions of the good, hence as matters of toleration. Because liberals typically frame these issues as concerns for equal dignity, they emphasize neutrality as the means of achieving justice for adherents of minority conceptions. However, proceduralists and nonproceduralists disagree about whether neutrality entails (1) a fundamental 'indifference to differences' (Patrick 2000: 34), or (2) differential treatment of differences in order to bring them into parity.

I then turn to Rawls's and Kymlicka's proposals as exemplars of these two approaches. I examine first Rawls's later theory of justice as fairness modified to account for the 'fact of reasonable pluralism' (*PL* xix). In *Political Liberalism* he argues for a basic political structure that is neutral among reasonable but incommensurable comprehensive moral views, but that secures social stability and promotes inclusiveness by achieving an 'overlapping consensus' on principles of justice by proponents of those views (15). Justice as fairness is also meant to secure citizens' abilities to realize their conceptions of the good by allowing for fair inequalities in social positions. Its principles are to secure for all citizens the chief 'social primary goods' of 'rights, liberties, and opportunities, and income and wealth,' and 'the social bases of self-respect' (Rawls 1999: 54; cf. *PL* 181).

Kymlicka's argument in *Multicultural Citizenship* for a liberal theory of minority rights can be read as a kind of extension of Rawls's political liberalism. In fact, it has been dubbed 'multiculturalism as fairness,' since it inquires into the requirements of justice given, as it were, the 'fact of multiculturalism' (Kukathas 1997: 406). Kymlicka concludes that as some citizens suffer social disadvantages because of their cultural differences, securing equal dignity requires granting some cultures special group-differentiated rights and other protections against discrimination and marginalization.

Both Rawls's and Kymlicka's arguments are compelling and highlight essential components of a successful liberal politics of difference. However, their focus upon differences in conceptions of the good and their political solutions of shoring up public neutrality to protect these differences obscure the manner in which disadvantages still accrue to social differences in ways that perpetuate oppression. I argue that if liberals are committed to ending oppression, we must supplement the political program of toleration, rights, and distributive justice with a social theory that addresses how we can reform everyday social relationships and practices in ways that secure the equal dignity, not only of citizens who endorse different conceptions of the good, but also those who bear different—and socially salient—collective identities.

I conclude this chapter by analyzing some implications of liberal oversights concerning difference. I contend that while liberal theory ought by no means to abandon neutrality, we must re-conceive it as something other than 'indifference to differences' or differential treatment to compensate for disadvantages. I offer an alternative conception of neutrality more consistent with the idea of equal dignity. I then outline the features of a liberal theory of recognition that acknowledges that attention to social attitudes is necessary for an effective liberal politics of difference.

## Contemporary Differences: Matters of Toleration?

The liberal impulse to treat contemporary claims for recognition as issues of toleration is easy to understand once we bracket collective identity differences. Arguably, emancipatory concerns *can* then be interpreted as minority group demands for rights and policies that secure their ability to realize their different but reasonable conceptions of the good. Contemporary demands have been subsumed under the *generalized* principle of toleration, the Enlightenment extension of the original, post-Reformation concept to include not only state non-interference in private matters of faith and conscience, but also state neutrality vis-à-vis religious and moral differences (Galeotti 2002: 26). Generalized toleration is a basis of the liberal distinction between the private and public spheres and, accordingly, between two roles occupied by social members: that of *private individuals* espousing various comprehensive moral doctrines and conceptions of the good, and that of *citizens* united around a set of shared political values.[4] Private individuals are guaranteed freedom to exercise their faith and conscience, but as citizens they can expect one another (collectively, as the state) to remain neutral in their treatment of different moral views, so that no one gains undue privilege or suffers discrimination because of them. Liberals accordingly treat claims of minority groups as matters of securing not only the freedom of private individuals to pursue their different religious, moral, and cultural ways of life—a right that is now more or less taken for granted—but also, and more pressingly, the right of citizens to find their different conceptions of the good treated equally in public.

Both Rawls and Kymlicka advance neutralist proposals that promote equal treatment without entailing the forced assimilation of minority groups to majority conceptions of the good. This is in keeping with the neutralist premise that 'forced homogenization of the citizen body or a simple repression of irreducible differences' is inimical to liberal democracy (Galeotti 2002: 29). However, again, neutralists disagree about what neutrality itself entails: indifference to differences, as the concept is traditionally understood, or differential treatment in order to bring differences into parity.

Rawls and other proponents of what he calls 'neutrality of aim' insist that justice is best secured by treating all citizens equally and fairly regardless of their moral differences (*PL* 193). A politics that acknowledges the fact of reasonable pluralism by seeking an overlapping consensus on political principles, thereby privileging no particular comprehensive moral doctrine over others, can be deemed legitimate by all reasonable members of a liberal polity, especially since such a politics addresses only the most basic principles required to secure rights and social stability. Advocates of neutrality of aim, that is, favor procedural liberalism. If a society wishes to compensate social members for institutionally driven social inequalities, then it must seek some means other than extending special rights to some social groups, since that would violate others' basic right to equal treatment.

By contrast, theorists who think that neutrality requires differential treatment for some citizens to ensure parity maintain that justice does require extending special rights and immunities to certain minorities. They tend to favor nonproceduralism, arguing that achieving social parity is a substantive good to be given due consideration relative to the right. By their lights, 'a liberal society singles itself out as such by the way in which it treats minorities, including those who do not share public definitions of the good, and above all by the rights it accords to all of its members' (*PoR* 59). Thus, while nonproceduralists maintain that basic individual rights must still take precedence over group rights, they nevertheless conceive of both as legitimate. In Taylor's words, 'There will undoubtedly be tensions and difficulties in pursuing these objectives together, but such a pursuit is not impossible, and the problems are not in principle greater than those encountered by any liberal society that has to combine, for example, liberty and equality, or prosperity and justice' (59–60).

Thus, procedural liberals hope to ward off social inequalities by means of a political procedure that can be uniformly applied. Nonprocedural liberals aim to reconcile provisions for special group rights with the liberal commitment to basic individual rights. Both neutralist positions clearly face substantial challenges.

## John Rawls: Political Liberalism

### Toward reasonable pluralism

In *PL* Rawls develops his later theory of justice as fairness, grounded in a thin theory of the good, by employing the procedural device of an original situation of equality confirmed by its amenability to an overlapping consensus. His thin theory of the good specifies the ends thought to be pursued by all reasonable citizens since they all presumably endorse three ideas implicit in the conception of liberal democracy: (1) 'society as a fair system of cooperation . . .'; (2) 'citizens . . . as free and equal persons'; and (3) 'a well-ordered society as a society effectively regulated by a political conception of justice' (*PL* 13–14). Thus, Rawls recommends a system of justice that secures the basic good of citizens subject to the constraint that *rational* principles of political organization, rather than any set of substantive ends citizens may wish to endorse (or 'thick' conception of the good), must govern their deliberations on the principles of justice.

This sets the general terms of Rawls's new original position: 'symmetrically situated' representative citizens assume a 'veil of ignorance' vis-à-vis other dimensions of their comprehensive doctrines and social positions (e.g., their class, religion, sex, ethnicity) in order to derive principles of justice solely on the basis of their rationality and knowledge of general facts about society and human psychology (24–25). Rawls presumes that diverse citizens representing a plurality of reasonable but incommensurable spheres of value can reach a consensus on principles derived through this procedure. The achieved consensus constitutes justice as fairness as both a 'free-standing' liberal politics (i.e., one not grounded in any single metaphysical or ethical doctrine) and legitimate (10; 133ff.). This substantively neutral politics that displays indifference to differences, even as it reflects some components of every reasonable citizen's comprehensive view, should be agreeable to all citizens.

Rawls's concern in *PL* with the 'fact of reasonable pluralism' corrects for his earlier error, in *A Theory of Justice*, of arguing for fairness and social stability ultimately by assuming citizen convergence on a single comprehensive doctrine (his Kantian-inspired contractarian theory) despite his acknowledgment that citizens actually endorse many different, incommensurable, and often conflicting comprehensive views (*PL* xviii). In the more distinctively 'political' rather than metaphysical project of *PL*, Rawls softens his neutralist position and endorses a substantive neutrality (still a neutrality of aim) instead of the strictly procedural neutrality of the earlier work. Now justice as fairness represents a plurality of moral and cultural perspectives rather than a method of *pure* proceduralism that overlooks substantive views entirely (306). Moreover, its perspective is now specific to no one in the sense that its principles presumably can be endorsed universally by reasonable citizens, even if for a number of different substantive reasons. In this way, the overlapping consensus of comprehensive moral doctrines becomes a key to social stability.

The outcomes of the deliberative procedure are two categories of principles of justice. First are principles for the basic structure of society, providing, in order of priority, for (1) the widest scheme of equal basic liberties possible for all citizens and (2) the just distribution of social and economic opportunities (291). Second are principles for individuals, including the duty of mutual respect (Rawls 1999: 95). All of the principles aim at securing the higher-order interests of citizens, including mitigating social injustices by ensuring a fair distribution of the 'chief' social primary goods and social bases of self-respect, which Rawls considers 'perhaps the most important social primary good' (386).

Rawls is confident that a consensus can be reached on these principles, although *demonstrating* it is a challenge. Political liberalism cannot simply be advanced as a *true* doctrine, since the profession of its truth might conflict with many reasonable doctrines (essentially the problem in *A Theory of Justice*); hence Rawls stresses political liberalism's character as a free-standing *political* conception. The principles, he writes, 'might be endorsed—so it is hoped—by all reasonable comprehensive doctrines that exist in a democracy regulated by it' (*PL* 375). This is not a demonstration, then, but a hope.

Invoking the fact of reasonable pluralism also reinforces the political conception of persons as *free*. Rawls observes that citizens, *qua* political beings, conceive of themselves as free in three senses: they possess 'moral power to form, revise, and rationally pursue a conception of the good'; are 'self-authenticating sources of valid claims'; and are 'capable of taking responsibility for their ends' (which 'affects how their various claims are assessed') (30–33). Political liberalism supports the first conception of freedom by acknowledging that an individual's possession of a conception of the good is essential to her freedom, but also that she can revise her favored doctrines over time without compromising her political identity as citizen. It supports individuals' second self-conception, as self-authenticating sources of valid claims, by not dictating political principles to them from above, but rather acknowledging they have their own reasons for both endorsing those principles and making claims against institutions founded upon them. This represents a contiguity of citizens' private and political reasons. Finally, political liberalism supports the third conception of freedom, as moral responsibility, by expecting citizens to be responsive to demands of rationality and reasonability in matters of justice.

## Problems generated by Rawls's approach to difference

At first glance, Rawls's proposals look promising as a means of both maintaining neutrality of aim and securing equal dignity. The theory aims at securing all citizens' chances to realize their conceptions of the good by deriving principles of justice through a procedure that rationally determines them. As a result all citizens are assured equal basic rights, fair equality of opportunity, a minimum standard of living, and the respect of their fellows on the basis of principles they presumably can embrace as both consistent with their reasonable comprehensive doctrines and as expressive of their status as free and equal persons.

However, two problems threaten the viability of political liberalism as a response to contemporary problems of difference. First, while Rawls's deferral of issues related to collective identity differences is certainly justified in light of his articulated aims, it is nevertheless problematic, since it is far from evident that, as he claims, the principles *can* eventually secure *de facto* justice and equality for ethnic minorities, women, and other disfavored groups. In particular, his account of the second principle of justice raises the question of whether social positions not defined in economic terms should also be considered socially relevant (Rawls 1999: 81ff.; *PL* 23ff.). Second, Rawls's similar bracketing of 'the claims of democracy in the firm and the workplace' (*PL* xxx) prompts the question of whether the processes through which social inequalities are generated by the basic economic structure of a presumably well-ordered society need to be addressed explicitly as part of the theory.

## The social and political relevance of collective identity differences

According to Rawls, our prospects for securing justice for bearers of collective identity differences by appeal to the principles of justice as fairness are akin to Lincoln's success in abolishing slavery by appeal to the Declaration of Independence. But the principles of the Declaration did not of themselves motivate emancipation; it required the willingness of citizens to apply the principles to African Americans. Similarly, we have little reason to expect the principles of justice as fairness themselves to secure social justice until such time as citizens willingly apply them and treat all others as equals. But we need an account of how citizens will come to do so.

Rawls rightly assures us that citizens of a well-ordered society will apply the principles, for not only do they have good laws, but they are motivated to apply them. He claims they have a higher-order interest in developing and exercising their sense of justice, meaning, among other things, that 'not only are they normally and fully cooperating members of society, but they further want to be, and want to be recognized as, such members' (81). That is well and good, but we need an account of how we progress from our current social and political practices to the rational standpoint of justice as fairness. How do citizens come to desire being recognized as having a sense of justice? In the absence of such an account, it is difficult to place full confidence in the theory.

For instance, the second principle aims specifically to redress injustices associated with social inequalities. Rawls treats only socio-economic differences as socially relevant because most other differences are the product of natural contingencies (e.g., sex and race) and not generated by the basic structure itself. He defines the least advantaged in society as citizens who either have income and wealth equivalent to or less than that of unskilled workers or who earn less than half the median income of all workers (Rawls 1999: 84). Of course, members of the lower economic classes *are* among the least advantaged in society, but they are not the only ones: the disabled, women, ethnic minorities, gays and lesbians, all of whom may be economically well-off, nevertheless suffer disadvantages because of prevalent social attitudes about their identities. Their disadvantage may not be indicated by *low* income, wealth, or positions of authority so much as by a *lesser degree* of income, wealth, and authority than that enjoyed by comparably talented and motivated members of majority groups.[5] In Rawls's ideal theory this inequity is ruled out, in the first instance, by citizens' guarantee of fair equality of opportunity. But we have in our current society laws and policies to promote fair equality of opportunity. The crucial difference between Rawls's well-ordered society and ours seems to lie in the fact that Rawls's citizens willingly and consistently apply the opportunity principle, whereas members of our society do not.

Rawls's ideal theory must be supplemented by an account of how we can attain the social- and self-understanding citizens of a well-ordered society possess, if we are to have confidence that we, too, may come to apply the principles of justice as fairness. In the interim, we must not rest assured that collective identity differences such as race and gender are *not* socially relevant. The fact of contemporary oppression attests to their relevance. My worry, then, is that our premature acceptance of Rawls's conclusions may actually frustrate our chances of attaining the standpoint of justice as fairness. In this case it *remains* an ideal theory—a hope—and contemporary oppression persists.

The potential for this unfortunate outcome is underscored by the potential inability of Rawls and other members of majority groups to perceive the social and political relevance of collective identity differences, in part because of their different experience of the salience of collective identity. The oversight may even stem, ironically, from a commitment to equal dignity. After all, difference-blindness has been held as an ideal of justice for many decades. But the ability *not* to perceive the social and political salience of collective identity differences may be a product of privilege enjoyed only by members of majority groups.

## The injustice of processes underlying the basic economic structure

A second problem generated by Rawls's theory is that it does not critically assess underlying social practices, including the determining principles and processes of the production of wealth and assignment of positions of prestige (*JPD* 20). Rawls admits that he does not intend to address such concerns, which he places in the same category as issues of collective identity differences—as a matter to be deferred (*PL* xxx). However, in addition to ensuring that all persons have equal access to positions, and that disparities in wealth actually benefit the least advantaged, the representative persons should make explicit that the conditions through which wealth is produced and positions assigned are themselves fair and equitable. Surely the workplace is implicated in the question of justice inasmuch as there must be some basic economic structure. The workplace is the primary domain within that structure through which socio-economic inequalities are generated in the first place.

Workplace democracy would therefore seem to play just as significant a role in securing self-respect as equal rights, the difference and opportunity principles, and mutual respect. Accordingly, it is not unreasonable to require that the representative citizens address explicitly the internal structures and processes of the marketplace. They might ask, for example, whether the hierarchical model of the division of labor is the most just and effective way to structure organizations. Are the jobs that lack prestige usually those that involve no opportunity to define one's own tasks or to share in corporate decision-making? Is that just? To ignore such questions is to ignore potential sources of injustice and oppression.

To illustrate, imagine that I earn the minimum living wage within an economic system in which I am assured that I am not compromised or exploited economically; positions and compensations are arranged so that I, the least advantaged, am never made worse off economically than I currently am. Moreover, there is fair equality of opportunity, so I have received an equitable education and know that many positions are open to me by law. Additionally, my associates practice mutual respect, which entails, among other things, that they are willing to consider my situation from my perspective. I argue that it is nevertheless the case that these principles do not rule out the possibility that my self-respect is undermined by workplace structures and norms.

For instance, I may be employed in a menial job that is only ever assigned routine tasks, such that I have no opportunity to acquire or develop other skills through which I might advance professionally. Moreover, I have no say in how my job tasks may be performed, or whether I can modify procedures to enhance productivity. Procedures are always dictated from above. Furthermore, because of the very nature and structure of organizations such as mine—typically hierarchical and authoritarian—I may be disposed to complacency. Thus even if my superiors were to consult me about my level of satisfaction, I might not express dissatisfaction, not because I am intimidated by these presumably respectful albeit authoritarian superiors (these categories are not inherently contradictory), but rather because I have good reason to believe that expressing dissatisfaction will not improve my position, which looks quite fixed. Thus, a condition in which pervasive organizational structures have a role in limiting my opportunities to cultivate my skills and talents may very likely undermine my self-respect, even if the income I am assured (by the difference principle), the respect of my peers and superiors, and my own acceptance of my situation would seem to secure it. For I may envision and desire a different plan of life for myself but fail to realize it because I have little evidence that such a plan is more than a fantasy. Rather than complain or struggle against this reality, I become reconciled to it.

The workplace—organizational relationships determined by social- and self-understandings—therefore emerges as one of the *sources* of social inequalities to be arranged for the benefit of the least advantaged. If the representatives were to take this idea seriously, the least advantaged might be defined not only in terms of income shares, but also in terms of power and authority shares. Thus, for instance, a menial laborer who exercised some authority in his job, and accordingly broadened his experience, might come to conceive of a wider array of life options as available to him. If so, a tradition of workplace democracy will have nurtured his self-respect.

In a just society, then, shares of power and authority might not be distributed hierarchically, such that the least advantaged would have to pursue higher social positions in order to possess them. Rather, it might ensure the least advantaged a measure of power and authority through democratic organizational structures. Workers could then develop skills and abilities through which to actualize facets of self, whether or not they aspired to other social positions.

## Conclusion: Rawls's political liberalism

Rawls's deferral of issues related to collective identity differences and workplace democracy may tempt us to ignore the social and political relevance of these differences—and this may actually cause us to miss the mark in attaining the standpoint of justice as fairness. His ideal theory ends up treating collective identity differences as the concern of 'private individuals' and not of 'citizens.' However, we *must* acknowledge the salience of collective identity in public life; victims of civilized oppression already possess formal rights and legal equality but are still treated as second-class citizens.

We are left wanting an account of how we can bridge the distance between where our society currently is in its thinking about justice—the very problem that prompted Rawls's construction of his ideal theory—and where we want to go. We need an account of how we prevent negative social attitudes from seeping back into public life even as we endorse justice as fairness. Despite Rawls's confidence that we all have the capacity to deliberate rationally, and *will* in a well-ordered society, he does not tell us how to actualize this implicit understanding we have, how we will come to express the standpoint of these truly rational and noble liberal democratic citizens. This will be one of the distinctive advantages of Hegel's account: Hegel provides us a 'ladder' to this new standpoint.

## Will Kymlicka: Multicultural Citizenship

Kymlicka, like Rawls, sees the liberal ideal of equality as substantially undermined by persistent social and economic injustice. In *Multicultural Citizenship* he pursues a 'comprehensive theory of justice for a multicultural state,' inquiring into the requirements of justice given the fact of multiculturalism (6). He also shares Rawls's conviction that the doctrine of equal basic rights requires supplementation by some measure capable of 'rectifying unchosen inequalities' (109). But Kymlicka extends justice as fairness on the basis of his further conviction that 'justice requires removing or compensating for undeserved or "morally arbitrary" disadvantages, particularly if these are "profound and pervasive and present from birth"' (126, quoting Rawls 1999: 82). He seizes on the latter point and goes beyond Rawls to address the specific problem of injustices related to *cultural* differences.

### Rationales for group-differentiated rights

As a liberal multiculturalist Kymlicka tries to reconcile two commitments: the multiculturalist conviction that cultural differences, that is, *group* differences, are politically salient, and the liberal belief that ultimately only *individual* differences are politically relevant. Accordingly, he conceives the contemporary problem of liberal justice, and that of multiculturalism, as the problem of specifying the political measures necessary to protect individuals against the injustices they suffer because of their group membership. He advocates for group-differentiated rights in order to benefit *individuals* as members of disadvantaged cultures, not to benefit *cultures*, since cultures do not have moral status. He establishes the connection between cultural membership and the need for group-differentiated rights as follows:

1. Individual autonomy is importantly nurtured by cultural membership, such that the survival and recognition of cultures are essential to individuals' full autonomy. (*MC* 83)
2. Some citizens are denied access to their cultures or suffer injustices because of their cultural membership; both of these conditions compromise individual autonomy. (101)
3. Group-differentiated rights can be designed so as to protect members of minority cultures against injustices that compromise their autonomy. (107ff.)

Kymlicka contends that, notwithstanding the provision of basic individual rights for all citizens, the link between the denigration of minority cultures and the compromising of their members' autonomy indicates the 'legitimate, and indeed unavoidable' need to supplement basic individual rights with special 'group-differentiated' rights (6).[6]

Kymlicka suggests that because the doctrine of individual rights presupposes an atomistic ontology and conceives neutrality as indifference to differences, it ignores the necessary function of cultural membership in facilitating individual autonomy. Individual freedom is bound up with cultural membership, he argues, because culture provides the context of meaning in and through which individuals both form their beliefs and acquire a sense of the value of those beliefs and of the courses of action they choose as a result. But Kymlicka ascribes this significance to a rather restricted sense of 'culture' as 'societal culture,' by which he means 'an intergenerational community, more or less institutionally complete, occupying a given territory or homeland, sharing a distinct language and history' (18).[7] A societal culture (and not necessarily a racial, ethnic, or other group), in providing a context of meaning, is politically relevant as a vital 'context of choice' through which individuals develop their capacity for autonomy (82).[8] This context extends 'across the full range of human activities, including social, educational, religious, recreational, and economic life,' and is 'institutionally embodied—in schools, media, economy, government, etc.' (76). The recognition and preservation of these cultural forms of life are therefore essential to citizens' full flourishing as autonomous agents.

We may grasp, from another angle, the significance of culture as a context of choice if we recall Rawls's (notion of the citizen's) conception of freedom as the ability to form and revise conceptions of the good. Kymlicka affirms this conception and suggests that a societal culture is the source of, and the ongoing context in which, individuals form and revise their substantive views and life plans (83). He therefore agrees with other critics that procedural liberalism's strict adherence to neutrality conceived of as indifference to differences, or what he calls the 'benign neglect' of difference (3), in ignoring this crucial relationship between societal culture and autonomy, erects a barrier to freedom for many individuals—in particular, the members of minority cultures.

That is, the 'benign neglect' of culture is a barrier to freedom for *some*, but not *all* citizens. The autonomy of members of a dominant societal culture tends not to be compromised, since these citizens have full access to their culture (109). The dominant culture is widely recognized and embraced. Minority cultures, by contrast, are frequently rendered invisible by procedural neutrality or, worse, misrecognized or rejected. Thus, for example, because English is the only official language in the US—and therefore until only very recently the only language spoken in schools, businesses, government offices, and other public spaces—Native Americans and other indigenous peoples have struggled to preserve their languages, an important component of their societal cultures. As younger generations have been pressured to become increasingly Americanized, native languages have become increasingly marginalized. In light of the fact that indigenous groups were in America long before the English, one might see this particular form of marginalization as definitely unjust. Meanwhile, Anglo-Americans have never faced this barrier to the survival of their culture. In this way we witness how the language of neutrality can obscure the fact that sometimes the neutral stands for the majority, who, accordingly, benefit from presumed indifference to differences. It turns out that this version of neutrality is truly indifferent only to the differences of those who are 'othered.'

The second problem with the doctrine of individual rights, according to Kymlicka, is that its language—concerning rights to freedom of conscience, free speech, and so on—is not sufficiently specific to advise us *how* to address the claims of minority cultures for rights that would grant them full equality: 'The right to free speech,' for example, 'does not tell us what an appropriate language policy is; the right to vote does not tell us how political boundaries should be drawn, or how powers should be distributed between levels of government' (5). Majority groups typically determine such policies, often at the expense of minority group interests (4–5). Thus, while this degree of generality in the doctrine of individual rights is in fact part of its appeal (for the further specification of the content of these rights can also result in greater exclusion), it does mean there is no guarantee that it actually secures equal justice, including the ability of everyone to exercise those very rights provided for. Again, Kymlicka sees this as evidence that if liberal democracies are to be truly just and are truly to secure the greatest measure of freedom for individuals (consistent with a similar freedom for others), the system of basic individual rights must be supplemented by a separate scheme of special group-differentiated rights for minority cultures.

## Kymlicka's proposals for group-differentiated rights

Of course, devising a legitimate scheme of group-differentiated rights is no simple matter. The outstanding feature of Kymlicka's analysis of minority group claims for rights is the careful distinction he makes between 'national minorities' and 'ethnic groups' (6), each of which makes different claims for special rights that have different bases of legitimacy.

A national minority is a cultural group that has at one time been an autonomous nation, that is, a 'societal culture' (11). An autonomous societal culture becomes a national minority through its incorporation into a larger nation in which there is another, dominant societal culture. Native Americans, native Hawaiians, and Puerto Ricans are examples of national minorities (and societal cultures) in the US.

By contrast, Kymlicka means by 'ethnic group' an immigrant culture formed by the voluntary migration of individuals and families into a new societal culture. In the US, European Americans, Asian Americans, and many (but not all) Latin Americans are members of ethnic groups. Their presence in a new societal culture is entirely a matter of choice; thus, *their* societal culture is the dominant culture, their new context of choice and source of at least some facets of their conceptions of the good. Of course, this does not mean that they must passively endure misrecognition of their cultural heritage. Quite the contrary, Kymlicka claims we must clarify the kinds of special rights to which immigrants should be entitled in order to insure their protection against violations of their dignity.

Kymlicka argues that the special rights a minority culture can legitimately lay claim to differs according to the circumstances under which it has come to be part of the dominant societal culture. He identifies three sources of justification for group-differentiated rights. The first is the liberal commitment to equality, and Kymlicka's 'equality-based arguments' for group-differentiated rights cite the necessity of cultural membership, and in some cases group political autonomy, for the autonomous agency and equal status of minority group members (8, 108–115). He thinks, for instance, that equality for members of ethnic groups requires 'equal access to the mainstream culture,' which entails that the societal culture concretely display receptiveness to cultural differences as a counter-measure against committing forms of witting and unwitting discrimination (114). By contrast, equality for members of national minorities, which were at one time fully autonomous within the given territory, entails that they are restored some degree of political autonomy in order to protect their cultures from political and economic endangerment by policies insensitive to their survival needs (109ff.).

A second source of justification, specifically for national minority rights, are the historical terms of their association with the dominant culture. Kymlicka's 'history-based arguments' appeal to national minorities' earlier sovereignty and treaties made with majority cultures for additional justification of their entitlement to special rights and immunities (8, 116–120).

Finally, Kymlicka contends that special rights for minority cultures are legitimated by the intrinsic value of cultural diversity in forming a richer context of free choice for *all* citizens of liberal democracies (8, 121–123). However, because diversity-based arguments appeal primarily to the 'enlightened self-interest' of the majority rather than to the requirements of justice, he acknowledges that they are insufficient to justify group-differentiated rights; rather, they should supplement equality-based and history-based arguments (123).

Just as we may distinguish different sources of justification for group-differentiated rights, so minority cultures may lay claim legitimately to distinct kinds of special rights. *Self-government rights* are pursued legitimately only by national minorities, who were forced to relinquish their original sovereignty as a result of colonization or conquest. That is, political autonomy is not appropriately pursued by ethnic groups, who as immigrants have voluntarily chosen the dominant societal culture as their own and who therefore should, and typically do, seek integration into it (27–30).

However, ethnic groups *are* justified, along with national minorities, in pressing for what Kymlicka calls *polyethnic rights*: typically legal protection against discrimination, certain immunities (e.g., exemption from 'blue laws'), rights to pursue cultural practices in public, and public support for programs that promote cultural appreciation (30–31). Both national minorities and ethnic groups may also pursue *special representation rights* that guarantee seats for their groups within the central institutions of the state (31–33).

Kymlicka therefore thinks there is ample justification for extending different programs of group-differentiated rights to minority cultures. However, to his mind such provisions ultimately are only legitimate, from a liberal point of view, if they do not compromise citizens' basic individual rights. A commitment to liberalism therefore entails placing two limitations on the extension of group-differentiated rights. First, while they are certainly legitimate as means of providing 'external protections' to minority cultures, that is, protection against the potentially destabilizing impact of the political and economic polices of the dominant culture, such protections are not legitimately pursued for the sake of exploiting or oppressing other groups, as, for example, in apartheid (35, 152). Second, minority rights are not justified when they place 'internal restrictions' upon the autonomy of individuals for the sake of preserving cultural traditions—as, for instance, when they endorse illiberal practices such as wife-beating (as an acceptable form of punishment) or compulsory arranged marriages. In other words, liberalism 'requires *freedom within* the minority group, and *equality between* the minority and majority groups' (35, 152).

Kymlicka concludes, then, that it is possible to justify the reconciliation of group-differentiated rights with the traditional doctrine of individual rights. However, special rights are justified, from a liberal perspective, only insofar as they are consistent with liberal autonomy.

## Criticisms of Kymlicka's program

This leads us to perhaps the most frequent objection raised against Kymlicka's argument: that he recommends a solution to the problem of difference that is actually inhospitable to difference since it is intolerant of non-liberal cultures. Kymlicka strongly suggests that non-liberal minority cultures should be 'liberalized' to embrace values such as autonomy (172). But he acknowledges that this is a complex and thorny issue, and he therefore distinguishes two questions: that concerning a liberal state's right to affirm or deny the legitimacy of claims to special rights, and that concerning the authority of a liberal government to impose its values on non-liberal minority cultures (164). While it is perfectly appropriate for liberal states to deny the legitimacy of 'un-liberal' claims to rights, the question of whether or not they possess the authority to impose liberal values on non-liberal minorities depends upon the type of minority. Liberal governments do have the right to 'compel respect' for liberal values from members of ethnic groups, since they have entered the liberal state voluntarily (170). However, they do not have the authority to impose liberal values on national minorities any more than they do with respect to foreign sovereign nations. Here, liberal governments must practice toleration. Nevertheless, a liberal society does have the right and responsibility to speak out against the illiberal practices of non-liberal national minorities and to support members within those cultures who try to reform them from the inside. That is, a liberal society should support the liberalization of such cultures and use whatever means it can to convince them to abandon practices that compromise the autonomy of their members.

Some critics charge Kymlicka with thereby failing to appreciate the 'authentic otherness' of non-liberal cultures (Parekh 1997: 59), but this does not seem entirely correct; for although Kymlicka, as a committed liberal, finds that he must indeed reject on principle practices that compromise individuals' autonomy, he does acknowledge that non-liberal sovereign cultures, including national minorities within liberal states, rightfully retain the authority to continue their 'authentically other' practices (*MC* 165). Thus, while he may not appreciate their otherness in the sense of *valuing* it, he does appreciate it in the sense of acknowledging and accepting it as a real difference that liberals have no right to impose upon. I am not sure that we can ask more of Kymlicka than that.

The problem I see with Kymlicka's emphasis upon autonomy is that he accordingly builds his argument for respecting cultures primarily on their role as a choice-context for individuals. He contends that cultures should be respected mainly because they are the crucial contexts in which individuals develop the capacity for choosing among life options, including the sense of which options it is meaningful to pursue. Kymlicka is correct to observe that nurturing autonomy is one of the great benefits of cultures, but he does not go far enough in accounting for the freedom-fostering function of cultures and presents a limited picture of what cultures contribute to society. We get a better picture—and one that corresponds more fully with liberal ideas of freedom—if we consult the reasons minority cultures themselves seek respect for their cultures.

Minority groups want their cultures respected, not simply as contexts of choice, but more precisely as *legitimate sources of identity*—as legitimate forms of life and styles of agency. The difference, though subtle, is noteworthy: it is the difference between autonomy as the liberty to choose a conception of the good, and autonomy as the ability to be author and addressee of justified claims and to *act* on the basis of such claims—to situate one's purposes in the world. I may enjoy some aspects of my autonomy privately, but when I *actualize* my purposes, they become in an important sense *public.* Minorities seek respect for their cultures because, even in the face of their many contributions to the societal culture, their identities are dismissed as illegitimate and accordingly are denigrated and disrespected to the point that they are oppressed. Moreover, minorities do not cite as the source of their oppression the majority's belief simply that their cultures do not foster choice and autonomy, but rather the majority's conception of their identities, including their modes of embodiment, as *on the whole inferior.* Therefore, to justify respect for cultures primarily on the basis of their choice-fostering role diminishes the full force of emancipatory claims.

In arguing for the value of cultures as legitimate sources of identity, then, I do not mean essentially as sources of a sense of belonging, which Kymlicka argues is a second reason cultures should be respected (89). He appropriately connects the sense of belonging to self-esteem and suggests that cultures should be respected because they are also, ultimately, sources of self-esteem. I agree that they are, but, strictly speaking, minority cultures do not seek respect for their cultural identities because denigration and disrespect undermine their sense of cultural belonging and, hence, their self-esteem. These forces may in fact strengthen their sense of cultural belonging. Rather, they seek respect because the denigration of their cultures has undermined their ability to be resiliently self-actualizing and in *this* respect compromises their self-esteem.

Minority cultures might ground the argument for respecting cultures partly on their status as legitimate sources of identity that inform their agency. That is, cultures *are* valuable as contexts of meaningful choice and a sense of belonging, but also as sources of identity through which individuals *actualize* their autonomy and contribute to societal culture.

## Conclusion: Kymlicka's proposals for multicultural citizenship

In the final analysis, Kymlicka is correct to stress that a program of group-differentiated rights is needed to rectify the social injustices that currently coexist with the liberal commitment to basic individual rights. He also rightly insists that such special rights are only legitimate insofar as they are compatible with individual rights. However, the objective of contemporary claims for recognition is not only to widen the sphere of rights, but also, and perhaps more importantly, to overcome social injustices that result not only from procedural politics (indifference to differences), but also from the majority's tendency to view differences with disfavor. Implicit social attitudes are so significant a source of injustice that it is not clear that even the provision of special group-differentiated rights can guarantee *de facto* equality for members of minority groups. Legal status must be supplemented by robust acknowledgement of the equal legitimacy of different cultures as sources of meaningful agency.

## Conclusion: Accommodating Differences—The Limits of Toleration

Both Rawls and Kymlicka argue vigorously that liberal justice requires addressing the facts of reasonable pluralism and multiculturalism and redressing social injustices that accrue to certain minority groups. They maintain further that procedures to ensure social inclusion and provide for distributive justice or special rights can be reconciled with the doctrine of individual rights. However, both treat the problem of difference as rooted in conflicts over differences in conceptions of the good, comprehensive doctrines, and cultural values. In this respect, they treat difference ultimately as candidates for toleration.

But it is of the utmost importance to see that contemporary conflicts over differences, unlike earlier historical contests that became matters of toleration, do not concern only differences in individuals' conceptions of the good, but also, in some cases, collective identity differences that are viewed with disfavor. Interpreting problems of difference as matters of toleration obscures the manner in which social and institutional practices of misrecognition that target the bearers of 'different' collective identities generate distorted social relationships among individuals and groups that persist despite liberal attempts to secure equal dignity. While the liberal concern with procedural justice and rights directs our thinking to legal status, the *de facto* denial of equal status wrought by social attitudes about identity differences continues to be 'ignored on principle' (Galeotti 2002: 5, 59–60).

A further problem with the model of toleration is that the very notion specifies an asymmetrical relationship—between tolerator and tolerated (20ff.). Issues of toleration emerge when differences are, specifically, *disapproved* of. The party that disapproves, usually the majority, becomes a tolerator when it opts to refrain from interfering with the practices (which it dislikes) of the tolerated and, in cases of generalized toleration, when it further agrees to act neutrally with regard to those differences. The power lies with the tolerator, either to desist from interfering or to persist in it, and either to act neutrally or to discriminate. The tolerated, by contrast, are in a position of relative passivity. But to the extent that political authorities in liberal democracies essentially represent majority groups, they for all intents and purposes advance the perspective of the majority, even when they purport to adopt the stance of neutrality.

Toleration is therefore not an unquestionable model for securing equal dignity. In fact, interpreting the problem of difference as an issue of toleration not only fails to address the problem fully but may actually exacerbate it. Insisting upon public indifference to differences in a social context in which differences nevertheless emerge as remarkable and therefore continue to be the target of social injustices, and in which majority cultures actually benefit from this indifference, allows social injustices associated with difference to persist, even to escalate. However, pursuing neutrality as differential treatment fares no better: for in a context in which identity differences are viewed with disfavor, such that those identities become both rooted in and circumscribed by distorted and oppressive relationships of misrecognition, programs of group-differentiated rights may offer valuable protections but may also generate resentment that leads to other forms of social injustice. How often do we hear that affirmative action unfairly privileges unqualified minorities, who steal the jobs of better qualified members of majority groups? Neither approach to neutrality, then, offers a reasonable guarantee that minority cultures will win *de facto* equality.

However, this does not mean we must abandon the ideal of neutrality altogether. Instead we need a different conception. Rather than conceive of neutrality either as blindness to differences or as the endeavor to compensate for disadvantages that accrue to the 'different,' we might think of it as the commitment to treating all cultural ways of life as equally legitimate insofar as they are sources of agency that contribute to collective social life. Genuine neutrality requires abandoning conceptions of majority identities as 'normal' and of minority identities as 'different' in favor of envisioning all cultures that are present and contributing to collective life as in some sense 'normal' (see also Galeotti 2002: 15). It requires allowing these different ways of life to be equally visible, not rendering some of them invisible or marginalized. On such an interpretation, a liberal state's commitment to neutrality means not only that it will not tolerate discrimination against individuals on the basis of their collective identities, but also that it will *positively promote* the equal inclusion of those identities.

Genuine neutrality would entail, for example, not deeming a student's decision to honor his culture by wearing a bolo tie as something remarkable, much less punishable. It would also entail conceiving of affirmative action, not as a thumb on the scale for minorities and women, but rather as the effort to optimize organizational performance by guaranteeing qualified individuals from diverse backgrounds fair and equal access.

Because this alternative conception of neutrality suggests the need to acknowledge differences in some positive sense, it points us in the direction of what scholars have been calling the *recognition* of differences. We might say, accordingly, that recognition involves, in the first instance, acknowledgment of the legitimacy of different ways of life, such that the bearers of identities labeled 'different' enjoy *de facto* equality. Let us call this the first provisional definition of recognition:

$R_{p1}$: *Recognition is acknowledgment of the legitimacy of different ways of life.*

The alternative conception of neutrality also indicates the second criterion to be met by a conception of recognition adequate to the task of overcoming oppression:

$CR_2$: An adequate conception of recognition elucidates how acts of recognition embody the notion of liberal neutrality as the commitment to treating different ways of life as equally legitimate.

I will argue that securing the equal dignity of all citizens entails that their collective identities enjoy public recognition in precisely this sense, since this is required to ensure them equal opportunities for resilient autonomy.

There is good reason, then, to think that the liberal discussion of rights and redistribution must be supplemented by a liberal social theory that features recognition. Such a theory would analyze the reasons underlying the problem of unjust social relations between citizens whose identities are considered the 'norm' and those who are designated 'different,' those facets of everyday social life that ultimately undermine liberal equality, justice, and freedom. I will argue, following Hegel, that what largely determine the quality of social relations among citizens are both their self-understanding and their understanding of others, which extend beyond the reach of strictly political procedures and special rights provisions. Greater attention by liberal theorists to the social implications of attitudes about difference—in which it is liberal ideals that are ultimately at stake—will surely advance this discussion and move us closer to a workable solution.

From this point on, I highlight the role a theory of recognition can play in a viable liberal politics of difference. The conception of recognition I develop will involve an appropriation of Hegel's theory and an analysis of the distinctive function of recognition in his theory of ethical life, since I take Hegel to have presented the most compelling portrait of a liberal society capable of securing freedom for its citizens. Before turning to Hegel, however, I adduce further evidence that public recognition is necessary to overcome oppression.

Chapter 4

# Beyond Toleration:
# Toward a Concept of Recognition

*Let me share with you how Sister Audrey would often introduce herself. She would say, 'I'm Audrey Lore [sic], a black woman, lesbian, feminist, poet, professor, mother.' And then she would say, 'I am all of that.'*

(Johnnetta Cole)*

*Due recognition is not just a courtesy we owe people. It is a vital human need.*

(Charles Taylor)*

The idea that social justice requires thinking beyond rights to consideration of the social conditions necessary to sustain just political institutions is not new. An impressive number of theorists, including liberals like John Rawls, have argued precisely that.[1] Many of them agree further that despite problems associated with the idea, extending some form of public recognition to the bearers of 'different' identities is a necessary condition of social justice. This thesis has become increasingly compelling in light of arguments by Axel Honneth and Charles Taylor that individual identity and freedom are conditioned by intersubjective recognition.[2] Both Honneth and Taylor advance versions of Hegel's social freedom thesis that individual freedom is socially mediated, since the formation and actualization of practical identity depend upon the freedom and recognition of others.

Whatever intuitions we have concerning the social freedom thesis, much perplexity surrounds the notion of recognition. This is partly because even given the abundance of theorizing about it, the meaning of recognition is usually assumed and not explicitly defined. For care ethicists, for instance, the term 'recognition' designates relationships of love and concern, whereas for discourse ethicists it often means acknowledgment of the 'particularity and equality' of discourse participants (*RMO* 18). Honneth's and Taylor's arguments are particularly helpful, however, in that they illuminate two crucial features of recognition: (1) the content of a meaningful notion of *public* recognition and (2) the processes through which citizens can extend it meaningfully to one another. In this chapter, I explore their idea, also advanced by Hegel, of a crucial continuity between private and public forms of recognition, since public forms are a natural and logical outgrowth of private ones and informed by them. Honneth and Taylor both follow Hegel in arguing that while identity is *forged* in the private sphere of primary relationships with significant others (e.g., partners, parents), it is further *secured* and *actualized* in public life, through relationships of legal respect and civic solidarity.

This continuity becomes evident if we follow Hegel, Honneth, and Taylor in seeking the justification of recognition not only as potential grantors of recognition, but also as self-actualizing subjects. That is, the shift in perspective from grantor to beneficiary of recognition perhaps makes clearer how our need for recognition extends continuously from our most intimate relationships to an ever-widening circle of intersubjective relations. If we can agree that the self-understanding and capacity for agency we acquire in primary relationships inform our interactions with others in the public realm, then adopting the perspective of the self-actualizing subject illuminates not only the meaning of recognition and its relationship to freedom, but also the nature of the social processes through which we meaningfully and legitimately extend it.

Honneth's and Taylor's arguments smooth the way for my later treatment of Hegel's notoriously dense discussions of recognition in the *Phenomenology* and *Philosophy of Right*, in part because both theorists appropriate Hegel's earlier Jena theory of recognition, expounded in the *System of Ethical Life* (1802/03) and the *Jena Lectures on the Philosophy of Spirit*, or *Realphilosophie* (1803–1806). In the following, I preface my analysis of Honneth's and Taylor's arguments with an overview of Hegel's early recognition theory in order to supply indispensable background for grasping the force of their versions of the social freedom thesis, for perceiving the interrelation between private and public forms of recognition in the project of self-actualization, and for considering the role of struggles for recognition in facilitating social progress. Turning subsequently to Honneth and Taylor, I find they reinforce my preliminary conception of public recognition as acknowledgment of the legitimacy of different ways of life ($R_{pl}$). However, closer evaluation of their proposals reveals that essential features of an adequate concept of recognition are missing from their accounts. I therefore must look beyond them for a viable concept.

# Hegel's Early Jena Theory of Recognition

In the *SEL* and *Realphilosophie* Hegel develops a theory of individual and societal development as fueled by struggles for recognition. An important impetus of recognition theory was his resolve to overcome both the abstract formality of Kantian notions of autonomy and the increasingly influential atomistic conception of the individual (*NL* 59ff., 64ff.). Accordingly, Hegel aimed to bridge the gap many falsely presumed to obtain between rationality and actual human experience, and to account for the formation of society out of a state of nature without depicting individuals as originally isolated. Inspired by accounts of the integrated social and political life of the ancient Greeks, Hegel envisioned the ideal society as likewise a unified community of 'ethically integrated' citizens, an 'ethical totality', their integration embodied in their customs and mores [*Sitte*] (*SEL* 102). For Hegel, neither formal legislation nor individuals' private morality is sufficient to ground freedom. Rather, freedom requires the cultivation of shared social understandings and attitudes expressed in customarily ethical (*sittliche*) intersubjective relationships. Still, an ideal community must also secure individual rights, so ethical life must also incorporate a legal system. Combining these features, Hegel conceives of society as a unity of universal and individual (objective and subjective) freedom.

## Hegel's system of ethical life

Hegel appropriates both Fichte's theory of recognition and Hobbes's concept of a struggle for self-preservation in his theory of societal development in the *SEL*. Conceiving of the state of nature as 'natural *ethical* life,' in order to stress the original interrelatedness rather than isolation of individuals, Hegel portrays subsequent stages of society as developing naturally out of this original condition toward an enriched 'ethical totality' (*SEL* 99–102; my emphasis). Most importantly, he shows how a simultaneous process of socialization and individuation—a growth of society and increase of individual freedom—results from this 'budding of ethical life' (*NL* 115).

In *Foundations of Natural Right*, Fichte had posited recognition as the relation of reciprocity between individuals implicit in all legal relations: as the 'common consciousness' manifested when individuals mutually 'summon' each other to 'act freely' while 'limit[ing] the sphere of those actions that [are] possible' for themselves for the sake of that other's free agency (2000: 41–42). Applying Fichte's conception to his own account of developing ethical life, Hegel conceives of its stages in terms of intersubjective relationships involving interaction partners, each of whom discovers himself as recognized by the other—that is, as worthy of the other's self-limitation—in virtue of certain of his own traits and abilities. These recognitive encounters, stabilized (temporarily) by the achievement of mutual recognition, foreground each subject's status as a particular individual, a distinct member of the community with certain acknowledged traits. At the same time, each relationship is itself revelatory of a dimension of selfhood of which subjects first become cognizant: for example, implicit in legal relations is the notion that individuals are entitled to make claims—they have rights. Subjects' awareness of each new dimension of selfhood motivates them to pursue confirmation (recognition) of that status and thus propels them toward the development of new stages of social life.

Thus is set in motion the unfolding of ethical life via a progressive cycle of 'reconciliation and conflict' among members of a community (*SR* 17). The relation entails conflict because of the ways, often unconscious, in which individuals pursue confirmation of their status. The particularity of individuals' claims, either explicit or implicit in their words and deeds, offend the established norms and self-understanding of the community, provoking the latter to resist.[3] To develop his account of conflict, Hegel appropriates Hobbes's notion of struggle. However, because Hegel portrays the stages of ethical life as relations of mutual recognition that are subsequently upset, rather than as various competitions over interests, he describes the conflicts as struggles for recognition rather than as struggles for self-preservation.

The development of society toward the integrated totality of ethical life proceeds through three general stages facilitated by individuals' efforts to satisfy their survival needs and confirm their evolving self-concept: the establishment of (1) familial bonds (*love*); (2) legal contractual relations and socio-economic cooperation among heads of households/property owners (*law*); and (3) an ethical state that, as the rational codification of the social order, secures their rights and well-being (*ethical life*). Love involves the recognition of 'practical feeling,' realized in intimate relationships between mature adults and between parents and children, who recognize each other mutually as biological, emotionally needy beings (*SEL* 102–116). They cultivate family life through the cooperative development and use of labor, tools, and language, which at the same time facilitate individuals' self-actualization. For example, the labor of child-rearing, while supplying dependent children's needs through loving care, simultaneously equips them for independence, which eventually supersedes the 'unification of feeling' (*SEL* 118). However, labor also facilitates individuals' development beyond this initial stage since it is implicated in the generation of private property.

The stage of love, then, passes naturally into that of law, which features recognitive relations among property owners as heads of households. Here, individuals' practical engagements are 'wrenched from their merely particular conditions of validity and transformed into universal, contractually established legal claims' (*SR* 18). They now recognize each other mutually as rightful claims-bearers. Through their contractual exchanges, they come to identify themselves as capable of *choosing* to accept or reject proposals and as not entirely determined by their biological needs. Thus legal status also represents the freedom to be 'the opposite of [themselves] with respect to some specific characteristic' (*SEL* 124). The needy concrete individual now becomes a claims-making *universal* (undetermined) person. However, only a limited advance is made toward self-actualization, since in being recognized publicly only as a universal legal person the individual's particularity goes unrecognized. Hegel maintains that society does not progress to ethical life until individuals *reclaim their particularity* and integrate it with their self-conception as universal persons.

The reclaiming of particularity begins when the stability of legal relations is upset. Here individuals, either explicitly or only implicitly 'aware' of new dimensions of their identities, assert claims that take the form of 'transgressions' (129). Hegel describes each offense as a reaction to the abstract, 'indifferent' character of the freedom achieved in legal contractual relations—a negation of the indeterminacy of formal laws (*ibid.*). He does not elaborate upon the motives of transgressors, but we may surmise that transgressors test the boundaries of legal relations by asserting their authority to violate them in particular circumstances—when the *need* arises, as it were—expressing an impulse to integrate particularity with the universal character of law. Insofar as the act transgresses established relations of mutual recognition under the law, it sets in motion a struggle—of the transgressor for recognition of his right of particularity (to meet his particular need even if it violates the law) and of the victim for the integrity, not merely of his rights as a recognized legal person, but of his '*whole* person' (137), his entitlement to both rights and needs.

The various modes of transgression compel communities to create positive laws and institutionalized customs and practices, and thus to enter the stage of integrated *ethical life* (142). In much the same way that mutual recognition generates individuals' awareness of their particularity, the transgression of mutual recognition stimulates consciousness of their dependence upon relations of intersubjective recognition. Hegel describes ethical life as characterized by 'mutual intuition,' meaning that 'each individual intuits himself as himself in every other individual' (144).[4] Individuals affirm one another's identities through recognitive relationships grounded in mutual concern and interest, thereby both supplementing and securing their merely formal contractual relationships. The result is their realization of ethical totality, wherein they 'mutually recognize one another as persons who are dependent on each other and yet also completely individuated' (*SR* 24).

Missing from the *SEL* is a detailed elaboration of the precise motives of individuals, explained from their perspective, in initiating conflicts. Hegel supplies this fuller articulation in the *Realphilosophie*, marking the beginning of his transition to the speculative philosophy of consciousness through which he derives the categories needed for a more complete account of struggles for recognition.[5]

## The Realphilosophie

Hegel's *Realphilosophie* covers the same social development treated in the *SEL*, but now his concern is the evolution of modes of consciousness as individuals are socialized. The focus is now on the progression of *consciousness*, from its cognition of objects to its awareness of self as totality, that is, as a 'unity of singularity . . . [and] universal multiplicity' (*FPS* 212), of particular individuality and universal personhood.[6]

As one example of this process, in *Realphilosophie II* Hegel depicts a dialectical development that first brings the subject to awareness of himself as a producer of 'the world' in cognition (as intelligence) and subsequently as a practical agent in work (as will). When the underlying truth of labor appears as the subject 'making himself into a thing' (*HHS* 103), it becomes evident that the subject can grasp his nature *as consciousness* only through an intersubjective encounter with another human. Here that other is woman, who embodies the passive mode of consciousness Hegel calls 'cunning' (104). Conveniently, then, he can portray the will as 'divid[ing] itself' into two shapes—masculine and feminine. We now have a natural intersubjective relationship—sexual desire—that has been explained in terms of modes of consciousness. Furthermore, when sexual love develops into mature love, each subject 'knows itself likewise in each other' in a mutually recognitive relationship of trust (107).

The goal of the *Realphilosophie* corresponds to that of the *SEL*: the actualization of an ethical totality. Viewed from the perspective of the subject, mutual recognition now designates relationships through which the subject attains cognitive awareness of *its* status as a totality, which finally occurs, Hegel says, when it 'recognizes itself as the totality that it is in another such totality of consciousness' (*FPS* 236), that is, when another subject whom it recognizes as possessing a certain self-understanding demonstrates that it likewise perceives the first subject as such an individual. Struggle is entailed by the fact that only through mutual provocation can individuals, who perceive themselves in each other, know that these others who mirror themselves back to themselves are likewise a totality—the only condition in which subjects obtain confirmation that they are themselves truly a totality. Hegel explains:

> [T]hat my totality as the totality of a single [consciousness] is precisely this totality subsisting, on its own account, in the other consciousness, whether it [my totality] is recognized and respected, this I cannot know except through the appearance of the actions of the other against my totality; and likewise the other must equally appear to me as a totality, as I do to him. (237, N. 46)

Here, as in the *SEL*, the interaction is prompted by the subject's awareness of a new dimension of her identity in each stage of mutual recognition, which makes her 'ideally' (or conceptually) a new totality. The subject pursues affirmation of this new self-concept by making a claim that provokes another, and now it is clear why: the reaction of the other to this provocation is the gauge by which the subject measures the accuracy of her new self-concept. When, finally, subjects establish recognitive relationships in which they are indeed able to intuit themselves as themselves in every other individual, they effectively grasp their own nature as totality, as a unity of particularity and universality.

In both the *SEL* and the *Realphilosophie*, then, Hegel reveals intersubjective recognition to be the ground of both individual self-actualization and social progress toward ethical life. Furthermore, his account makes plain that public forms of recognition are logically dependent upon private forms. Subjects establish legal relations to secure private needs for property, and ethical life to secure not only legal rights but also well-being through mutual concern and interest. These core ideas re-emerge in Honneth's formal conception of ethical life, in Taylor's arguments for recognition, and in Hegel's later theory of recognition in the *Phenomenology of Spirit* and *Philosophy of Right*.

## Axel Honneth's Critical Social Theory of Recognition

Honneth's interest in developing a social theory grounded in recognition was, he says, a natural consequence of his earlier conclusion, reached in

*The Critique of Power*, that social theory needed a philosophical account of 'morally motivated struggle' (*SR* 1). He found inspiration in Hegel's early Jena texts, 'with their notion of a comprehensive "struggle for recognition,"' perceiving in them a central concern with intersubjective recognition (*ibid.*). However, he believed Hegel abandoned this focus upon intersubjectivity when he became preoccupied with the speculative analysis of consciousness. He therefore dismissed Hegel's *Phenomenology* theory of recognition, opting instead to naturalize the early theory of the *SEL* and the *Realphilosophie*.[7] In more recent essays, 'Recognition and Moral Obligation' and 'Grounding Recognition: A Rejoinder to Critical Questions,' Honneth draws out the moral implications of these findings and offers a more precise formulation of his concept of recognition.

My discussion of Honneth's recognition theory begins with his reconstruction and naturalization in *The Struggle for Recognition* of Hegel's early speculative theses, in which he appeals to the social psychology of George Herbert Mead, object-relations psychoanalytic theory, and modern historical developments to ground Hegel's theory empirically. The result is Honneth's 'social theory with normative content' grounding his own 'formal conception of ethical life' (*SR* 1). He posits struggles for recognition as the driving force of emancipatory conflicts aimed at securing both individual freedom and societal progress. Individuals' normative expectation is that these struggles will culminate in the three modes of mutual recognition Hegel identified—on Honneth's formulation, 'love, law, and solidarity'—through which they can cultivate, in private and in public life, the corresponding 'practical relations-to-self' ('basic self-confidence, self-respect, and self-esteem') required for full autonomy and self-actualization (*SR* 76, 92ff., 128–131). Accordingly, Honneth argues that corresponding forms of disrespect, or *mis*recognition—violence, the denial of rights, and the denigration of ways of life—constitute moral injuries, giving evidence that recognition is a moral obligation and a requirement of social justice.

Next, I examine Honneth's later elaborations, in 'Recognition and Moral Obligation' and 'Grounding Recognition,' of the status of recognition as a moral requirement. I then explore the implications of Honneth's more 'precise and general' conception of recognition (*GR* 499) for our understanding of both the concept and the possibility of public recognition.

## Honneth's naturalization of Hegel's early recognition theory

Three core theses of Hegel's early work ground Honneth's critical social theory. First, identity formation, understanding oneself as an 'autonomously acting, individuated' self, presupposes mutual intersubjective recognition (*SR* 68). Second, individuals experience a sequence of recognitive relations—love, law, and ethical life—in which they increasingly reinforce each other's self-conceptions as autonomous and individuated persons. Third, that sequence of relations represents a logical development fueled by moral struggles. In Honneth's words, 'In the course of their identity-formation and at their current stage of integration into the community, subjects are, as it were, transcendentally required to enter into intersubjective conflicts, the outcome of which is the recognition of claims to autonomy previously not socially affirmed' (68–69).

Thus Honneth appropriates from Hegel the idea that the formation and continued actualization of practical identity occurs through an agonistic developmental process that begins in an individual's private experiences of mutual recognition (i.e., love) and progresses logically through an expansion of recognitive relationships (i.e., law and ethical life) in public life. Because I am concerned mainly with highlighting the necessity of both private and public recognition for freedom, I concentrate mainly on the second and third theses. I combine them into the following formulation:

> Identity formation and full self-actualization require that individuals experience sequentially three forms of recognitive relationship—love, legal status, and solidarity within an ethical community—the attainment of which is mediated by intersubjective struggles.

Honneth finds this thesis empirically confirmed by G. H. Mead's social psychology, but especially by object-relations theory and historical developments. He posits all three forms of recognition—love, rights, and solidarity—as stations on the way to full freedom, since each is the necessary condition for the development of the self-confidence, self-respect, and self-esteem required for self-actualization (128–129). Because recognition is accordingly a legitimate normative expectation, individuals react to failures of recognition with feelings of moral indignation (if they think others are at fault) or shame (if they blame themselves) (136ff.). Emancipatory struggles for recognition originate in these feelings of moral indignation at being 'disrespected' (misrecognized) in three ways corresponding to the modes of recognition: being the target, respectively, of violence, the denial of rights, or the denigration of a way of life. Moreover, Honneth views collective emancipatory struggles as facilitating, not only opportunities for individuals' self-actualization, but also social progress toward a more just society—toward ethical life.

**Love and basic self-confidence**

Honneth observes that Hegel's characterization of love as the 'being of oneself in another' (*SEL* 110) highlights a significant feature of healthy love relationships: that in them partners to interaction strike a balance between dependence and independence. Recall in particular that Hegel posits familial love as the first form of mutual recognition, insofar as family members acknowledge each other as individuals with needs. As parents meet the needs of their dependent children they simultaneously facilitate their independence. Honneth notes that object-relations theory stresses similarly that the cultivation of feelings of love in early childhood involves an agonistic process through which children and their primary caregivers mutually achieve a relationship characterized and sustained by a balance between 'symbiotic self-sacrifice and individual self-assertion' (*SR* 96).[8] He interprets this account as one in which the love between 'mother'[9] and child emerges as the most primary, agonistically achieved relationship of mutual recognition. The two begin in a symbiotic state, but as the child develops it learns to identify its own needs *as* its own and to assert them communicatively. The parent and child's concurrent, agonistic processes of 'ego-demarcation' and 'ego-dissolution,' their experiences of independence and mutual dependence, culminate in the mutually recognitive relationship of love, perceiving each other as independent beings with needs (101–107).

The child's ability to sustain this delicate balance of dependence and independence in mutual love is the basis not only of its basic self-confidence as an autonomous agent, but also of its ability to cultivate additional relationships of mutual love and friendship with a wider circle of others. Basic self-confidence equips one to enter the world certain of one's ability to communicate one's needs to other autonomous agents in ways that provoke their willing responses. One learns not merely to *manipulate* others' behavior, but rather to *harmonize* one's needs and actions with those of others. This latter thesis is confirmed by G. H. Mead, who suggests that by the time children progress to participation in competitive, rule-governed games, they are prepared to integrate the norms and action-expectations of a whole group, that is, a 'generalized other' (*SR* 77). They allow rules of interaction to govern their behavior, evidence of their sensitivity both to the efficacy of their own agency and to the needs of others. Thus the primary experience of mutual love lays the foundation for their cultivation of mutually recognitive relationships in the public realm: in Honneth's words, 'it constitutes the psychological precondition for the development of all further attitudes of self-respect' (106–107).

Honneth claims that just as the legacy of emotional recognition is confidence in one's efficacy in harmonizing one's desires with those of others in order to meet one's needs and preserve one's bodily integrity, the denial of emotional respect can cause one to lack basic self-confidence. This can happen in early childhood or at some later time, such as when an adult becomes the target of physical violence, which erodes his sense that he can 'coordinate [his] own body' (132). Honneth describes acts of physical violence (e.g., rape and torture) as the 'most fundamental sort of personal degradation' in virtue of the lasting psychological damage victims may suffer as a result (132–133). His analysis therefore corroborates Young's thesis that violence is a mode of oppression that can (but does not necessarily) constitute the virtually complete unmaking of a self.[10]


## Legal status and self-respect

Drawing upon Mead's analysis of socialization, and in particular of property relations, Honneth describes individuals' capacities for mutual legal recognition as proceeding from their ability to integrate the perspective of the generalized other. Mead explains that if, for instance, I proclaim, 'This is my property, I shall control it,' I presuppose 'an organized attitude with reference to property which is common to all the members of the community'; thus I both expect and do elicit 'normal' responses that 'must be the same in any community in which property exists' (1962: 161). Legal relations presuppose a shared understanding of norms, and being accorded legal status means one is recognized as a morally responsible person who understands and is willing to conform to those norms.

Conversely, the individual with legal status expects to have her own claims acknowledged and respected, not just by significant others, but by the community in general. In Honneth's words, 'Rights are . . . the individual claims about which I can be sure that the generalized other would meet them' (*SR* 79). Thus he agrees with Rawls that legal recognition is the primary basis of self-respect, conceived of now as an individual's own acknowledgment of her status as a morally responsible agent and bearer of rights.

Honneth also cites historical evidence of both the necessity of legal status for autonomous agency and of its achievement through struggle. Our very association of legal recognition with autonomy and right is, he claims, a distinctively modern achievement that could 'only emerge in the course of a historical development,' namely, the transition from 'tradition-bound' to 'post-traditional law' (108). He cites the eighteenth-century decoupling of the notions of respect and social esteem from the traditional notion of honor as the source of our contemporary sense of the value of self-respect; for only in the wake of Enlightenment challenges to the notion of class-bound honor did the idea of respect for persons, owed to all in virtue of our universal humanity, gain currency. Furthermore, because Enlightenment thinkers argued convincingly that 'persons' are capable of self-legislation and must be self-legislating in order to be free, they inspired revolutions that culminated in the according of legal status to all citizens equally.[11] Thus the expansion of rights resulted from struggles for recognition.

But Honneth observes further that the modern association of personhood with *recognizable* claims-making capacity has facilitated further historical expansions of legal rights, insofar as it has called attention to both the background conditions required for the exercise of that capacity and our changing notions of who counts as 'persons.' He cites sociologist T. H. Marshall's thesis of a three-phase historical expansion of basic individual rights since the eighteenth century: *basic individual rights* were emphasized and developed in the eighteenth century, *political rights* (participation rights) were expanded in the nineteenth century, and *social rights* were emphasized in the twentieth century. All emerged as a result of pressure from marginalized groups and appealed to the same normative principle employed in the original justification of individual rights: 'the moral idea that all members of society *must have been able* to agree to the established legal order on the basis of rational insight, if they are expected to obey the law' (*SR* 117; my emphasis). Thus political and social rights came to be institutionalized because marginalized groups argued convincingly that they were denied the requisite *preconditions* for 'equal participation in a rational agreement,' most notably 'a certain social standard of living' (117).

The assurance of legal status through rights has therefore become a basis of self-respect inasmuch as rights signify a community's affirmation of individuals' moral accountability and commitment to ensuring their opportunities for political participation.[12] By contrast, being denied rights constitutes an injury to self-respect.[13] It amounts to denying one's dignity as human and one's moral responsibility. In particular, it 'deprives one of . . . the cognitive regard for the status of moral responsibility that *had to be so painstakingly acquired* in the interactive processes of socialization' (134). This latter observation throws light on the magnitude of such an injury when it is motivated, not by the targeted persons' voluntary lawlessness or disregard for social norms, but rather by community contempt for their *non*-voluntary social group membership.

Because legal recognition acknowledges only an individual's status as a 'person' like all other persons, Honneth maintains, as did the early Hegel, that this leaves an important dimension of selfhood—particularity—unrecognized in the public sphere. In Honneth's words, because before the law 'one necessarily shares the capacities thus entailed with all of one's fellow citizens, one cannot yet, as a legal person, relate positively to those of one's characteristics that precisely distinguish one from one's partners in interaction' (80). In Hegel's terms, this deficiency means that individuals will inevitably struggle to 'recover' their particularity, to have it publicly recognized as well.

**Solidarity and self-esteem**

Honneth sees Hegel as having argued that individuals, in order to experience their 'whole persons' as recognized and free, must enjoy not only familial love and legal status, but also public recognition of their personal capabilities and traits. Honneth therefore distinguishes the social life of the ethical community from the domain of formal law. The law features the universal humanity of persons, but social esteem requires 'a social medium that must be able to express the characteristic *differences* among human subjects in a universal and, more specifically, intersubjectively obligatory way' (122). Social esteem, that is, presupposes some normative standard whereby differences are acknowledged not only as 'worthy,' but also as in some sense necessary for the community's success and flourishing. Individuals are therefore encouraged to make their special contributions and thereby win recognition.

Therefore, just as Hegel argued that individuals need to find themselves unified with an ethical community that shares mutually acknowledged laws, customs, and norms, Honneth claims that individuals require the experience of solidarity within a community of shared values in order to be socially esteemed and to develop self-esteem, their own sense of the worth of their particularity. Solidarity is necessary, he explains, because 'self and other can mutually esteem each other as individualized persons only on the condition that they share an orientation to those values and goals that indicate to each other the significance or contribution of their qualities for the life of the other' (121). Thus, 'solidarity' designates the existence of a shared evaluative framework (122).

As with legal status, Honneth adduces historical evidence that self-esteem is necessary for self-actualization and is achieved through struggle. He sees the de-coupling of the concepts of respect and esteem from that of honor as also giving birth to new social conceptions of esteem. Premodern individuals only earned the measure of honor appropriate to their social class, determined by birth and accorded on the basis of their conformity with class standards. Honneth therefore observes that in traditional, 'corporative' societies, in contrast to his (and Hegel's) notion of ethical life, the esteemed qualities of individuals were 'not those of a biographically individuated subject but rather those of a culturally typified status group' whose value was indexed to its collective contribution to social welfare (123). In corporative societies, *groups* were recognized in their particularity, not *individuals*. Individuals therefore still had a developmental task.

The problem is that moderns still associate esteem with social status—with group membership—even if status is not indexed to birth. Honneth observes that when groups are the beneficiaries of social esteem, asymmetrical relationships tend to form among them that motivate struggles for recognition (123). In Chapter 3 I noted that asymmetrical social relations based on distinctions between 'normal' and 'different' identities are a source of social injustice. Of course, an asymmetry of external relationships does not entail that the relations are unjust. But in modernity *struggles* for status are more prevalent than quiet acceptance of social rankings, since individuals typically strive to achieve or sustain high social status. Struggles ensue partly because members of higher classes resist upwardly mobile individuals. In Honneth's words, they 'try to deny non-members access to the distinguishing features of their group, in order to monopolize long-term chances for high social prestige' (124).

However, Honneth notes that although corporative understandings of esteem are still largely with us, they have been transformed such that they impel individuals to pursue the developmental task of reclaiming their particularity. With the concept of 'human dignity' came the idea that *all* persons are valuable. However, since what is valued are only shared human features, not distinctions, modern individuals struggle for recognition of their uniqueness: 'persons can *feel* themselves to be "valuable" only when they know themselves to be recognized for accomplishments that they precisely do not share in an undifferentiated manner with others' (125; my emphasis). Post-conventional moderns also believe that individual achievements, as well as social class, determine personal distinctness and worth. Accordingly, the concept of prestige, the social esteem a person garners by virtue of her particular contributions to social welfare, has replaced that of honor. But, Honneth stresses, individuals win prestige through their conformity with 'society's *abstractly* defined goals,' since the 'value-horizon' of most post-conventional societies is largely undefined (126; my emphasis).

The notion of prestige therefore generates a tension, because *some* particular value system must determine the bases of prestige. What is to be the content of that value system, and who is to determine it? Honneth says we may interpret contemporary *struggles* for recognition as struggles of marginalized groups for inclusion of their values in the value-horizon of the larger society—that is, along with the majority's values, which dominate that value-horizon. To the extent the marginalized succeed, they participate in determining societal goals and standards that are the bases of social esteem; they partly determine how their contributions to society will be evaluated.[14] Emancipatory struggles for public recognition can clearly be seen, then, to be struggles for *self*-determination.

However, Honneth detects a problem: collective movements for recognition of cultural values will likely result in the recognition of groups rather than of individuals (128). Social esteem, then, may be barely distinguishable from class honor. On the other hand, he argues, *within* groups individuals can, on the basis of their solidarity, express esteem for each other's contributions to social welfare. Moreover, because their contributions are at the same endeavors to realize their own life plans, the esteem individuals garner for them plainly supports their self-actualization.

However, Honneth acknowledges that the very esteem nurtured by group solidarity may be compromised when nonmembers denigrate the group's way of life. Being treated as 'inferior or deficient' undermines one's confidence in the value of one's contributions (134). Denigration leads to feelings of worthlessness. Again, the magnitude of this insult is disquieting: attributes such as ethnicity, sex, and sexual orientation do not determine individuals to fail to contribute to society. The fact that members of those groups do contribute means they are the targets of *arbitrary* insults and humiliation (because some others just happen to dislike those identities) that effectively thwart their chances for self-actualization and full social membership.

### Recognition as a moral requirement

Honneth has so far advanced a compelling argument for mutual recognition. Hegel's speculative proposals, corroborated by social-psychology and historical evidence, suggest that intersubjective recognition grounds not only individuals' self-actualization, but also society's progress towards ethical life, a society in which citizens find themselves both respected as legal persons and esteemed as distinctive contributors to societal welfare. Moreover, practices of misrecognition are unjust because they constrain self-actualization: '[U]nless one presupposes a certain degree of self-confidence, legally guaranteed autonomy, and sureness as to the value of one's own abilities, it is impossible to imagine successful self-realization, if that is to be understood as a process of realizing, without coercion, one's self-chosen life-goals' (174).

If practices of misrecognition are unjust, then recognition is a moral requirement. In 'Recognition and Moral Obligation,' Honneth derives the moral requirement of recognition from the 'anthropological premise,' established in *SR*, that humans are morally vulnerable because their identity formation depends on practical relations-to-self that they only acquire intersubjectively (*RMO* 37–38). Accordingly, he defines morality as 'the quintessence of attitudes we are mutually obligated to adopt in order to secure jointly the conditions of our personal integrity,' namely, the recognitive attitudes of love, moral respect, and solidarity (28–30). The range of our moral obligations—the range of persons to whom we owe recognition—is determined by the nature of each recognitive relationship. Only moral respect is owed by all persons to all others equally. Love and care are owed only to persons with whom we share an affective bond. Similarly, we owe solidarity only to the more local communities of value of which we are members (30).[15]

Honneth acknowledges, moreover, that these different duties may conflict in concrete situations. In such cases, individuals must assume responsibility for resolving the tension. However, the universal character of moral respect places a normative restriction on decision-making: moral respect must always take precedence over love and solidarity since 'we have to recognize all human beings as persons who enjoy equal rights to autonomy,' and we must never choose courses of action that result in the violation of such rights (33).[16]

Honneth further clarifies the moral character of recognition in 'Grounding Recognition.' Recognition is distinctively *moral*, he explains, because it involves action in which, in Kant's words, 'the representation of a worth [or value': *Wert*] . . . infringes upon my self-love' (1996: 56, n. 2). This echoes Fichte's and Hegel's ideas of recognition as finding another worthy of one's own self-limitation. A human *value* compels us to determine our actions non-egoistically. Accordingly, Honneth concludes: '[T]he reason why acts of recognition must be moral acts is that they are determined by the value or worth of other persons; acts of recognition are oriented not towards one's own aims but rather toward the evaluative qualities of others' (*GR* 513).

By 'evaluative qualities,' Honneth means those dispositions or attributes of individuals that are the object of valuation by others.[17] Those attributes compel recognition. Honneth delimits three such attributes, or 'sources of morality,' corresponding to the three modes of recognition he identifies as actually specified 'in our lifeworld,' or shared culture: (1) *singularity*, or physical integrity, the value of an individual's well-being that is the object of love; (2) *autonomy*, or the value of rational and moral agency that is the object of rights and respect; and (3) *particularity*, the value of individual capability, the object of solidarity (511–513). These evaluative qualities and the modes of recognition accorded them constitute the core normative content of Honneth's critical social theory. Members of a just society *ought* to recognize one another's singularity, autonomy, and particularity.

### Conclusion: Honneth's concept of recognition

Honneth admits that in *SR* he presented only his 'vague intuitions' about recognition rather than a 'precise and general' conception (*GR* 499). Now, in *GR*, he clarifies the fundamental concept underlying all three modes of recognition:

> [W]e are to understand 'recognition' as a behavioural reaction in which we respond rationally to evaluative qualities that we have learned to perceive [in human beings], to the extent to which we are integrated into the second nature of our lifeworld. (513)

This formulation of the concept is meant to capture five features. First, recognition is a *behavioral* reaction: Honneth stresses its character as an *action* and not only a perception or judgment (505–506). Second, recognition is a *response* to an already present *evaluative quality* that is at the same time an *attribution* of that very quality (506ff.). Such a claim raises several questions, not the least of which concern the ontological status of such a quality and how a response to a quality already present can be at the same time an attribution of that quality. With regard to ontological status, Honneth endorses moderate value realism, according to which the qualities—for example, autonomy—are not conceived as objectively existing values ('substances') in humans. Rather, they are judgments made on the basis of 'lifeworld certitudes,' the shared interpretive and normative frameworks of a society, its space of reasons (507–508). As for recognition's Janus-faced character, Honneth means it in the same sense that the early Hegel does: recognition is one's acknowledgment of a certain evaluative quality—of a judgment that can be made concerning an individual—an acknowledgment that *actualizes* that quality, brings it about that the recognized individual affirms that judgment herself and expresses it as part of her identity.[18] In this way, recognition is an according of status that facilitates an individual's self-actualization.

The third feature of recognition Honneth's definition highlights is that it is a response to qualities we have *learned* to perceive insofar as we have been socialized into a culture. Again, it is not a reaction to objectively existing values but rather to perceptions of dispositions and behaviors individuals have come to interpret consistent with societal norms. Related to this, recognition is, fourth, a *rational* response insofar as the grantor of recognition affirms those evaluative qualities that the culture has come to acknowledge as embodying freedom (508–509). That is, Honneth acknowledges that the affirmation of evaluative qualities varies across times and cultures; he sidesteps relativism by positing a notion of progress according to which we can judge that 'dominant norms of recognition' are those that have universal validity because they further freedom (517). For example, it is rational for twenty-first-century Westerners to value moral autonomy, but not medieval class-based honor, as a basis of recognition. Finally, Honneth stresses that recognition is a distinctively *moral* action, because it is a *normative* response to *evaluative* qualities. Simply put, there are social norms for acknowledging individual traits, abilities, behaviors, and so on. It is rational to acknowledge those that further and embody freedom. Therefore, we *ought* to acknowledge them.

Honneth therefore urges us to comprehend contemporary struggles for recognition, whether between private individuals or between social groups, not merely as competitions for goods or for the securing of material interests, but rather as fundamentally moral endeavors of individuals and groups to win acknowledgment of their identities as the kinds of subjects that they both have come to see themselves as being through earlier mutually recognitive relationships with others, and wish to actualize consistent with the notion of freedom. Their self-actualization depends upon their ability to cultivate basic self-confidence, self-respect, and self-esteem, but they can only develop these relations-to-self in the context of relationships in which they are accorded recognition of their singularity and physical integrity, autonomy as rational and morally accountable persons, and particularity as distinctive contributors to the life of a community. Accordingly, Honneth concludes, 'The forms of recognition associated with love, rights, and solidarity provide the intersubjective protection that safeguards the conditions for external and internal freedom, upon which the process of articulating and realizing individual life-goals without coercion depends' (*SR* 174). In addition to offering a clear conception of recognition, Honneth has illuminated the crucial fact that a continuity exists between private and public forms of recognition; both are required for genuine freedom.

## Charles Taylor's Politics of Recognition

Hegel's and Honneth's influences are apparent in Taylor's landmark essay on multiculturalism, 'The Politics of Recognition'—for instance, in Taylor's assertions that 'our identity is partly shaped by recognition or its absence, often by the *mis*recognition of others,' and that 'due recognition is not just a courtesy we owe people . . . [but] a vital human need' (*PoR* 26). In this section, I review Taylor's elucidation of the meaning of recognition and evaluate his proposal for a form of public recognition facilitated by inter-cultural dialogue and culminating in a Gadamerian 'fusion of horizons': a form of mutual perspective-taking through which individuals cultivate greater self- and mutual understanding (67; Gadamer 1989: 306–307).

   The strong conception of recognition that Taylor entertains in 'The Politics of Recognition,' in response to (as he understands it) the demand of postmodern multiculturalists for recognition of the equal value of dif-ferent cultures, is fraught with difficulties that have been the target of numerous attacks. However, notwithstanding the question whether Taylor has accurately represented the demand, I contend that critiques of his response that assume he endorses such a strong form of recognition actu-ally express precisely Taylor's stance: that the demand to recognize the equal value of actualized cultures is misguided, as are any attempts to meet it. A better alternative is to pursue recognition of the equal human *potential* present in all cultures, a thesis I take Taylor to elaborate more fully in an earlier essay titled 'Comparison, History, Truth.'[19] There he elucidates the full process through which fusions of horizons occur. By reading Taylor's two texts together, we may see more clearly why he maintains that the idea of a fusion of horizons illuminates the possibility of a viable form of public recognition.

### The politics of recognition

Taylor begins 'The Politics of Recognition' by noting, as Honneth does, the significance of the eighteenth-century decoupling of the notions of respect and social esteem from the concept of honor. He highlights that the result is the modern conception of humans as possessing universal *dignity* and individual *distinctness*. Accordingly, the traditional desire for honor has evolved into the modern desire for acknowledgment of one's dignity as an equal rational and moral person and one's distinctness as an authentic, *self*-realizing individual.

With regard to the recognition of individuals, then, Taylor agrees with Honneth: individual dignity is best secured by the provision of equal rights, a form of *public* acknowledgment, whereas individual authenticity is importantly facilitated by *private* recognitive relationships of love and caring with 'significant others' (*PoR* 36).[20] In particular, he endorses the idea that identity is not only *forged* dialogically through intimate recognitive relationships—the 'crucibles of inwardly generated [i.e., authentic] identity'—but also *sustained* by them over a whole life, since their influence 'continues within us as long as we live' (33, 36). So far, this view corresponds neatly to the ideal of toleration: individual dignity is secured by equal rights, whereas individual distinctness and authenticity are recognized privately.

However, *group* demands for recognition have now emerged proclaiming that these traditional modes of acknowledgment do not adequately secure freedom for all social members. Many are treated unjustly because of their distinctness, which Taylor notes, 'has been ignored, glossed over, assimilated to a dominant or majority identity,' forms of misrecognition that constitute 'the cardinal sin against the ideal of authenticity' (38). In fact, Taylor grants that given the dialogical character of ongoing identity formation, the denial of public recognition to some individuals, through 'the projection of an inferior or demeaning image' of them, may indeed be a 'form of oppression' (36). The demand for public recognition of these groups is therefore legitimate. The question is how to recognize collective identities.

Taylor reasons that two forms of group recognition are possible, corresponding to the two dimensions of personhood acknowledged by modernity: recognition of their equal dignity and their distinctness. He suggests that recognition of group dignity amounts to an acknowledgment of the 'universal human potential' present in all cultures, that is, 'the potential for forming and defining one's own identity . . . as a culture' (42). However, he sees emancipatory movements as making a more forceful demand for recognition of their *distinctness*, the 'accord[ing of] equal respect to actually evolved cultures' (42). He makes this more challenging demand the focus of his analysis. He treats two examples: (1) claims by national minorities, such as the Québècois in Canada, for special rights and immunities to secure their cultural survival against the homogenizing effects of assimilation; and (2) demands by minority groups for acknowledgment of the equal value of diverse cultures, which has figured prominently in the recent debate over multicultural education.

Since I have already addressed, in Chapter 3, the issue of special rights for national minorities,[21] I concentrate here on the latter claim for public recognition of the equal value of different cultures. Taylor observes that the expansion of the canon of Western classics to include contributions by women and minority cultures has been promoted as a counter measure against the 'demeaning picture' marginalized groups are given of themselves by the exclusion of their contributions—'as though all creativity and worth inhered in males of European provenance' (65). He interprets this as an *immediate* demand to recognize the *a priori* equal validity and value of all cultures. He acknowledges that the demand has some legitimacy, especially given the prevalence of attitudes such as that he attributes to Saul Bellow: 'When the Zulus produce a Tolstoy we will read him' (quoted in *PoR* 42). Taylor remarks that the cultural arrogance of such claims smacks of the fundamental denial of human equality essential to cultural imperialism; majority cultures 'entrench their hegemony by inculcating an image of inferiority of the subjugated' (*PoR* 66). He sees proponents of multicultural education as arguing for recognition of the equal value of different cultures in order to reverse the oppressive effects of cultural exclusion. Taylor supports the idea of according positive significance to cultural identities, because this seems entailed by the liberal commitment to equal dignity: in this case, 'we give due acknowledgement only to what is universally present—everyone has an identity—through recognizing what is *peculiar to each*. The universal demand powers an acknowledgement of specificity' (39; my emphasis). But he considers the demand for *immediate* recognition of the *a priori* equal value of actualized cultures to involve, problematically, 'something like an act of faith' (66). To recognize cultures meaningfully would seem to require that their accomplishments be *appreciated*, hence, examined and evaluated so that their genuine value can be comprehended.[22] Simply to posit their equal value would seem to be as presumptuous as merely positing their inferiority and would be equally a failure of recognition.

Therefore Taylor seeks a solution that lies 'midway between the inauthentic and homogenizing demand for recognition of equal worth, on the one hand, and the self immurement within ethnocentric standards, on the other' (72). Perhaps the most reasonable path to genuine cultural appreciation begins with the presumption of the equal value of cultures that have 'animated whole societies' over time, since they presumably 'have something important to say to all human beings' (66). Note that this is a normative claim: Taylor is suggesting that, at the very least, we should recognize the equal human potential inherent in diverse cultures, an idea consistent with the principle of equal dignity. To do otherwise would seem ethnocentric, marginalizing and excluding others solely on the basis of what is in truth a limited understanding.

By contrast, beginning with the presumption that other cultures have something valuable to offer, we open ourselves to the possibility of increased understanding. In this case, Taylor recommends engaging in intercultural dialogue aimed at achieving a fusion of horizons. In such an encounter we acquire 'new vocabularies of comparison' that inform our judgments of different cultures (67). We may discover much to admire in them, even if we also find much to reject. The important thing is that we will have broadened our understanding such that we can legitimately test our initial presumptions. Only from this enriched standpoint can we evaluate cultural differences meaningfully.

Taylor correctly stresses the importance of intercultural dialogue in resolving conflicts concerning cultural differences. A number of critical theorists, inspired by Habermasian discourse ethics, have similarly emphasized the value of reasoned, respectful dialogue.[23] However, the brevity of Taylor's discussion of fusions of horizons in 'The Politics of Recognition' has made him the target of several objections. For example, Anike Schuster (2006) worries about who 'we' are who are approaching cultures to be studied. If 'we' are distinct from 'them,' there is a potential problem. The distinction perpetuates dichotomistic thinking, which tends to undermine mutual understanding and recognition. A minority culture conceived of as distinct from the national culture is patronizingly treated as a remarkable object and marginalized in the very process of so-called recognition. Schuster is right to note by caveat that positing a distinction between 'us' and 'them' is hardly avoidable, since, after all, there *is* a difference to be cognitively grasped, hence a subject who studies a culture that is the object of study. Nevertheless, both concerns about cognitive exclusion (e.g., not *thinking* of African American culture as American culture) and exclusive objectification (e.g., treating Native American culture merely as a 'remarkable' object) are valid worries.

A second problem with Taylor's account as presented so far is that it is not yet clear that a fusion of horizons does not amount to an effort to assimilate the other culture to sameness. One of the dangers of trying to *understand* the other is that we may seek to apprehend otherness solely through our own categories—in fact, even if we broaden our perspectives by appropriating aspects of the other's perspective, the resulting understanding is still ours. It would seem, then, that the pursuit of a fusion of horizons might cause us to overlook the fact that the other may be *irreducibly* other.

Furthermore, the irreducibility of difference would suggest that a culture's worth does not lie in its ability to speak to all humanity, for non-members may not be able to comprehend much of what makes a culture valuable to its members.[24] And surely many Western cultural products do not speak to all humanity—Descartes' *Meditations* may not 'speak to' a Tibetan Buddhist, for instance—but they are nevertheless valuable and important to many Westerners for good reasons. These more 'local' reasons, once communicated, might form the proper basis of others' recognition, not the presumption that they have universal appeal. In this case, what is recognized is not the equal value of different cultural products to *everyone*, but rather the equal *legitimacy* of different cultures as valuable forms of life for members.

At this point I must note that Taylor addresses these very problems in earlier essays (to which he directs readers). I call special attention to 'Comparison, History, Truth' in which, among other things, he elaborates more fully the process of achieving fusions of horizons.

## Clarifying the sense of a 'fusion of horizons'

Taylor addresses 'Comparison, History, Truth' to comparative studies scholars, who, he observes, share common 'zones of puzzlement,' including issues of comparison itself:

> How does the home culture obtrude? Can we neutralize it altogether, and ought we to try? Or are we always engaged in some, implicit if not explicit, comparison when we try to understand another culture? If so, where do we get the language in which this can be nondistortively carried out? If it is just our home language, then the enterprise looks vitiated by ethnocentrism from the start. But whose language, if not ours? And isn't the language of science 'our language'? (*CHT* 147)

Taylor observes insightfully that the first step in approaching another culture is to reflect on the manner of approach. Are we adopting a neutral stance? Is that possible? Is it desirable? Self-examination is crucial for scholars, because our stock in trade is rational and reflective discourse. Our language *is* science.

But our desired goal—understanding a different culture—may not be fully accessible to us in our home language. We may require new vocabularies.

Is there any role, then, for our own language and understanding? Taylor cautions against thinking we must bracket our language and understanding and seek neutrality. Adopting the view from nowhere may be appropriate in the natural sciences, but in the human sciences, which aim to make human beings intelligible, our practical understanding of human agency 'sets the forms and limits of intelligibility' (149). We *must* therefore employ it. If our goal is indeed a *fusion* of horizons, we must bring our own horizon to the encounter.

Our home language and understanding are our media of interpretation, but our objective must be to broaden that understanding by accessing the other culture in a way that 'englobe[s] the other undistortively' (151). We accomplish that by inviting the other culture to present itself in its own language, on its own terms. Taking up aspects of the language and understanding of the other culture, we acquire necessary tools of comprehension. This does not mean we abandon our own perspective. Quite the contrary, if we try to interpret the other culture solely through *its* language and understanding, we undercut a vital source of critical reflection; we have only adopted a new position without illuminating it (Taylor 1995c: 117). Our aim is to achieve an understanding of the other that is mediated by our home understanding.

Thus our objective is to engage in dialogue and, in the process, to reflect critically upon our own culture as well as that of the other—to take note of contrasts that emerge. Ideally, these contrasts compel us to make explicit the assumptions, purposes, and motives underlying our own practices. In Taylor's words, 'we place the strangeness opposite some piece of our lives . . . and we go to work on it to make sense of this difference' (*CHT* 152). Taylor calls this dialogue the 'language of perspicuous contrast,' one outcome of which should be a robust sense that ours is just one way of being in the world, even if we have, upon reflection, good reasons to consider it more effective for certain purposes than other ways (1995c: 125). However, another outcome should be a greater sense that others do things differently for *reasons* of their own. What was formerly completely unintelligible to us may now begin to be, at the very least, comprehensible.

A third outcome of dialogue may be our awareness that a different cultural practice seems strange or unintelligible to us only because we have fixed a characterization of it that blocks understanding: 'Sometimes the way we place it impedes our understanding. Our location reflects some limit we can't get around, which would have to be overcome to understand it' (*CHT* 152). Taylor cites the example of our understanding of magic. Social anthropologist J. G. Frazer categorized magic as a practice aimed at controlling events, analogously to the way we use technology. On this interpretation, magic is a faulty and confused 'technology' that erroneously posits causal relations among superficially connected forces and events. Frazer therefore dismissed magic as an archaic practice reflecting a primitive and inferior knowledge of the world.

But Frazer misunderstood magic. Taylor urges that if we instead first articulate and then question our presuppositions about unfamiliar practices and invite practitioners to explain their motives and purposes in their own terms, we gain access to the intelligibility of their practices. We may learn that magic is not a 'technology' for its practitioners but a way of interpreting or expressing moral significance. Now we begin to comprehend:

> These people no longer seem just wrong, inferior to us in knowledge. Now there are things they know how to do, perhaps ways to come to terms with and treat the stresses of their lives, ways we seem to have lost and could benefit by. The balance of superiority is not all on one side. (153)

By placing the other cultural practice differently through dialogue, we not only render the practice intelligible but may also appreciate its effectiveness in achieving the purposes at which it is actually aimed. We may not resort to practicing magic, but we may comprehend its benefits as a creative means of resolving moral problems. Accordingly, a fusion of horizons liberates both us and the other, who is now released from 'a demeaning or contemptible picture of themselves' (*PoR* 25; *CHT* 164).

Thus when Taylor recommends that 'we' study cultures that have been misrecognized, he means we should engage in intercultural dialogue that culminates in a fusion of *two* horizons. From *our* perspective, as members of one culture seeking to understand another in order to cease misrecognizing it, our objective is to reach an undistorted understanding. Recognition is possible, not because we find the other to be like us, but because we grasp the other culture's significance and legitimacy rendered intelligible to us partly in the other's own terms and partly in ours. A bridge to understanding has been erected, but there remain contrasts in both our respective practices and understandings. What has changed is that now we can acknowledge 'two goods where before we could only see one and its negation' (*CHT* 163).

In light of the 'irreducible otherness' of the other culture, it is also worth noting that Taylor does not suggest that intercultural dialogue will be non-agonistic, involve error-free transmission, or culminate in complete understanding. Because we must approach the other through our home understanding, breaking through to that other understanding may be difficult. Moreover, even if we do break through, it is still mediated by our understanding. Thus we may find that we still distort the other, in which case we should continue dialogue: 'We must try to identify and place in contrast the new limit, and hence "let the other be" that much more effectively' (150).

The crucial point is that we have checked our original understanding of the other culture, through which we misrepresented and misrecognized it. But we have also enhanced our self-understanding (149). Ultimately, Taylor thinks that liberal democracies as a whole benefit from the diversity of *mutually* recognizing representatives of different ways of life: 'Since each life can only accomplish some small part of the human potential . . . we can benefit from the full range of human achievement and capacity only if we live in close association with people who have taken other paths' (1998: 153).

## Conclusion: Taylor's concept of recognition

Starting from the thesis that individual identity is importantly shaped dialogically, Taylor explores the crucial question of the meaning and possibility of the public recognition of cultural distinctness. His investigation leads him to distinguish four kinds of recognition: of (1) individual dignity; (2) individual distinctness, or authenticity; (3) cultural dignity; and (4) cultural distinctness. The first two are unproblematic insofar as individual dignity and distinctness are secured by basic individual rights and private forms of recognition, respectively. However, when these aspects of personhood are compromised by social and institutional misrecognition of cultures, we may argue for public recognition of cultural dignity and distinctness. Taylor argues for three kinds of public recognition: (1) the *a priori* presumption of the universal human potential located in cultures, in order to acknowledge their equal dignity; (2) the extension of special rights and immunities to certain national minorities to secure the survival of their cultural distinctness; and (3) the *a posteriori* acknowledgment of the equal value of cultures in their distinctness, comprehended through intercultural dialogue.

Taylor rightly contends that the demand, by contrast, for recognition of the *a priori* equal value of cultures is misguided. However, arguably proponents of multicultural education do not seek that form of recognition. They seek the abolition of institutional practices that misrepresent, marginalize, exclude, and denigrate the identities of minority cultures. They do not ask majorities to make strong evaluative judgments *moreover* of their cultural practices. Quite the contrary, they likely agree with Taylor that the demand for *a priori* recognition of equal value makes no more sense than demanding 'that we find the earth round or flat, the temperature of the air hot or cold' (*PoR* 69). But then neither do they seek patronizing nods of approval or grudging concessions that they are as good as the majority.

Rather, the push for multicultural education seems to be, at least partly, a demand for acknowledgment of the *fact* that modern Western liberal democracies are the very product of diversity—our national cultures are themselves the result of the creative agency of many different groups including, but not limited to, Western European, Christian, heterosexual, able men. The contributions of all groups should be duly acknowledged, but, more importantly, no groups should suffer injustice, especially given what they have contributed to society *by means of* their differences. Therefore the important question to bring to the study of other cultures is not whether these cultures are equally valuable but *to whom* they are valuable and *why*. Are these groups part of *our* collective culture and, in fact, valuable to us even though we do not acknowledge this? And can those groups convince non-members of the value to members of facets of their cultures that may not 'speak to' non-members? Still, we need not pose any of these questions to recognize the *legitimacy* of other cultures. Our commitment to equal human dignity is reason enough to acknowledge the human potential inherent in other cultures and therefore to accord them equal basic respect—and this may be all they ask.

Underlying the three forms of public recognition that Taylor endorses is a conception of recognition as *acknowledgment of the legitimacy (dignity) and, through dialogue, the value (distinctness) of diverse forms of life*. This is the foundation of a viable notion of public recognition and the core idea of recognition I take emancipatory movements to advance.


## Conclusion: Toward a Concept of Public Recognition

Hegel's, Honneth's, and Taylor's arguments concerning the relation between recognition, identity, agency, and self-actualization corroborate my thesis that recognition is a necessary supplement to rights in overcoming contemporary oppression. Far from treating differences with indifference or as disadvantages to be compensated, all three suggest that in a just society, citizens positively acknowledge the legitimacy, and perhaps over time the value, of differences. They have not only argued convincingly the need for recognition, but also affirmed my alternative notion of neutrality and corresponding preliminary conception of recognition ($R_{p1}$) as *acknowledgment of the legitimacy of different ways of life*.

I conclude this chapter by critically evaluating Honneth's and Taylor's proposals in order to clarify further the central features of a viable concept of public recognition. First, I integrate their perspectives into a somewhat more refined preliminary conception ($R_{p2}$). Then I address two difficulties in their accounts that compel me to look beyond them for a more adequate conception.

Honneth's definition of recognition may be reformulated as follows:

$R_{H}$: *Recognition is a rational response to evaluative qualities (singularity, autonomy, and particularity) that we have learned to perceive (as conducive to freedom) insofar as we have been socialized into a culture.*

From Taylor, we have the following:

$R_{T}$: *Recognition is acknowledgment of the legitimacy (dignity) and, through dialogue, the value (distinctness) of diverse forms of life.*

Integrating the two with $R_{p1}$, I modify my provisional conception of recognition:

$R_{p2}$: *Recognition is an act expressing social members' acknowledgment of the legitimacy of the singular, autonomous, and particular ways of life (dignity and distinctness) of individuals and cultures.*

This is a general conception that covers both private and public forms of recognition. Public forms, of course, do not acknowledge the singularity of individuals (private forms do), but rather their autonomy and particularity, their rational and moral accountability (dignity), and their worth as contributors to the life of a community (distinctness). A provisional conception of public recognition would therefore be:

$R_{p3}$: *Recognition is an act expressing social members' acknowledgment of the legitimacy of the autonomous and particular ways of life (dignity and distinctness) of individuals and cultures.*

However, there are two notable problems in Honneth's and Taylor's treatments of recognition. The first concerns Honneth's claim that while individuals' autonomy (rational and moral accountability) can be recognized publicly by a whole society, collective identities can only be recognized more locally, within particular communities of shared value. The second concerns Taylor's mere supposition of our motivation to pursue intercultural understanding. Both Honneth and Taylor leave unanswered the question of how a society, as a whole, can come to recognize cultural differences.

Recall Honneth's suggestion that because the recognition of cultures tends to result in the recognition of groups rather than individuals, this pursuit is practically indistinguishable from the pursuit of class honor. Intra-group solidarity, by contrast, is clearly distinguishable from the system of honor. However, intra-group solidarity is not an adequate solution to individuals' need for public recognition of their distinctness. Honneth has noted but not answered a core concern of emancipatory movements to secure marginalized groups against denigration by majority groups. Moreover, minorities seek inclusion of their cultural values in the shared value-horizon of their society as a whole. As Honneth observes, in the absence of recognition from the wider society, marginalized groups are still vulnerable to having their ways of life denigrated insofar as they are disfavored by majorities whose values stand in for the value-horizon of the community. The result is the persistence of an asymmetry that often culminates in oppression. Integrating the diverse value systems into a single shared value-horizon is challenging but necessary.

On the other hand, Taylor's intercultural dialogue proposal promises a solution. Here is an account of how social members not sharing some values in common may come to appreciate the legitimacy of each other's forms of life. The problem is that Taylor's account presupposes, and does not explain, their motivation to pursue fusions of horizons. Not all will be moved by the claim that recognition is a vital human need.

To achieve a concept of recognition that can secure collective identities against contemporary oppression, I first challenge Honneth's assumption that solidarity can only be cultivated within local communities of value and not on the basis of a shared value-horizon of a whole society. Drawing upon Taylor, we might say that one evaluative quality of cultures is the universal human potential found in them. In this case, we simply acknowledge the legitimacy of all cultures as sources of identity, and in this respect as conducive to freedom.

I have already suggested that emancipatory movements seek precisely this form of recognition of their legitimacy as sources of identity. However, they also seek acknowledgment of their legitimacy as sources of identity *through which they contribute to collective life*. We therefore need an account specifically of how a whole society can affirm, in solidarity, the dignity *and* distinctness of diverse cultures as sources of identity through which their members both are self-actualizing and contribute meaningfully to collective life. Accordingly, a third criterion of an adequate conception of public recognition has emerged:

CR$_3$: *An adequate conception of public recognition indicates the means by which a whole society affirms, in solidarity, the dignity and distinctness of cultures— their legitimacy as sources of identity through which they contribute to collective life.*

The desired concept will accordingly suggest how diverse cultural values can be integrated into the shared value-horizon of the larger society. I contend that CR$_3$, and the other criteria I specified in Chapters 1 and 3, are satisfied in Hegel's later theory of recognition developed in the *Phenomenology of Spirit* and applied in the *Philosophy of Right*. Hegel reveals how and why a society can, in solidarity, come to embrace difference as a shared social value.

Chapter 5

# Hegel's Theory of Recognition in the *Phenomenology*: Recognitive Understanding and Freedom

*[H]ow we conceive of ourselves determines how we conceive of others, and vice versa. If we conceive of ourselves as self-identical, and we conceive of identity as opposed to difference, and we conceive of anything or anyone outside of the boundaries of ourselves as different, then we will conceive of anything different or outside of ourselves as a threat to our own identity . . . Hostile relations will lead to hostile actions, and the result will be war, domination, and torture . . . [I]t is important to examine and diagnose our self-conceptions as they affect our conceptions of others and relationships, and our actions toward and in them.*

*(Kelly Oliver)**

*It is the self-awareness of individuals which constitutes the actuality of the state.*

*(Hegel)**

I have argued that emancipatory demands for recognition should be understood as legitimate claims for public recognition of different identities, with recognition understood provisionally as:

$R_{p3}$: *An act expressing social members' acknowledgment of the legitimacy of the autonomous and particular ways of life (dignity and distinctness) of individuals and cultures.*

Insofar as minority groups are not recognized in this sense, but rather are targets of systemic *mis*recognition, they are oppressed. Recognition is therefore indicated as a means of ending oppression.

Arguably, it is comparatively easy to acknowledge the legitimacy of individual and cultural expressions of autonomy (rational and moral accountability, or responsiveness to reason-giving). But how do we assess the legitimacy of particularities? How, in their ordinary interactions, do social members decide whether distinctive cultural practices promote freedom or undermine it? Hegel offers a compelling answer in his *Phenomenology* theory of recognition. Reading the *Phenomenology* as centrally concerned with epistemology, I follow Hegel in conceiving recognition not primarily as a mode of valuation, but as crucially dependent upon a kind of knowing—an understanding of the nature of identity. I call this knowledge *recognitive understanding*, subjects' awareness of both (1) their universality as rational and moral 'persons' and members of a community with shared norms and (2) the particularity of all their actions and judgments. Subjects who attain recognitive understanding acknowledge that conscientious expressions of particularity promote freedom. Recognition just is an act affirming this understanding and is in *this* way acknowledgment of the *distinctive* evaluative (freedom-promoting) qualities observable in individuals and cultures. Integrating this feature of recognition into my preliminary conception, I derive an enriched definition that satisfies two of three criteria of an adequate conception of public recognition:

CR$_1$: It specifies the means by which acts of recognition undermine or reverse social and institutional modes of oppression.

CR$_2$: It elucidates how acts of recognition embody liberal neutrality, understood as the commitment to treat different ways of life as equally legitimate and viable.

The real nature and significance of recognition emerges through my analysis of Hegel's elaborations of the 'pure concept of recognition [*der reine Begriff des Anerkennens*]' (*PhS* ¶185; *PhG* 147) and of subjects' later achievement of mutual recognition. Both are essential components of his *Phenomenology* theory that have been largely ignored or misinterpreted.[1] For instance, many postmodern and critical theoretical discussions of Hegel's theory of recognition still conceive it as exhausted by the struggle for recognition that culminates in mastery and slavery.[2] However, far from encapsulating the theory, the relation of mastery and slavery is manifestly a *deficient* mode of the pure concept of recognition—a *failure* of recognition that Hegel attributes to the erroneous self-understanding of that dialectic's warring subjects. For Hegel, the concept of recognition is 'spiritual *unity* in its doubling' (*PhS* ¶178; *PhG* 145; translation modified). He later explains that according to the concept 'each is for the other what the other is for it' (*PhS* ¶186; *PhG* 148). Mutuality is therefore essential to the concept. Because the relation of mastery and slavery clearly fails to realize the pure concept, it cannot be said to represent Hegel's considered theory of recognition.

Hegel develops his theory over the course of three chapters of the *Phenomenology*. He shows in Chapters IV through VI how self-consciousness works through increasingly adequate forms of social and self-understanding to apprehend the truth of its own nature and the world. This development is Hegel's chronicle, at times explicitly historical, of a dialectical evolution of theoretical and normative systems of thought. Through this *Bildung*, involving a series of struggles for recognition, consciousness comes to actualize the pure concept of recognition in an act of mutual recognition (*PhS* ¶¶632ff.; *PhG* 464).[3]

Because mutual recognition depends upon the attainment of recognitive *understanding*, in this chapter I highlight three features of Hegel's recognition theory illuminated by a focus upon the *Phenomenology's* epistemology.[4] First, Hegel suggests in his Preface and Introduction that recognition, as a form of *cognition*, is absolutely central in the dialectic of spirit since its achievement is, in one sense, spirit's penultimate achievement.[5] This throws important light upon the structure and significance of recognition. Second, consistent with his objective to trace the dialectical 'path of natural consciousness . . . *through the series of its own configurations*' (*PhS* ¶77; *PhG* 72; my emphasis), Hegel attributes the failure of recognition in mastery and slavery to the necessary, inwardly dialectical unfolding of spirit's *knowing*—in this case, its erroneous self-conception as *abstract* 'pure self-consciousness' (*PhS* ¶189; *PhG* 150). Neither pure recognition nor its failure stems primarily from subjects' desire to dominate one another but rather from spirit's *understanding*. Third, and related to the second issue, the shape of knowing adequate to successful recognition is recognitive understanding.

I elaborate these three features of Hegel's theory in the first three sections of this chapter and show that, for Hegel, mutual recognition grounded in recognitive understanding generates relations of moral equality and reciprocity—even if they always retain an element of tension. For, significantly, mutual recognition preserves the 'absolute' *difference* of subjects even as they are reconciled with one another (*PhS* ¶671; *PhG* 493). Spirit is finally resolved into a unity, but it is a *differentiated* unity, one constituted of diversity.

In the section titled 'Two Challenges to Hegel's Recognition Theory,' I answer two objections raised recently against Hegel's recognition theory. Kelly Oliver and Patchen Markell both suggest that Hegel's account, and the politics of recognition generally, are blind to the ways in which the pursuit of recognition necessarily culminates in relationships of domination. Both objections are important but depend upon flawed understandings of

Hegel. I urge more careful attention to what transpires in the *Phenomenology* beyond 'Mastery and Slavery.'

Finally, in the 'Conclusion' section of this chapter, I reconstruct Hegel's concept of recognition, cashing out 'spiritual unity in its doubling' in contemporary terms and addressing the resulting definition's satisfaction of two criteria of an adequate conception. Recognition is not only *consistent* with liberal principles and responsive to emancipatory claims, but the *fulfillment* of both, inasmuch as it is, to borrow Robert Pippin's phrase, Hegel's answer to the question concerning the nature and possibility of freedom (2000: 155).

# The Centrality of Recognition in the *Phenomenology*

Hegel's clear statements in the Preface and Introduction that the text is centrally concerned with epistemology already signal the central role that recognition (*Anerkennung*, with its root *kennen*, 'to know') will play in the dialectic. It is recognition, as an act marking the attainment of a crucial form of knowledge, that brings forth the highest shape of spirit, absolute spirit.

### The phenomenology as a theory of knowledge

In his advertisement for the *Phenomenology*, Hegel claims that his chief aim, to demonstrate the necessity of the historical development of 'spirit' as it pursues 'pure knowledge,' makes it possible to arrange all of its appearances into a 'scientific order':

> [The *Phenomenology*] includes the various shapes of spirit within itself as stages in the progress through which spirit becomes pure knowledge or absolute spirit . . . The apparent chaos of the wealth of appearances in which spirit presents itself when first considered is brought into a scientific order, which is exhibited in its necessity, in which the imperfect appearances resolve themselves and pass over into the higher ones constituting their proximate truth.[6]

Hegel's presentation of the *necessary* order of the unfolding configurations of self-developing spirit is precisely what he takes to be the distinctive feature of the work: he purports to demonstrate and systematize the logic internal to the emergence of the all of the major modes of human knowing, a demonstration that he calls 'Science' (*PhS* ¶1; *PhG* 11). The demonstration begins with the most immediate form of thinking, 'sense-certainty,' and shows how consciousness's critique of this and subsequent modes of knowing generates a dialectic that guides consciousness (later spirit) to absolute knowing.

In the *Phenomenology*, consciousness is cognition, the thought activity, or knowing, of individual cognizers as they 'take up' the world. Sense-certainty, perception, and understanding are all modes of cognition in which a cognitive subject investigates the nature of objects. Accordingly, *self*-consciousness is the cognitive subject's knowledge of self, its investigation and conceptions of its own nature. Specifically, it is the subject's conception of its nature *as a knower*, for self-consciousness 'appears' in the *Phenomenology* when the subject, as the shape of knowing called Understanding, is compelled to reflect on its own activity of representation and to give an account of itself as the source of representations.

*Spirit*, in contrast to consciousness and self-consciousness, designates the shared theoretical and practical understanding of a *community* of self-conscious knowers and agents. In Terry Pinkard's words, it is 'a form of life that has developed various social practices for reflecting on what it takes to be authoritative for itself,' or 'a fundamental *relation* among persons that mediates their *self-consciousness*, a way in which people reflect on what they have come to take as authoritative reasons for themselves' (1994: 8–9). Finally, *absolute spirit* is a unity of shapes of spirit in which these *different* shapes have achieved, and now express, a shared understanding of their essential nature as theoretical and practical knowers and agents in and of a world. They express this understanding sensuously in art, emotionally in religion, and conceptually in philosophy. Significantly, shapes of spirit become absolute spirit when they mutually recognize each other (*PhS* 670; *PhG* 493). Their final achievement is absolute knowing, 'Spirit that knows itself as Spirit' (*PhS* ¶808)—absolute spirit's *conceptual* and authoritative account of the unity of the knowing subject with all reality.

Understanding the terms 'consciousness,' 'self-consciousness,' 'spirit,' and 'absolute spirit' in this way as different modes of dialectically evolving theoretical and practical knowing illuminates the unity of the text and the sense of Hegel's claim in his Introduction that a 'self-moving' dialectic motivates the necessary unfolding of these shapes out of each other as spirit strives for self-knowledge. Cognitive frameworks evolve necessarily from earlier, less adequate frameworks through an ongoing process of *self-critique* incited by apparent contradictions inherent in those earlier frameworks. Thus, for example, the progression from consciousness to self-consciousness in Chapter III to Chapter IV requires a transition from purely theoretical to practical philosophy when consciousness discovers the limits of theoretical knowing.

## Recognition as spirit's aim

If one grants that the *Phenomenology* is importantly concerned with knowing, then the centrality of recognition in the dialectic becomes clearer. First, Hegel plainly conceives of 'recognition' and 'absolute spirit' as relations among knowers. Second, spirit's desire for self-knowledge, which fuels the dialectic, only begins to be satisfied when spirit accomplishes mutual recognition.

Consider Hegel's conception of recognition as 'spiritual unity in its doubling' (*PhS* ¶178; *PhG* 145–146). If spirit is a community of knowers, then recognition is a unity of two (or more) *distinct* communities of knowers—a '*spiritual* unity in its *doubling*.' The ground of their unity is signaled by Hegel's claim that the mutual recognition achieved by two shapes of spirit brings forth absolute spirit (*PhS* ¶670; *PhG* 493), which I have defined as communities' *shared* understanding of their essential nature as knowers and agents. In recognition, distinct communities form a unity constituted of a shared, more fundamental understanding of the nature of identity, knowledge, and agency.

Spirit's achievement of mutual recognition is the penultimate achievement of the dialectic in the sense that the appearance in recognition of absolute spirit in its immediacy means the only task remaining is the further development of this immediate self-knowledge into full conceptual expression as absolute knowing. In one way of looking at it, then, the entire dialectic aims at the achievement of recognition. Having suggested how this is so in terms of definitions of 'recognition' and 'absolute spirit,' I now show how it is so *structurally*.

In the Preface, Hegel explains that the entire dialectic is, unbeknownst to the natural spirit that experiences it, constituted of the attempt to actualize the true nature of knowing as the unity of subjectivity and objectivity. However, natural spirit primarily experiences the pursuit of truth as the quest for certainty about the nature of objects. Accordingly, throughout most of the dialectic, spirit stubbornly and erroneously persists in *opposing* subjectivity and objectivity, when in fact the *unity* of subjectivity and objectivity is implicit in knowing itself. In ¶¶18–21, Hegel describes this problem of natural spirit's perspective and how it will only be corrected when spirit accomplishes the 'unifying reflection' of recognition. He explains how and why the dialectic is set in motion, introduces the basic structure of the stages of self-developing spirit, and indicates the means by which the dialectic will be completed. He begins with the dialectic's starting point in the absolute as the concept of knowing:

> This Substance is, as Subject, pure, *simple negativity*, and is for this reason the bifurcation of the simple; it is the doubling which sets up opposition, and then again the negation of this indifferent diversity and of its antithesis [the immediate simplicity]. (*PhS* ¶18; *PhG* 23)

Hegel's first point is that the absolute is a subject, or thinking itself, which has begun in pure immediacy (the simple, or immediate simplicity) as pure essence: a pure, abstract universal that is the concept [*Begriff*] of thinking. However, as thinking it is 'pure, simple *negativity*,' since thinking entails differentiating, opposing subject and object. The outcome of the absolute's self-differentiation is its bifurcation into two modes that Hegel refers to here as 'diversity,' and elsewhere as 'difference' (see, e.g., *PhS* ¶167; *PhG* 138). The moments of difference (throughout the text) are (1) *actuality*, or the posited *appearance* of spirit, and (2) *essence*, or the *concept* that corresponds to that appearance of spirit.

We who look onto this first movement, the bifurcation of the simple absolute (the concept of thinking), can see that each of the moments of difference—the absolute as essence and its appearance as actual thinking—in a sense express the absolute 'truly.' However, the absolute must be grasped as both moments together, as the *unity* of essence and actuality. This can only be achieved through the important act of unifying reflection that negates the opposition of essence and actuality. Thus, Hegel continues:

> Only this self-*restoring* sameness, or this reflection in otherness within itself—not an *original* or *immediate* unity as such—is the True. It is the process of its own becoming . . . and only by being worked out to its end, is it actual. (*PhS* ¶18; *PhG* 23)

That is, we must understand (*pace* Kant, for instance) that the True is not only essence, or the thing-in-itself, but the unity of noumenal and phenomenal, of the universal and particular. '[T]he True is the whole,' Hegel urges (*PhS* ¶18; *PhG* 23). Essence alone cannot be taken for the True because it is a pure universal. But universals are empty concepts, having no real content: just as the expression '"*all* animals" . . . cannot pass for a zoology,' Hegel writes, so universals, such as 'the Divine' or 'the Absolute,' being *immediate*, fail to 'express what is contained in them' (*PhS* ¶20; *PhG* 24–25). The absolute is actual only insofar as it is thinking, which necessarily entails its differentiation into a concrete, *actual*, determinate mode of thought—into 'a *becoming-other* that has to be taken back, or is a mediation' (*PhS* ¶20; *PhG* 25). This requirement, that it 'be taken back,' expresses, again, that only through reflection that unites essence and actuality does spirit apprehend the True.

It is a long, difficult road to spirit's accomplishing this unifying reflection. Indeed, the repeated revelation that shapes of spirit are not true knowledge but only 'appearances,' or semblances, of it means we experience the quest for truth more often as 'the way of despair' (*PhS* ¶78; *PhG* 72). This is because, in the first place, it is not readily apparent to natural spirit that its modes of knowing are really only partial perspectives. Throughout most of the dialectic, it posits only essence as the True. However, experience makes spirit aware of the limitations of this perspective, for it invariably confronts objects whose actual features are in tension with its conceptions of them. This failure of thought to correspond to world reveals that spirit's way of representing the world is self-undermining[7]; natural spirit is revealed, time and again, 'not to be real knowledge' (*PhS* ¶78; *PhG* 72). This insight compels spirit to critique its own standpoint through reflection that seeks a more adequate conception of the True. Through this process it accomplishes an *Aufhebung*, the simultaneous undermining (or canceling) of the untrue aspects of its mode of knowing and 'taking up,' or preservation, of what is true in it. Spirit thereby transforms itself into a new shape in its endeavor to apprehend the True, which, if it is truly to be *knowing* being, it *must* do.[8]

However, to the extent that consciousness persists in conceiving of essence and actuality as distinct in both its theoretical and practical reasoning, it fails to apprehend the True. 'Reason is . . . misunderstood,' Hegel writes, 'when reflection [itself actual] is excluded from the True, and is not grasped as a positive moment of the Absolute. It is reflection that makes the True a result, but it is equally reflection that overcomes the antithesis between the process of its becoming and the result' (*PhS* ¶21; *PhG* 25).

Unifying reflection is precisely what two crucial shapes of spirit, 'conscience' and the 'beautiful soul,' accomplish in mutual recognition. Their unity is constituted of their mutual negation of the difference between essence and actuality—they reconcile universal and particular willing, and pure thought and concrete action. It is especially because of conscience, a particularly 'negativizing' and 'unifying' shape of self-certain spirit that 'acts and preserves itself in the unity of its *essential* and *actual* being' (*PhS* ¶646; *PhG* 476), that this reflection occurs. Moreover, in asserting with conviction the authoritative agency of the individual, conscience is the first to *posit* the unity of essence and actuality, and thus is the source of the 'reflection that overcomes the antithesis between the process of [the True's] becoming and the result' (*PhS* ¶21; *PhG* 25). Conscience's claim attains objective validity when the 'beautiful soul' acknowledges it in mutual recognition.

If unifying reflection is the goal of the dialectic, and conscience and the 'beautiful soul' accomplish this in mutual recognition, then the dialectic of spirit is, in one sense, a striving toward mutual recognition. Clearly recognition is central role in the phenomenology of spirit.

## The Pure Concept of Recognition and its Failure in 'Mastery and Slavery'

Within the dialectic, the origin of the need for recognition is self-consciousness's desire to actualize its self-conception as an independent, authoritative knower. As 'Desire,' the subject conceives of itself as an all-encompassing, independent, essential being, a 'simple universal' (*PhS* ¶174; *PhG* 143). It acquired this self-conception in its earlier shape as 'Understanding,' when it grasped that it somehow itself generates appearances of objects (*PhS* ¶163; *PhG* 134). Accordingly it conceives of all objects as contingent, inessential beings that exist solely for self-consciousness. This perception seems corroborated by the fact that although objects have an inner life and subsist in themselves (*PhS* ¶168; *PhG* 139), they are not, like self-consciousness, *for* themselves, or knowing beings. Taking itself, then, to be the only essential being, self-consciousness 'comes forward in antithesis to the *universal* substance [the world of objects], disowns this fluent continuity with it, and . . . preserves itself by separating itself from this its inorganic nature, and by *consuming* it' (*PhS* ¶171; *PhG* 141; my emphasis).

Desire is really after a concrete demonstration that it is the essential being. In Michael Monahan's excellent way of putting it, 'I, as an agent in the moment of Desire, seek . . . a clear and unambiguous answer to the question of the nature of my own existence. The easiest way to approach this most fundamental of questions is through a negation of difference.' In this way, my 'status as independent, necessary, and "simple" is affirmed over and over again' (2003: 51–52). So, Desire vanquishes objects, making them *manifestly* for it (*PhS* ¶174; *PhG* 143). It believes it thereby demonstrates that there is no other independent being whose existence undermines its self-conception as all-encompassing and absolutely independent.

In consuming objects, Desire does concretely manifest that they are *for it*; it effectively 'abolish[es] the "otherness of the other." '[9] However, it eventually confronts an unsettling truth: that it is dependent upon its object. Desire's self-certainty is conditioned by the object, because it is satisfied only *through* the object's negation. Satisfaction therefore depends on the object's presence but brings about the object's absence. Accordingly, desire for the object reproduces itself; self-consciousness experiences the object as essential. Thus Hegel concludes: 'It is in fact something other than self-consciousness that is the essence of Desire' (*PhS* ¶175; *PhG* 143). The *object* is the essence of desire, not the *self*.

This marks a crucial turning point. Self-consciousness has learned that it only has self-certainty so long as there *exists* this other for it to *vanquish*, an apparent contradiction that must be resolved. Self-consciousness must transcend its desire to negate objects, but it must also somehow appropriate them, for Hegel says that self-consciousness realizes its nature 'only by "taking up" the object [*durch Aufheben des Gegenstandes*]; and it must experience its satisfaction, for it is the truth' (*PhS* ¶175; *PhG* 143; translation modified). The present challenge is to figure out *how* to appropriate the object, demonstrating the independence of self-consciousness and the dependence-despite-independence of the object, but without negating the object. Hegel concludes that 'on account of the independence of the object,' the only solution is the object's *self*-negation (*PhS* ¶175; *PhG* 144). Stated differently, the issue inherited from consciousness as Understanding is to establish for consciousness *how* it is the 'origin' of objects of appearance. This requires a negation that makes explicit the *unity* of subject and object in consciousness, but in a way that reveals consciousness to be authoritative. The object *must* therefore be somehow negated before the subject, but not through the subject's action, for that would exhibit the subject's dependence on the object for self-certainty. The negation therefore requires the object's own action, yet in such a way that the object is nevertheless preserved for the subject; otherwise the subject cannot sustain its self-certainty.

Of course, if the object can negate itself, this reveals it to be a subject too (*PhS* ¶177; *PhG* 145). Thus, on Hegel's account, to win self-certainty self-consciousness must be in relation to another *subject*: 'Self-consciousness achieves its satisfaction only in another self-consciousness' (*PhS* ¶175; *PhG* 144; cf. *HHS* 104). This is the origin of the need for recognition.

## Elucidation of the pure concept of recognition

The dialectic of recognition begins with Hegel's elucidation of the concept in ¶¶178–184. It is crucial to see that these passages describe the *pure* concept of recognition and the process by which it is achieved. Hegel is not introducing only the struggle that ends in mastery and slavery. These paragraphs are Hegel's overview of the 'detailed exposition of the Notion of spiritual unity in its doubling,' which is 'the process of Recognition' (*PhS* ¶178; *PhG* 145). This process is actualized not in Chapter IV, but in Chapter VI, when two shapes of spirit really do '*recognize* themselves as *mutually recognizing* one another' (*PhS* ¶184; *PhG* 147).

At the beginning of Chapter IV, self-consciousness requires an encounter with another subject through which it can resolve two apparent contradictions: first, between its *conception* of itself as absolutely independent of its objects and its *experience* of itself as actually dependent upon them; and, second, between its *conception* of the object as dependent on consciousness and its *experience* of the object as independent. Of course, the subject's experience of being somehow dependent upon the world yet somehow independent is very much the human condition. We are influenced and shaped by external forces and yet distinct from them. Self-consciousness's challenge is to discover the conditions under which it can experience itself as both independent *and* dependent in relation to its objects.[10] Hegel maintains that it is in intersubjective recognition, when the subject finds itself related to, but not determined by or determining, another subject.

Hegel introduces the dialectic of recognition in ¶177 by noting that the original encounter between two subjects introduces us to the concept of spirit: an ' "I" that is "We" and "We" that is "I" ' (*PhS* ¶177; *PhG* 145). Indeed, the structure of the relation between self-consciousness, which desires to realize its nature as an authoritative knower, and the other self-consciousness required for this knowledge, reflects the structure of recognition as '*spiritual unity* in its doubling' (*PhS* ¶178; *PhG* 145; my emphasis), the achievement of a shared understanding between subjects concerning their essential nature. At this point, Hegel writes, 'Self-consciousness exists in and for itself when, and by the fact that, it *so* exists for another' (*PhS* ¶178; *PhG* 145; my emphasis). Self-consciousness can only know itself *as* self-consciousness, as authoritative knower, when another self-consciousness acknowledges its cognitive authority. But this requires the first self-consciousness to affirm the cognitive authority of the second; otherwise it cannot accept the second's *acknowledgment* as authoritative.

According to Hegel, mutual recognition does not occur immediately, in the initial moment of encounter, but is an achievement, the outcome of a process constituted of six moments detailed in ¶¶179–184:

1. First, self-consciousness perceives that its nature is conceptualized by another human. In this moment it becomes concerned not with this other's existence *per se*, or even with the other's subjectivity, but only with the fact that it is being conceived by another and therefore somehow 'exists' outside itself. That is, self-consciousness is fundamentally concerned with its own alienated being, its self as it 'exists' in the thinking of the other, or its own 'otherness' (*PhS* ¶179; *PhG* 146).

2. To achieve self-certainty as an independent, 'essential being' (*PhS* ¶180; *PhG* 146) self-consciousness must restore its sense of its fundamental unity and identity. It must 'appropriate [*aufheben*] this otherness of itself'—*take up* its otherness into its own consciousness again—by appropriating the perspective of the other 'independent' self-consciousness. Hegel adds that, in doing so, self-consciousness 'appropriates' itself, 'for this other is itself' (*PhS* ¶180; *PhG* 146; translation modified).

3. Self-consciousness, in 'taking up' the perspective of the other, recovers itself in two senses. First, through its own action of embracing its unity with the other, 'appropriating *its* otherness,' it 'receives back its own self.' Second, the other self-consciousness, through *its* action of voicing its conception—'giv[ing self-consciousness] back again to itself'— supports the first self-consciousness's self-recovery. It 'lets the other again go free' (*PhS* ¶181; *PhG* 146).

4. The two comprehend that this 'liberating' relation comes about only through mutual action, for both are independent subjects and not mere objects to be used for each other's own purposes: 'Each sees the *other* do the same as it does; each does itself what it demands of the other, and therefore also does what it does only insofar as the other does the same' (*PhS* ¶182; *PhG* 146–147).

5. Their mutual action of appropriating each other's perspective in order to recover self therefore constitutes a single act inasmuch as (1) the first self-consciousness cannot actually appropriate the other's perspective if the other does not freely offer it (and vice versa), and (2) not only does the other allow its perspective to be appropriated, but it does so partly by appropriating the perspective of the first self-consciousness: 'The action is indivisibly the action of one as well as the other.' This simultaneous articulation and appropriation of conceptions constitutes a joint actualization of subjectivities and is the 'middle term' between the two subjects (*PhS* ¶183; *PhG* 147).

6. The two do not thereby become an identical, single mind but remain
   as distinguishable 'extremes,' each 'an immediate being on its own
   account,' even as they become so through a mutual action, the 'middle
   term,' of self-mediation-through-other (one might say that the 'middle
   term,' *qua* action, inheres in the extremes, since action is always *of* an
   *agent*). In this act, '[t]hey *recognize* themselves as *mutually* recognizing
   one another,' two independent beings in mutual dependence (*PhS* ¶184;
   *PhG* 147).

To illustrate, imagine that you and I are these subjects. When you and I
first encounter each other (moment 1), you understand that I am forming
a conception of you, and vice versa. What concerns you in this moment
is not me, but *my conception of you*. The fact that I form judgments about
you means that you are not a completely self-identical, independent being.
There is a 'you'—a conception of your nature—that 'exists outside' you, in
my thinking, and it is not a forgone conclusion that my conception of you
affirms your self-concept.[11]

To achieve self-certainty, your sense that your self-conception as independent and authoritative is legitimate, you must solicit and appropriate
my conception of you (moment 2). You establish a relationship of cognitive
*unity* with me. This does not entail that you aim to 'appropriate' me in the
sense of dominating me in order to control my judgments of you.[12] In this
context it seems more plausible to think that you want simply to take up my
idea of you; for if you take up my conception of you, incorporating it into
your self-conception, you appropriate your 'alienated' self. If, by contrast,
you aim to control my idea of you, my conception still remains alienated
since you cannot *really* control it. I can always change it, so at best you
enjoy only a semblance of control. Instead, the point is to reconcile the
two senses of 'you'—mine and yours—in *your* self-conception, which only
becomes truly yours if you endorse it.

Appropriating my conception of you therefore furthers your freedom
(moment 3). In identifying with my perspective, you come to embrace a
formerly unacknowledged dimension of your selfhood; you generate a new
self-concept that is truly *your* self-concept. Thus offering my conception of
you, rather than withholding it from you or otherwise making your self-
understanding problematic, supports your self-actualization.

Moreover, we both acknowledge that this is the activity of two *independent
subjects* who are both undergoing the same process (moment 4). Even as
you appropriate my conception of you, I am appropriating your conception
of me. We also both acknowledge that we have offered up these ideas of

each other freely for each other's appropriation—that we are not ordinary objects of desire that we can 'utilize for [our] own purposes' without each other's consent (*PhS* ¶182; *PhG* 146).

However, it is also the case that the moment is not only 'binary,' involving two agents, but also a singular, mutual act (moment 5). For not only is your appropriation of my conception of you at the very same time my offering up of that conception, but it is also an offering up of my subjectivity, which you also appropriate—and likewise for me in appropriating your conception of me. The subjectivity of both of us has been *actualized* in and through each other.

Although Hegel speaks of our mutual action, our self-mediation-through-other, as a 'middle term,' he says we remain 'extremes' (moment 6) (*PhS* ¶184; *PhG* 147). Our mutual acknowledgment of each other's subjectivity— finding each other's *different* perspectives worthy of appropriation—makes explicit for both of us our status as authoritative subjects: We '*recognize* [our] selves as *mutually recognizing* one another' (*PhS* ¶184; *PhG*, 147). Equally importantly, in 'recovering' our subjectivity through mutual recognition, we come to understand our own subjectivity not as simple universality but as necessarily mediated. In Monahan's words, '[I]n "bridging" this divide between self and other, the other need no longer confront one as an obstacle to be overcome, but rather can be understood . . . as an extension of and contribution to the self' (2003: 60).

Hegel reiterates that he has just described the 'pure concept of recognition' (*PhS* ¶185; *PhG*, 147) and that he will proceed to elaborate the process as it unfolds in the actual experience of self-consciousness. The *first* experience, he says, will end in the *unequal* recognition of mastery and slavery.

### 'Mastery and Slavery' as a failure of recognition

Because 'pure' recognition entails mutual acknowledgment, any intersubjective relation that lacks this characteristic mutuality is not genuinely recognitive. Hegel suggests that mutual recognition is the ideal goal of intersubjective encounters, but stresses that in experience self-consciousness's first attempt will fail: 'At first, it will exhibit the side of the inequality of the two, or the splitting-up of the middle term into the extremes which, as extremes, are opposed to one another, one being only *recognized*, the other only *recognizing*' (*PhS* ¶186; *PhG* 148). I stress that this first pursuit *must* fail as the necessary consequence, not of their enmity, but of their erroneous self-conceptions, their belief that they are *essentially* 'simple universals,' *abstract* 'pure self-consciousness' (*PhS* ¶189; *PhG* 150).

In their first encounter, two self-consciousnesses form conceptions of each other, but not of each other as subjects, for '[t]hey have not as yet exposed themselves to each other in the form of pure being-for-self, or as self-consciousness' (*PhS* ¶186; *PhG* 148). Each posits itself as authoritative but not the other. The other is just a consciousness immersed in Life, not a 'simple universal' like itself (*PhS* ¶186; *PhG* 148). This is one sense of Hegel's earlier claim that self-consciousness 'does not see the other as an essential being' (*PhS* ¶179; *PhG* 146). Thus Hegel is careful to distinguish their present relation from recognition, which requires *both* subjects to actualize 'pure being-for-self,' their subjectivity, an event that is yet to come:

> For it would have truth only if its own being-for-self had confronted it as an independent object, or, what is the same thing, if the object had presented itself as this pure self-certainty. But *according to the Notion of recognition this is possible* only when each is for the other what the other is for it, *only when each through its own action, and again through the action of the other, achieves this pure abstraction of being-for-self.* (*PhS* ¶186; *PhG* 148)

The present question for self-consciousness is *how* to raise this certainty to truth. It must discover how to resolve the apparent contradiction of its, and the other's, simultaneous independence and dependence. At this early stage, it thinks it must do so in such a way that it both appropriates the other's perspective through the other's own self-negation, and manifests its own true nature as independent, authoritative knowing. Hegel has said this must occur through the action of two self-consciousnesses. Both take the required action to be *mutual* self-negation, for each comes to see that it must also negate *itself.* They take this to mean the staking of bodily existence:

> The presentation of itself . . . as the pure abstraction of self-consciousness consists in showing itself as the pure negation of its objective mode, or in showing that it is not attached to any specific existence, not to the individuality common to existence as such, that it is not attached to life. (*PhS* ¶ 187; *PhG* 148)

Self-consciousness's act of staking its life expresses its indifference to *anything other than the actualization of self-consciousness as pure, authoritative knowing.* Its sole desire is to actualize its conception of its essence as *pure rationality.*

To enact their mutual self-negation, the two subjects wage a battle to the death: 'just as each stakes his own life, he must seek the other's death, for it values the other no more than itself' (*PhS* ¶187; *PhG* 149). However, insofar as these subjects believe that staking their physical existence is the action required to manifest their essential nature as pure rationality, the two *must* fail to realize their desire—for mutual recognition cannot be the outcome of a struggle that has the staking of life as its aim. First, both must survive the struggle if they are to achieve *mutual* recognition; if one or both die, the intersubjective relation evaporates as does the possibility of actualizing their true nature. However, second, if they give up the fight for the sake of survival, they cannot say they have truly staked their lives. One of the subjects eventually grasps the inherent contradiction, that staking his life for the sake of actualizing pure rationality entails that he should die but nevertheless survive. At the same time, he confronts the *real* possibility of death; his 'whole being is seized with dread,' and 'everything stable and solid has been shaken to its foundations' (*PhS* ¶194; *PhG* 153). Thus, Hegel writes, 'In this experience, self-consciousness learns that life is as essential to it as pure self-consciousness' (*PhS* ¶189; *PhG* 150). Embodiment is essential to subjectivity. This subject surrenders and becomes the slave of the other, for he has only demonstrated his attachment (enslavement) to life. The other becomes his master, for he has demonstrated only indifference to anything other than the actualization of pure self-consciousness.

As the dialectic progresses, Hegel makes evident that the master–slave relation fails to actualize the authoritative subjectivity of either subject. It is in virtue of *this* failure that we perceive clearly Hegel's conception of their relation as a deficient mode of recognition. The master is only in a superficial sense 'recognized' by the slave, who does acknowledge the master as an essential, 'independent' being, but still appears to the master as an 'ordinary consciousness' immersed in Life. The slave's way of regarding the master is at best a meaningless pseudo-recognition. To treat another only as object and not as authoritative subject is to undermine one's own authority. Hegel puts the point differently by noting that the shape of consciousness a subject confronts as object 'constitutes the *truth* of his certainty of himself' (*PhS* ¶192; *PhG* 152). He suggests that the true measure of our self-certainty is the self-certainty we confront and affirm in our interaction partners.

By contrast, consistent with this idea that the consciousness one confronts as object constitutes the truth of one's self-certainty, the truth of the slave's self-certainty is independence, inasmuch as he has the image of the master's independent consciousness as his object. Hegel portrays

the slave as the consciousness that transcends desire and begins to actualize his subjectivity through his creative labor for the master. Still, the
slave does not achieve self-certainty any more than the master does, since
although his subjectivity is situated in the world, it is not recognized by
another subject.

It seems clear, then, that Hegel, in keeping with the stated aims of the
*Phenomenology*, is concerned in 'Mastery and Slavery' with demonstrating its *failure* as a mode of recognition. The attempts of abstract self-
consciousnesses to realize their nature *qua* knowers as 'simple universals'
necessarily culminates in unequal recognition so long as they conceive of
that nature as realizable only in complete abstraction from bodily nature.

Accordingly, Hegel advances two important theses. First, actualized subjectivity is necessarily *intersubjective*. Hegel has exposed the self-undermining
character of the atomistic models of subjectivity featured in the tradition
from Descartes to Kant. If we understand the problem of self-consciousness
as the subject's epistemological problem of grasping and actualizing its
status as the source of appearances, we see Hegel showing how the subject only achieves this, first, by exiting the purely theoretical realm of
Understanding and entering the practical realm of Desire—that is, by dis-
covering the role of desire in its activity of representing the world. But the
subject actualizes self-consciousness, second, only by establishing a relationship of unity with other subjects.

Hegel's second thesis concerns the necessity with which the shape of self-
consciousness develops in this dialectic from its most abstract configura-
tion, in which both subjects conceive of their essential natures *qua* knowers
as pure rationality, toward a conception of self as necessarily embodied. In
proclaiming that 'life is as essential . . . as pure self-consciousness' (*PhS* ¶189;
*PhG* 150), and showing the slave, and not the master, to be the consciousness through which the dialectic progresses, Hegel clearly attacks conceptions of human nature as essentially pure intellect, portraying them as not
only self-undermining, but as potentially *oppressive*.


## The Achievement of Mutual Recognition through Recognitive Understanding

Between 'Mastery and Slavery' and the dialectic of conscience lie series
of struggles for recognition: for instance, in the self-actualizing efforts of
the pleasure-seeker, the 'heart-ruled' individual, and the competing proponents of 'virtue' and the 'way of the world' in section B of Chapter V.[13]

In section C, the community members of the 'spiritual animal kingdom' struggle with the 'honest consciousness' for recognition of their entitlement to a share in his work upon the 'matter in hand.' In Chapter VI, 'Spirit,' the struggle for recognition emerges first in Hegel's famous references to Antigone and Creon. We might also interpret the self-actualizing attempts of the 'legal' persons of Roman antiquity, the 'self-alienated' individuals of French culture and enlightenment, and, finally, the moralizing figures of modern 'conscience' and the 'beautiful soul' as struggles for recognition.[14]

I devote particular attention to the final struggle, for it is there, in the last stage of Hegel's discussion of morality, 'Conscience. Evil, the Beautiful Soul, and its Forgiveness,' that mutual recognition is achieved. Conscience and the 'beautiful soul' are two shapes of moral spirit that reach a difficult impasse while trying to realize their different visions of duty.[15] Conscience is convinced of the legitimacy of her actions done from conviction. However, she is challenged by the judging 'beautiful soul' who proclaims that insofar as her actions necessarily bear the mark of particularity—of her purposes and inclinations—they clearly are not done from pure duty and so lack moral worth; in fact, they are 'evil.' Hegel illuminates the path from this struggle to the reconciliation of these two positions in a way that vindicates particularity and difference.

### The objective of 'conscience': resolving the antinomy of Kantian morality

Conscience emerges in the dialectic as the resolution of a contradiction:

> The antinomy of the moral view of the world, viz. that there is a moral consciousness, and that there is none, or that the validation of duty lies beyond consciousness, and conversely, takes place in it.
>
> (*PhS* ¶632; *PhG* 464)

The source of this antinomy is Kantian 'moral consciousness' (*PhS* ¶601; *PhG* 444), the common progenitor of conscience and the 'beautiful soul.' Both shapes of spirit understand themselves as members of a society with customs, institutions, and laws they endorse as rational.[16] They feel compelled to uphold these 'universal duties' (*PhS* ¶599; *PhG* 442–443), not by an external authority but by their own reason. They live for the sake of the law, but it is a law that they, as autonomous subjects, give themselves.

However, the moral consciousness that will become conscience is aware that its determination to *act* as an autonomous subject runs in tension with its conception of moral action as motivated solely by respect for universal duty. It 'sees only an *occasion* for acting,' Hegel writes, 'but does not see itself obtaining, through its action, the happiness of performance and the enjoyment of achievement' (*PhS* ¶601; *PhG* 444), since moral action entails denying this very thing. The moral consciousness is therefore dissatisfied, both with this 'state of incompatibility between itself and existence' and with 'the injustice which restricts it to having its object merely as a *pure* duty' without allowing for its *self*-actualization (*PhS* ¶601; *PhG* 444). It concludes that it is in fact impossible to live up to this moral ideal and actually *do* anything: 'There is no *moral, perfect, actual* self-consciousness' (*PhS* ¶613; *PhG* 452). For action always entails the expression of individual purpose, of a particular interest in creating some reality other than the present one, even if at the same time it is universal in virtue of being conceived in terms of community norms. Therefore Hegel claims that 'action is nothing other than the actualization of the inner moral purpose, nothing other than the production of an actuality *determined by the purpose,* or of the harmony of the moral purpose and actuality itself' (*PhS* ¶618; *PhG* 454). Hegel maintains, *pace* Kant, that respect for the moral law must be united with a particular interest—that is, it must become a *purpose*—if it is to generate action.

Facing the impossibility of morally perfect agency, the Kantian moral spirit is plunged into the 'antinomy of the moral view of the world': again, 'that there is a moral consciousness, and that there is none, or that the validation of duty lies beyond consciousness, and conversely, takes place in it' (*PhS* ¶632; *PhG* 464). The meaning of the first part of the antinomy is clear: Kantian morality asserts its reality, but experiences its unreality, since moral consciousness cannot be actualized. In the second part, 'that the validation of duty lies beyond consciousness, and conversely takes place within it,' Hegel criticizes Kant's notion of the noumenal self, said to be capable, because it is purely rational, of determining pure duty. However, the claim that the noumenal self is 'beyond' the phenomenal self and yet somehow integral to the agency of the phenomenal self entails a contradiction.

Hegel claims furthermore that the Kantian moral spirit originally does not assume responsibility for resolving this contradiction. Instead, it 'shift[s] onto a being other than itself,' that is, upon a transcendent moral legislator that stands beyond human moral struggle, this responsibility (*PhS* ¶632; *PhG* 464). This will not suffice for Hegel; the spirit that will attain absolute knowing can discover for itself the means by which all apparent contradictions are resolved. As Dean Moyar explains, for Hegel 'the endpoint or telos of human activity must be seen as constitutive rather than as a hypothesized task. Kant did not go far enough in divinizing the human agent, in allowing no barriers to our responsibility for our action and for our happiness' (2002: 278). Instead, Kantian morality forecloses the very possibility of our action and happiness (in this life). Conscience emerges dialectically from the moral spirit's determination to resolve the antinomy of Kantian morality and discover how a morally valid action *is* possible: how a duty is in fact validated from within and beyond the individual.

## The nature of conscience: the authority of the self and unifying reflection

Conscience begins to resolve the antinomy by positing the two require-ments of external and internal moral validation as 'intrinsically the same' (*PhS* ¶632; *PhG* 464–465). This move is justified, to Hegel's mind, by the notion that 'pure duty, *viz.* as *pure knowing*, is nothing else than the *self* of consciousness, and the self of consciousness is *being* and *actuality*' (*PhS* ¶632; *PhG* 465). That is, pure duty, as knowledge of what one ought to do, is the knowledge (thinking) of a concrete, individual self. Therefore, unlike the original Kantian moral spirit, conscience does not conceive of pure duty as distinct from actuality. Pure duty just is concrete human thought; it just *is conscience* itself, the form of *self*-knowledge informing one's deepest sense of the right.

Hegel notes next the implication of conscience's identification of the two seemingly opposed moments, external and internal validation:

> [B]ecause what is supposed to lie beyond *actual* consciousness is nothing else than pure thought, and thus is, in fact, the self—because this is so, self-consciousness, *for us* or *in itself*, retreats into itself, and is aware that that being is its own self, in which what is actual is at the same time pure knowing and pure duty. (*PhS* ¶632; *PhG* 465)

Conscience identifies duty as its own thought, and so posits the moral authority of the self.[17] *This is a pivotal moment of the dialectic of spirit*, for conscience hereby accomplishes the unifying reflection that finally brings together essence—here, the concept of pure, universal duty—and actual-ity, the concrete thinking ('being and actuality') of conscience. Conscience is '*concrete* moral Spirit' for which 'pure duty, as also the Nature opposed to it, are appropriated [*aufgehobene*] moments' (*PhS* ¶634; *PhG* 466; trans-lation modified). However, at this moment conscience is merely *certain* of this unity and that it is 'in its contingency completely valid in its own sight' (*PhS* ¶632; *PhG* 465).[18] For Hegel, the truly glorious moment is the actualization of conscience's merely posited unity in the mutual recognition of conscience and the 'beautiful soul.'

Conscience, in positing the authority of the self, conceives of herself distinctively as 'a *self-actualizing* being' whose action is 'immediately something *concretely* moral' (*PhS* ¶634; *PhG* 466). She takes her actions to be truly moral because any action she takes *qua* conscience is, to her mind, '[a]ction *qua* actualization' of 'the pure form of will' (*PhS* ¶635; *PhG* 466), in this case the willing of duty. Thus conscience is the source of the 'reflection that overcomes the antithesis between the process of [the True's] becoming and the result' (*PhS* ¶21; *PhG* 25), since by committing her moral purpose to action, and thereby *actualizing essence*, she embodies the insight that 'becoming is also simple, and therefore not different from the form of the True which shows itself as *simple* in its result' (*PhS* ¶21; *PhG* 25).

Let us consider carefully this notion of moral action. Earlier Hegel draws an important distinction between 'pure' and 'actual' moral consciousness, noting that

> *actual* moral consciousness . . . is one that *acts*: it is precisely therein that the actuality of its morality consists. But in the very doing or acting, the place [given to actuality] is *dis*placed; for the action is nothing other than the actualization of the inner moral purpose, nothing other than the production of an actuality *determined by the purpose*, or of the harmony of the moral purpose and actuality itself. (*PhS* ¶618; *PhG* 454)

This claim, too, suggests that conscience's moral action is the *actualization* of her will to transform a present reality into one shaped by her purpose and activity. Through this *activity* of actualization, conscience gives concrete, sensuous being to moral purpose. Most importantly, the process of actualizing this new sensuous being *just is* the *being* of conscience. She invests a present reality with her very being; she 'pours her *self*' into this transformative work.[19] This is the point of Hegel's claim that 'in the very doing or acting, the place [given to actuality] is *dis*placed.' The accomplished *deed* is no longer considered the locus, or the actuality, of morality. The actuality of morality resides instead in the knowledge and purpose of an agent, expressed in the moral action *qua* actualization. Thus Hegel reiterates (again *pace* Kant) that moral action always bears the mark of the agent, asserting that the action is, in fact, 'determined by the *interest* of the consciousness knowing it' (*PhS* ¶635; *PhG* 467; my emphasis).

These facts taken together mean that conscience does not find herself torn among conflicting duties. Quite the contrary, as authoritative and self-affirming, conscience takes herself to *know* in a given instance what is right: what is right is what *she* determines is right according to both her knowledge *and* interest—that is, according to her *purpose* (the unity of knowledge and interest). Hegel explains:

> Conscience does not split up the circumstances of the case into a variety of duties. It does not behave as a *positive universal medium*, wherein the many duties would acquire, each for itself, a fixed substantial nature. If it did, then *either* no action could take place at all, because each concrete case involves an antithesis in general . . . and therefore by the very nature of action one side would be injured, one duty violated: *or else*, if action did take place, there would be an actual violation of one of the conflicting duties. Conscience is rather the negative One, or absolute self, which does away with these various moral substances; it is simple action in accordance with duty, which fulfills not this or that duty, but knows and does what is concretely right. (*PhS* ¶635; *PhG* 467)

In calling conscience the *negative* One, Hegel refers to conscience's ability to *determine* the right: her authority to negate, or eliminate, possibilities of action. Conscience is the shape of spirit who determines herself what her duty is and does it.

At the same time, conscience knows that her duty is creative and positive; she is called to convert a 'reality that merely *is* into a reality that results from *action*,' to leave her mark on the world. The positive performance of *this specific action*, and not just the adherence to abstract pure duty, is the true duty of conscience. For conscience knows 'that pure duty consists in the pure abstraction of thought, and has its content only in a specific reality, in a reality which is the reality of consciousness itself' (*PhS* ¶637; *PhG* 468). *Abstract* pure duty can only be the *form* of action. As the *content* of action, duty must always be formulated as the concrete purpose of an individual: 'The content of the moral action is the doer's own immediate *individuality*' (*PhS* ¶637; *PhG* 468). Moreover, the *form* of conscience's action is *conviction*: 'this self as a pure movement, *viz.* as [the individual's] knowing' (*PhS* ¶637; *PhG* 468).

We can now say that duty as the *content* and *purpose* of conscience's action is her *knowledge* of 'universal duties' (of the community's rational norms and standards) united with her particular *interest* in the concrete case. Conviction, as the *form* of duty, is the mode in which conscience expresses duty. In fact,

conviction distinguishes the action of conscience from other kinds of action, as the expression of both the conscientious agent's knowledge of the community's rational norms and her interest in a given case. For what conscience implies in claiming that her action stems from conviction is that *all* rational persons would choose this action if they were in the same circumstances.

The legitimacy of conscience's agency from conviction is what is to earn recognition. Accordingly, Hegel ascribes a crucial role to language as the medium through which conscience actualizes her conviction, making others aware of the 'universality' of her action, its rationality.[20] Hegel stresses that the action is 'valid as duty solely through the conviction being *declared*' (*PhS* ¶653; *PhG* 479). Otherwise, in the absence of clearly articulated conviction, the action of conscience appears to others as just an ordinary action motivated by inclination and desire.

Having argued that the duty of conscience is the very self of conscience, 'the *self that knows itself as essential being*,' Hegel concludes that for conscience, 'Duty is no longer the universal that stands over against the self . . . It is now the law that exists for the sake of the self, not the self that exists for the sake of the law' (*PhS* ¶639; *PhG* 469 and *PhS* ¶653; *PhG* 479). Conscience knows that in every concrete case of moral action, her duty is to actualize what she determines to be concretely right in that case. Duty is now *manifestly* the product of her own thought and being: she both determines and actualizes it herself. The fact that conscience determines duty herself might make her action appear arbitrary: she may simply do whatever she proclaims *with sincerity* is her duty. But conviction does not equate to sincerity; rather, it is grounded in conscience's knowledge of the community's norms and her commitment to acting in accordance with them: 'In calling itself *conscience* . . . it calls itself a universal knowing and willing which recognizes and acknowledges others, is the same as them' (*PhS* ¶654; *PhG* 480). Again, in proclaiming that her action is her duty, she expresses her confidence that every rational social member can acknowledge this duty.

However, although conscience is *certain* of her legitimacy, she is not for that reason infallible; but neither does she take herself to be. Conscience knows that she cannot know all the circumstances surrounding a particular case. Or it may be that she must choose among apparently *conflicting* duties. Still, as conscience she *must* act and is convinced of her authority to do so. As the 'negative One,' she is confident that she will determine the best course of action: her 'relation to the *actual* case in which [she] has to act is . . . that of *knower*' (*PhS* ¶642; *PhG* 471), even if one of the things she knows is that her knowledge of the case is finite. Therefore she acknowledges that she can only apply her '*own* knowledge' to the case but deems this '*incomplete* knowledge' to be 'sufficient and complete' insofar as she has weighed the circumstances, both to the best of her ability and 'for *others*,' acknowledging the community's standards (*PhS* ¶642; *PhG* 472). This 'strength of [her] own self-assurance' Hegel calls '*self-determination*' (*PhS* ¶646; *PhG* 476). It is 'the majesty of absolute autarky, to bind and to loose' (*PhS* ¶646; *PhG* 476).

Of course, given the complexity of the concrete case, others may interpret the matter differently than conscience has. For example, others' judgment of conscience's 'cowardice' may be, from conscience's perspective, 'the duty of supporting life [namely, her own] and the possibility of being useful to others' (*PhS* ¶644; *PhG* 474). Thus conscience is also aware that when she acts, she creates a new concrete reality that is inescapably *public*. She has invested her self in a reality that is now subject to others' conceptualization. This, then, is the basis of the recognitive encounter. Because it is not a foregone conclusion that conscience's action will accord with others' convictions, it is only deemed *objectively* valid when acknowledged as such by the others. Analogously to his earlier insight that self-consciousness requires recognition by another self-consciousness, Hegel now proclaims that '[t]he *existent reality* of conscience . . . is . . . the spiritual element of being recognized and acknowledged' (*PhS* ¶640; *PhG* 470). Both conscience and her community must become fully cognizant of the legitimacy of her actions.

## The beautiful soul and the struggle of conscience for recognition

It is here that conscience meets the judging 'beautiful soul.' The 'beautiful soul' emerges dialectically from one of the moments of conscience as a member of a community that celebrates its essence, the moral purity of conscience, at the expense of actuality (*PhS* ¶¶655–664; *PhG* 481–488). Thus the 'beautiful soul' does not act but conceives of morality as adherence to pure duty (which Hegel has said can only be the bare form of action) and calls attention to the particularity of ostensibly moral actions (*PhS* ¶669; *PhG* 492). Such a judging spirit, 'in order to preserve the purity of its heart . . . flees from contact with the actual world' (*PhS* ¶658; *PhG* 483). Accordingly, when conscience proclaims with conviction that her action is her duty (*PhS* ¶653; *PhG* 479), the hard-hearted 'beautiful soul' denounces her as *evil*, 'because of the disparity between [her] *inner being* and the universal' (*PhS* ¶660; *PhG* 485)—between her purpose, tainted by her personal interest, and universal duty. As far as the 'beautiful soul' is concerned, conscience is wholly in violation of moral law in acting from her own sense of what is right, even from conviction. He furthermore accuses conscience of hypocrisy for daring to call her particular action a duty, when it 'clearly' is done from interest (*PhS* ¶660; *PhG* 485).

Again, conscience openly acknowledges the particularity of her action and is aware of its contingency, its potential for committing unwitting harm. She 'admits, in fact, to being evil by asserting that [she] acts, in opposition to the acknowledged universal, according to [her] *own* inner law and conscience' (*PhS* ¶662; *PhG* 486). Moreover, she grants that 'when anyone says that he is acting according to his *own* law and conscience against others, he is saying, in fact, that he is wronging them' (*PhS* ¶662; *PhG* 486). However, conscience is also convinced that she has acted in a manner consistent with universal duty, the rational standards and laws of the community. She declares her action to be 'an *acknowledged* duty' (*PhS* ¶662; *PhG* 486). The issue at hand is therefore whether the agent can be *recognized* as conscientious, as legitimately asserting the rightness of her action-from-conviction.

It is crucial to note that although conscience knows the particular action is, in one sense, the actualization of her self, she also knows that she is more than her deeds. As the 'negative One,' conscience herself determines her actions to be right. The actual being of conscience is therefore not the action *qua* specific accomplished deed but, rather, the action *qua rightness of determination* by conscience. In Hegel's words: '[Conscience's] *immediate* action is not that which has validity and is actual; what is acknowledged is not the *determinate* aspect of the action, not its intrinsic being, but solely the self-knowing *self* as such,' which unlike the deed has 'permanence' (*PhS* ¶651; *PhG* 478). Accordingly, Hegel adds, 'it is only self-consciousness that is acknowledged and that obtains actual existence' (*PhS* ¶651; *PhG* 478). The actuality of my conscience lies not in my petition of protest against the war, but in *my judgment* of the rightness of protest in this case. What is really at stake for conscience, then, is acknowledgment of her legitimacy *as* an authoritative, conscientious agent.

The crucial question with which I opened this chapter now re-emerges: How do we assess the legitimacy of particularity, distinctness? On what grounds should the 'beautiful soul' acknowledge the legitimacy and authority of conscience? Why should *anyone* recognize particularity in this sense? Hegel answers, in effect, 'because it is *conscientious*.' He writes, 'Whether the assurance of acting from a conviction of duty is *true*, whether what is done is actually a *duty*—these questions or doubts have no meaning when addressed to conscience' because of conscience's unshakeable certainty concerning her judgments, which always make reference to the rational standards of the community (*PhS* ¶654; *PhG* 480).

The impasse between conscience and the 'beautiful soul' can only be overcome when both willingly appropriate each other's conceptions of their natures. In this case, both come to see and accept the limitations and validity of the particular agency of conscience and the particular judgments of the 'beautiful soul.' Conscience is the first to manifest this recognitive understanding. Although the 'beautiful soul' thinks he has laid claim to the moral high ground, taking his judgments to be characterized solely by universality, conscience declares him to be hypocritical, 'pass[ing] off such judging, not as another manner of being wicked, but as correct consciousness of the action . . . wanting its words without deeds to be taken for a superior kind of *reality*' (*PhS* ¶666; *PhG* 489). The 'beautiful soul' thinks he escapes particularity by refusing to act and refusing to endorse conscience's action. However, conscience grasps that the judge is also expressing his own sense of what in this case is duty and his own judgment of conscience's purpose. If, for example, conscience becomes famous as a result of her action, the 'beautiful soul' may judge the action as motivated by 'a *desire* for fame' (*PhS* ¶665; *PhG* 488). If the action befits a person of a higher social status, then even if conscience does not achieve that higher status, the 'beautiful soul' may judge her action ambitious (*PhS* ¶665; *PhG* 488). The 'beautiful soul's' judgment, as 'a positive act of thought,' always has, like the action of conscience, 'a positive content' (*PhS* ¶665; *PhG* 488).

Conscience therefore acknowledges two senses in which she and the 'beautiful soul' are alike: both voice convictions grounded in a commitment to the community's norms, and pronounce particular judgments in cases of moral action. Hegel comments that conscience, in adopting this reflective stance, has 'expressly appropriated its particularity, and in so doing posited itself in continuity with the other as universal' (*PhS* ¶667; *PhG* 490; translation modified). Conscience confesses this insight, expecting the 'beautiful soul' likewise to confess.

The 'beautiful soul' is silent. He neither confesses nor recognizes conscience. Hegel declares that the 'beautiful soul's' failure to give actuality to his being, either by acting or by acknowledging his common identity with agents, causes him to waste away 'to the point of madness' (*PhS* ¶668; *PhG* 491). What is required to liberate him as well as conscience is 'the breaking of [his] hard heart' (*PhS* ¶669; *PhG* 492), acknowledgment of his own hypocrisy and 'evil': the hypocrisy of professing commitment only to universality while expressing with conviction his particular judgments, and the evil of asserting his own will and conviction when doing so inevitably wrongs *someone*.

## The achievement of mutual recognition

Ultimately, the 'beautiful soul's' self-renunciation does come, not as a confession but, rather, in the form of 'forgiveness which it extends to the other' (*PhS* ¶¶669, 670; *PhG* 492). His forgiveness as *self-renunciation* means he acknowledges his own particularity rather than insisting upon his self-conception as pure universality. Still, in assuming a reflective stance, he posits his unity with conscience as universal. Thus he manifests, with conscience, recognitive understanding, his awareness of both their universality, as members of a community with shared, rational norms, and the particularity of their actions and judgments. As forgiveness *of conscience*, in particular, it is recognition of the legitimacy of conscientious agency. The beautiful soul 'acknowledges that what thought characterized as bad, *viz.* action, is good' (*PhS* ¶670; *PhG* 492).

Conscience and the 'beautiful soul' mutually recognize each other, and the antinomy of Kantian morality is resolved: conscience actualizes moral agency, and it is validated from within and beyond herself. The two exchange 'the word of reconciliation'—a 'reconciling *Yea*' that is 'the *objectively* existent Spirit, which beholds the pure knowledge of itself *qua universal* essence, in its opposite, in the pure knowledge of itself *qua* absolutely self-contained and exclusive *individuality*—a reciprocal recognition which is *absolute* Spirit' (*PhS* ¶670; *PhG* 493). We witness, then, the final achievement of spirit's unifying reflection, the *actualization* of the unity of essence and actuality in the word of reconciliation. Conscience and the 'beautiful soul' both achieve their 'completed form' as 'actual conscience' (*PhS* ¶662; *PhG* 486). In this singular unifying moment, the 'wounds of the Spirit heal, and leave no scars behind' (*PhS* ¶669–671; *PhG* 492–494).

Moreover, in claiming that the reconciling *Yea* is 'the objectively existent Spirit,' Hegel means that mutual recognition, as a speech act that affirms the recognitive understanding of two shapes of spirit, is the concrete linguistic object that embodies *absolute* spirit. It is the verbal articulation of a community's shared understanding of their essential nature as *universal*—as a community with 'universal duties'—and as *particular*, as self-determined individuals realizing ends of their own in that communal context. They acknowledge their dependence-and-independence. This conception squares with Hegel's introduction to the concept of spirit:

> Spirit, being the *substance* and the universal, self-identical, and abiding essence, is the unmoved solid *ground* and *starting-point* for the action of all, and it is their purpose and goal, the in-itself of every self-consciousness expressed in thought. This substance is equally the universal *work*

produced by the action of all and each as their unity and identity, for it is the *being-for-self*, the self, action. As *substance*, Spirit is unshaken righteous self-identity; but as *being-for-self* it is fragmented being, self-sacrificing and benevolent, in which each accomplishes his own work, rends asunder the universal being and takes from it his own share. (*PhS* ¶439; *PhG* 325)

Spirit, in other words, is simultaneously the shared political community taken as a whole and as the ground of its members, and the collection of individual members, each contributing distinctively to the community as they pursue their own ends. Spirit is ' "I" that is "We" and "We" that is "I" ' (*PhS* ¶177; *PhG* 145).

Thus the unity of absolute spirit is, significantly, constituted of *difference*. Hegel writes that in their unity conscience and the beautiful soul 'are different; and the difference is absolute' (*PhS* ¶671; *PhG* 493). Absolute spirit, then, is a unity constituted of identity and difference, and the difference is comprised of these two distinct shapes of spirit that must perpetually be present in the political community: conscientious agents and judging 'beautiful souls' engaged in ongoing struggles for recognition. When they are reconciled through recognitive understanding, both win acknowledgment of their status as authoritative rational subjects and their right of self-determination; for not only does this understanding liberate acting conscience for truly free action, but it affirms the 'beautiful soul' in his role as a conscientious judge of particular cases of agency. The 'beautiful soul' *must* judge, for conscience can only be realized *as* conscience when it is recognized by another conscientious self-consciousness, that is, by one that judges her action conscientiously.

## Implications of recognitive understanding

More should be said about the normative implications of the special knowledge that facilitates mutual recognition. As individuals' awareness of both their universality and particularity as knowers and agents, recognitive understanding is simultaneously a social understanding and a self-understanding—a unity of spirit and self-consciousness, of community and individuality, that Hegel calls *absolute* spirit.

With regard to their *social* understanding, individuals who possess recognitive understanding grasp the centrality of dialogue in constituting the concrete life of a community with shared norms. They comprehend that language is the medium of spirit, the means by which individuals give expression to rationality, and the primary means by which they appropriate the perspectives of others. This has two important consequences. First, they comprehend that their opportunities for self-actualization are socially mediated. Second, they establish their norms through dialogical struggles for recognition, through achieving fusions of horizons. Conscientious social members voice convictions and invite community deliberation on them. Recognitive communities, then, value and encourage public discourse, comprehending that it is always by nature agonistic insofar as it entails the production of arguments and counterarguments—the presentation and evaluation of *reasons* for action. Discourse entails struggles for recognition.

With regard to their *self*-understanding, individuals who, against the background of their self-certainty as conscientious beings, become aware of their particularity acknowledge the contingency of both their actions and their judgments of others' actions. Evangelia Sembou states it nicely: 'In an "absolute" community humans are conscious of the fact that each one of them finds himself to be at one time the agent who has committed some wrong in the eyes of the others and at another the judge of some individual action' (2003: 273). Thus judges can forgive actors on the basis of their acknowledgment that their judgments themselves are always particular judgments. This affirmation of particularity frees individuals to go forth as agents and judges of actions. In fact, recognitive understanding is what finally liberates individuals *concretely*, since their actions and judgments only attain objective validity when they are expressed and affirmed in their particularity.

## Two Challenges to Hegel's Recognition Theory

I hope by now to have corrected some misconceptions of Hegel's recognition theory: for instance, that it is exhausted by 'Mastery and Slavery' and that recognition suppresses difference. I turn now to two poignant criticisms raised by Kelly Oliver and Patchen Markell.

### Oliver on the neglected subjectivity of the other

In *Witnessing: Beyond Recognition*, Kelly Oliver challenges the assumption that emancipatory social struggles are fundamentally struggles for recognition. She is critical of recognition on the grounds that it 'merely repeats the dynamic of hierarchies, privilege, and domination,' particularly if we envision recognition as conferred upon minorities by majorities (2001: 9).

She claims this model instantiates rather than resolves the Hegelian 'warring' struggle and its result: 'The very notion of recognition as it is deployed in various contemporary theoretical contexts is . . . a symptom of the pathology of oppression itself,' such that 'struggles for recognition and theories that embrace those struggles may indeed presuppose and thereby perpetuate the very hierarchies, domination, and injustice that they attempt to overcome' (11).

Oliver maintains that the oppressed do not seek recognition anyway, but rather aim to bear witness to 'horrors beyond recognition' that can only be remedied through 'retribution and compassion' (8). The politics of recognition cannot fix on this aspect of emancipatory struggles partly *because* it treats the oppressed, the 'other,' solely as object of recognition. Recognition theories overlook the other's *subjectivity* just as the Hegelian model in 'Mastery and Slavery' privileges the master's subject position. Oliver is criticizing not only liberal, but also critical and postmodern approaches to recognition, 'populated with subjects warring with others, often referred to as *objects*. Subjects still dominate in spite of their dependence on dialogue with their "others" and "objects"' (5).

Furthermore, according to Oliver, Hegel and his followers incorrectly suggest that the other's subjectivity is *formed* only through the experience of being subordinated. Accordingly, they obscure not only the fact that the other is already a subject, but also that relationships of subordination actually damage subjectivity rather than form it (7). She maintains that subordination is itself 'part of what makes subjectivity othered . . . not part of what makes subjectivity subjectivity' (*ibid.*). Recognition theories, in ignoring that the other is already a subject, render the other invisible and silence him.

Oliver stresses, last, that not only is the other's subjectivity *not* formed in the first instance by compulsory labor, but labor is not the primary means by which subjectivity is restored. Quite the contrary, '*witnessing* is the essential dynamic of all subjectivity, its constitutive event and process,' which captures the 'address-ability and response-ability' characteristic of subjects (*ibid.*). Moreover, in witnessing, subjects are enabled both to give 'eye-witness testimony' to what can be known 'on the basis of first-hand knowledge' and to '[bear] witness to something beyond recognition that can't be seen' (16). It permits subjects not only to reflect upon and speak of what is commonly experienced and hence familiar, but also to discover, reflect upon, and convey what is rare or radically *different*. It is this ability to give testimony to both what is familiar and what is new and different that enables the oppressed to restore their damaged subjectivity. Thus Oliver argues that a theory of witnessing avoids the pitfalls of recognition theory by spotlighting the 'address-able' and 'response-able' subjectivity of the other, who testifies of the horrors of subordination and domination. We end oppression by addressing and responding to the other's subjectivity.

Hegel might agree with most, if not all, of Oliver's observations concerning a conception of recognition based upon the struggle in 'Mastery and Slavery.' Hegel, too, is critical of the flawed ideal of recognition the struggle's protagonists assume, and he would agree that this model only 'repeats the dynamic of hierarchies, privilege, and domination' (Oliver 2001: 9). However, it should be clear from the foregoing that Hegel does not deny the subjectivity of the other. *Two* self-consciousnesses, that is, two cognitive subjects, wage the struggle to the death. While Hegel does claim, in the passages leading up to the struggle, that *for self-consciousness* the other at first appears as an 'ordinary object' (*PhS* ¶186; *PhG* 148), this is the perspective of self-consciousness (not of Hegel) and only the case because the other has not yet *displayed* his subjectivity.

Furthermore, while it is true that mastery and slavery result in the 'objectification' of the slave, with only the master having subjectivity ascribed to him, again this is how *they* see their situation, by virtue of their erroneous identification of subjectivity with mastery. It is not how Hegel intends *us* to see it. The slave discovers his subjectivity through his labor, but we have witnessed it all along. What the slave recovers through labor is not his subjectivity but his *awareness* of it. Of course, it is because the slave becomes aware of his subjectivity that the dialectic progresses, even to the point where Hegel can show two subjects again confronting each other, this time becoming fully aware of each other's nature as subjects and legitimizing that subjectivity in mutual recognition.

Moreover, Hegel's analysis of mutual recognition gives evidence that he also ascribes a role to witnessing—in Oliver's sense of giving testimony to both what is seen and not seen—in the fulfillment of mutual recognition. Language is the medium through which subjects convey their recognitive understanding. Conscience attests to what has not been seen by the 'beautiful soul,' namely, their shared identity and the idea that their 'hypocrisy' is in some sense 'good' insofar as it makes possible the actualization of duty. Moreover, the confession and forgiveness of conscience and the 'beautiful soul' affirm the address-ability and response-ability of both subjects in a way that promotes mutuality and equality.

Oliver's highlighting of the tendency toward 'subjectivity blindness' among' recognition theories is important and echoed in comments by Nancy Fraser and Patchen Markell concerning the dangers of treating minority groups as less than full subjects and as passive beneficiaries of recognition. They, too, caution against emphasizing too much the ways misrecognition damages subjectivity without acknowledging the inner resources through which the subordinated restore their damaged subjectivity and sometimes resist damage in the first place. As Markell observes, 'there is . . . something troubling about making psychic deformation into a constituent feature of injustice, for this seems to deny that people may experience severe forms of social and political injustice without finding themselves 'crippled' or 'scarred' by the experience' (2003: 18). Fraser stresses that this tendency among recognition theorists to 'constitute some actors as inferior, excluded, wholly other, or simply invisible, hence as less than full partners in social interaction' is another form of misrecognition (2001: 24). I agree that while misrecognition all too often compromises the subjectivity and agency of the subordinated, often to the point of thwarting chances for resilient autonomy, it is crucial to acknowledge the address-ability and response-ability of these *subjects* who do resist and overcome the damaging effects of oppression.

### Markell on the self-undermining character of recognition

Patchen Markell targets more squarely an important internal tension in Hegel's recognition theory. He argues, in *Bound by Recognition*, that Hegel rightly criticizes the desire for recognition in 'Mastery and Slavery' and is appropriately sensitive, in his analyses of 'Mastery and Slavery' and *Antigone*, to the finitude and contingency of action (2003: 99ff.). Nevertheless, Hegel proceeds to advance a conception of *mutual* recognition in the *Philosophy of Right* that, like all desires for recognition, stems from a delusional desire for sovereignty: 'the condition of being an independent, self-determining agent' and of experiencing 'uncompromising self-sufficiency and mastership' (Markell 2003: 11; Arendt 1998: 234). Markell thinks Hegel is therefore still largely blind to the way in which the pursuit of recognition fails to acknowledge our fundamental finitude and vulnerability. Recognition's aspiration for sovereignty cuts against our awareness of our finitude and vulnerability, culminating in simply a different kind of domination. Markell argues instead for a politics of acknowledgment, since he sees social injustice as rooted, not in the misrecognition of identities but rather in our failure to 'acknowledge [our] own basic situation and circumstances,' our finitude and 'intersubjective vulnerability' (2003: 7, 14).

Markell is correct to acknowledge Hegel's sensitivity to 'our basic situation' and the contingency of action. Hegel expresses this in what

Markell calls his 'diagnostic' voice, underlying the basic approach of the *Phenomenology* (92). Markell observes, for instance, that Hegel highlights the faulty understandings underlying the desire for sovereignty exhibited by the protagonists of the struggle to the death. However, he thinks that in the *Philosophy of Right* Hegel 'tries but fails' to harmonize this diagnostic voice, in his analysis of the contradictions driving that dialectic, with his 'reconciliatory' voice, which promises a final 'redemption' of 'contradiction, division, and suffering' in the mutually recognizing community of *Sittlichkeit* (92–93). Thus, for example, Hegel's reconciliatory voice supposes recognition to be a precondition of sovereign agency, but his diagnostic voice acknowledges that 'action forever outruns the relations of recognition out of which it emerges' (94). The outcome of Hegel's failure to harmonize these two understandings is the perpetuation in the *PR* of the *problem* of recognition: relations of subordination (such as the exclusion of women from the public sphere) that are the legacy of the desire for sovereignty and the denial of our finitude and vulnerability.

Markell concludes that we should therefore understand social relations 'not in terms of the failure of recognition, but in terms of the failure of *acknowledgment*—that is, the failure to acknowledge one's own finitude, rooted in the condition of human plurality' (95). He thinks Hegel attributes problems of subordination in *Sittlichkeit* to failures of recognition and proposes mutual recognition as their solution; but they are actually failures to acknowledge our finitude and vulnerability.

Markell's observation about the persistence of social injustice in *Sittlichkeit* (e.g., in the treatment of women) is apt and rightly pinpoints a problem in Hegel's application of his theory that I will take up in Chapter 7. For now I wish to point out that his account of Hegelian recognition omits Hegel's crucial culmination of the theory in the dialectic of conscience, which (I will show in Chapter 6) Hegel presupposes in his account of *Sittlichkeit*. It should be clear by now that Hegel's sensitivity to finitude and vulnerability is fully evident in his account of the standoff between conscience and the 'beautiful soul' and their agonistic achievement of mutual recognition. But Markell does not discuss this account, and so he does not acknowledge that although Hegel is optimistic about the prospects of mutual recognition for individual freedom, and although we may conceive this as a kind of desire for sovereign agency, Hegel's idea of sovereign agency is by no means Markell's 'antidote to the riskiness and intermittent opacity of life' (5). Quite the contrary, it presupposes an ongoing process of interaction in which individuals admit the fallibility of even conscientious action, leaving them vulnerable to the judgments of others, who may deny their legitimacy in acting. Thus, while the desire for recognition, in Hegel's view, is indeed the desire for the legitimation of one's authority as an agent, this does not entail that one expects this to end all conflict. Nor is the desire for freedom the desire for absolute independence. Hegel makes clear that while freedom entails the ability to actualize one's particularity, we only experience genuine freedom through acknowledging our mutual dependence. We must indeed understand freedom as an intersubjective achievement rather than as a feature of 'unencumbered' selves (12).

I maintain, then, that Hegel's treatment of mutual recognition in the *Phenomenology* harmonizes his diagnostic and reconciliatory voices successfully. In fact, Markell's notion of acknowledgment is implicit in Hegel's conception of recognition.

# Conclusion: Hegel's Theory of Recognition in the *Phenomenology*

I have argued that in the *Phenomenology* Hegel advances a theory of recognition that recommends a conception of public recognition capable of redressing contemporary oppression. He enriches the provisional conception of recognition I derived from Honneth and Taylor by advancing a notion of it as the mutual acknowledgment, by two or more interaction partners, of the legitimacy of their conscientious agency. I end this chapter by reformulating Hegel's definition of recognition, showing how it satisfies two criteria of an adequate conception, and exploring its relevance to our concern with overcoming oppression.

## Reformulating Hegel's concept of recognition

I have interpreted Hegel's conception of recognition—as 'spiritual unity in its doubling' (*PhS* ¶178; *PhG* 145–146)—as indicating a *unity achieved by two distinct shapes of spirit* (i.e., two distinct communities of subjects advancing conceptions of their natures as knowers and agents) *constituted of their now shared understanding of their essential nature as authoritative, rational subjects.* Recognitive understanding is required to attain this knowledge of oneself as authoritative, since an individual can only *actualize* her authority through recognition by another subject whom she recognizes as authoritative. The process involves their appropriation of each other's perspectives through dialogue such that their self-conceptions as authoritative subjects are legitimated *through each other* in two ways: (1) in their affirmation of each other's subjectivity, expressed by their willingness to appropriate each other's perspective; and (2) in the specific conception of each subject formed by the other, which each subject finds worthy of appropriation. Their reconciling '*Yea*' is the speech act signifying their achievement of spiritual unity, their affirmation of their recognitive understanding. Thus, I translate Hegel's pure concept of recognition into more contemporary (albeit provisional) terms:

$R_{p4}$: *Recognition is an act expressing the mutual acknowledgment of two (or more) distinct subjects of their shared understanding of themselves as authoritative subjects.*

I now enrich this definition by taking into account the nature of recognitive understanding as achieved by two shapes of *conscientious* moral spirit. As a form of social understanding, recognitive understanding expresses individuals' awareness that their freedom to act is mediated by others' recognition of their rationality (the social freedom thesis). As a form of self-understanding, it expresses their knowledge of themselves as conscientious, albeit *particular* knowers and agents. Accordingly, recognition, as the mutual affirmation of a shared recognitive understanding, is the mutual acknowledgment by subjects of the legitimacy their conscientious, but particular and *different*, styles of agency. By '*styles* of agency' I mean their different ways of performing actions and formulating judgments, largely informed by the interests, desires, and understandings entailed by their different forms of life and conceptions of the good. Incorporating this notion into $R_{p4}$, I now say that, for Hegel (and finally),

$R_f$: *Recognition is an act expressing subjects' mutual acknowledgment of the legitimacy of their conscientious, albeit particular and different, styles of agency.*

Let us compare $R_f$ to $R_{p3}$, which I derived based on Honneth's and Taylor's conceptions:

$R_{p3}$: *Recognition is an act expressing social members' acknowledgment of the legitimacy of the autonomous and particular ways of life (dignity and distinctness) of individuals and cultures.*

Both $R_f$ and $R_{p3}$ posit recognition as acknowledgment of the legitimacy of differences. Moreover, in both conceptions the content of the acknowledged differences is the same: for Hegel, it is conscientious agency, and for Honneth and Taylor it is autonomy and particularity (or dignity and distinctness). Recall that in $R_{p3}$ 'autonomy' refers to rational and moral accountability, and 'particularity' designates worth as a contributor to the life of a community. These are precisely the characteristics of Hegel's conscientious agent, whose rational and moral authority, actualized in a concrete, public action, is acknowledged by another as legitimate.

The only essential difference between the two conceptions is that $R_f$ stresses the mutuality of recognition, whereas $R_{p3}$ does not. According to Hegel, *genuine* recognition is never unilaterally granted. This is important, for we sometimes conceive recognition as extended unilaterally by majority groups to minorities. Hegel's conception enables us to see that genuine recognition entails that both groups recognize each other, that *both* attain recognitive understanding.

## Satisfaction of two criteria of an adequate conception

In the preceding chapters, the problems of contemporary oppression and of theoretical responses to it gave clear indications of some of the work to be done by an adequate conception of recognition. The first two criteria are:

$CR_1$: It specifies the means by which acts of recognition undermine or reverse social and institutional modes of oppression; that is, through legislation, institutional reform, the cultivation of a different moral understanding, or other means.

$CR_2$: It elucidates how acts of recognition embody liberal neutrality, understood as the commitment to treat different ways of life as equally legitimate and viable.

With regard to $CR_1$, Hegel's conception $(R_f)$ clearly indicates that acts of recognition, which are in the first instance dialogical affirmations of a shared understanding, undermine or reverse modes of oppression primarily by cultivating a moral understanding that transforms social relationships of moral subordination into ones characterized by equality and reciprocity. In this way, recognition *fulfills* the social relationship expectations of individuals. While $R_f$ says nothing about legislation or institutional reforms, it does not preclude such measures as expressions of recognition. Legislation and reforms may be secondary manifestations of citizens' mutual recognition, since laws and institutions are, in Hegel's view, the concrete actualizations of social rationality.

It is also clear that $R_f$ satisfies $CR_2$, the requirement that it support a conception of neutrality as treating differences equally in public. Hegel's definition plainly states that recognition is mutual acknowledgment of the legitimacy of conscientious, albeit different, styles of agency. Of course, these styles of agency are informed by different forms of life and conceptions of the good. The suggestion, then, is that individuals possessed of recognitive understanding are capable of conceiving of liberal neutrality, not as indifference to differences, nor as the commitment to compensating for differences, in which case they may be viewed as disadvantages. Rather, acknowledging the particularity of their actions and judgments (including their own), social members can acknowledge the *positive* value of difference as sources of identity and agency, hence, as equally legitimate.

## Conclusion: applying the dialectic of conscience to our contemporary situation

Hegel's theory of recognition is an especially promising candidate for *our* appropriation, both by virtue of its insight into the relationship between recognition and genuine freedom, and insofar as the bipolarity of struggles for recognition in his account is analogous to that of contemporary struggles. We might read the final struggle for recognition between conscience and the 'beautiful soul' as the demand, on one hand, of social groups for recognition of their authoritative agency as co-creators of what are in fact *multicultural* societies versus the demand, on the other hand, of majority groups for recognition of their forms of life and their norms as of 'universal value' and hence as the most rational modes of social and political life. Conscience does affirm the authority of the larger community to establish norms and hold community members accountable to them. However, conscience, too, is part of that larger community. As such, she demands the freedom to contribute to the determination of its norms just as she determines her actions in accordance with them. She only solicits the others' acknowledgment of her conscientiousness. This idea resonates with my Chapter 4 claim that emancipatory movements are struggling to have their values integrated into the value-horizon of the larger society to which they contribute.

Thus, the shape of spirit represented by conscience, like contemporary emancipatory movements, affirms and proclaims the legitimacy of conscientious actions that necessarily express particularity and difference. They demand acknowledgment of their legitimacy by equally self-assured, universalizing, and judging majority groups. Only then can *both* experience their agency as *objectively* valid and free.

In fact, Hegel's conception of recognition ($R_f$) makes clear that absent such acknowledgment of their legitimacy, minority groups are *unjustly* denied full freedom and potentially oppressed. That denials of recognition are unjust follows from the thesis that recognition is a requirement of morality. That they can be oppressive is also shown by $R_f$: wherever subjects are denied acknowledgment of their legitimacy as agents, they lack assurance that they can act unconstrained by others. The situation is oppressive if their legitimacy is denied in sufficiently many domains that their opportunities for resilient autonomy are thwarted. Moreover, if the mutuality condition of $R_f$ is violated, the result is either unequal recognition or mutual disregard. The first case culminates in moral subordination. The second forecloses self-actualization.

In light of the mutuality condition, I stress furthermore that only when the 'beautiful soul' is challenged by conscience is he able to overcome the inefficacy of his judging-without-acting and his failure to manifest concretely his unity with others. By analogy, the demands of emancipatory movements for recognition might be read as a summons to majority groups, not only to cease allowing their values to parade as universal, but also to acknowledge their unity with minority groups. For to achieve *their* freedom, members of majorities must actualize their essential natures as members of a *shared* community, existing in a state of interdependence with minority groups. Their willingness to acknowledge this fact is just as much a condition of minorities' acknowledgment of *their* legitimacy as is their willingness to extend recognition to minorities. Absent recognition of their legitimacy, majority groups only enjoy the semblance of sovereignty appropriate to deluded masters and wasted beautiful souls.

Chapter 6

# Recognition in the *Philosophy of Right*: Particularity and Its Right

*In modern times people have been concerned to consider the state, to determine how it should be organized and governed. They have so to speak, sought to build the upper floors, but have neglected or demolished the foundations . . . But an organization cannot hang in the air. The ethical must exist not only in the form of the universality of the state, but also essentially in the form of particularity.*

*(Hegel)\**

In his *Elements of the Philosophy of Right* and associated lectures (*LNR* and *VPR*), Hegel suggests that the form of liberalism we have instituted so far represents the first budding of a truly liberal society. History, Hegel says, is the progression of human societies toward greater freedom, and ethical liberal modernity is the fulfillment of this progression.

In ethical liberal modernity, freedom is secured not merely negatively, by protecting individual rights from infringement, but also positively by publicly recognizing citizens' 'right of particularity' (*PR* §154), their liberty to actualize their different identities through conscientious agency. Hegel claims that in a genuinely liberal polity, 'the right of individuals to their *particularity* is . . . contained in ethical substantiality, for particularity is the mode of outward appearance in which the ethical exists' (*ibid.*). That is, although, in one sense, an ethical community exists by virtue of its norms, laws, and so on, it also exists because of the particularity of its agents. They should therefore find their right to particularity secured by the community's institutions and practices. The citizen can find her *distinctness* recognized via the practices and institutions of a shared public life.

In this chapter and the next, I examine Hegel's portrait of a society in which the public recognition of difference, instantiated in liberal institutions and social practices, is understood by social members as a necessary condition of freedom. In the *PR* Hegel establishes the necessity of the right of particularity by means of a speculative analysis of the core concept of liberal institutions: *freedom of the will* (§4). He begins with the concept's most abstract form—the universal freedom emphasized in abstract legal right—and analyzes each stage of its logical development from that abstract shape to its most enriched manifestation—the unity of universal (objective) and particular (subjective) freedom that is ethical life. The progression is fueled by the unmasking of the logical presuppositions of each stage, which expose their deficiencies as complete systems of right. Thus, the universal freedom of abstract right is revealed to presuppose the subjective freedom of morality, since the actuality of right as universal will presupposes individual wills (free subjectivities) that actually affirm it (§82A, 104, 104A). Morality, in turn, is shown to presuppose ethical life, by virtue of its implicit notions that the good can be actualized and that subjectivity can actually be good (§141, 141R).

The outcome of Hegel's analysis is the revelation that ethical life is the rational basis and principle of the highest form of social and political organization: a liberal institutional structure that, as the unity of abstract right (objective freedom) and morality (subjective freedom), is the actuality of *concrete* freedom. Furthermore, as a structure that recognizes the rights of both universality and particularity, of the community and individuals, ethical life not only accommodates the public recognition of difference but encourages it. For Hegel not only thinks that individuals can be free in the liberal state to express their moral, cultural, and individual differences in public, but he sees the conscientious expression of individuality as a necessary condition of both individual freedom and social stability. The conscientious expression of difference should not be merely tolerated but welcomed.

Hegel's theory of ethical life in fact presupposes recognition and specifies two crucial conditions of the possibility of publicly recognizing difference: (1) an arrangement of mutually supporting social and political institutions that facilitate and secure the conscientious expression of particularity; and (2) the recognitive understanding presupposed by members of such institutions, their awareness of both their universality as members of a shared community and the particularity of their spheres of value. I stress that Hegel's speculative analysis of civil society, in particular, highlights the crucial issue of achieving social justice through public recognition in everyday social life, such that Hegel's liberalism avoids the major pitfall of contemporary liberal theorizing about difference: it reaches beyond the concern with political rights and distributive justice and asserts the need for solid ethical bonds among citizens through which they form relationships characterized by moral equality and reciprocity. Hegel contends that such bonds are necessary for the actualization of freedom.

I begin, in the section titled 'Recognition in the Philosophy of Right,' by justifying my appeal to Hegel's *PR* for a model of a liberal society that can publicly recognize difference. One might worry that the *PR* is the wrong place to look for such a model in view of Hegel's controversial claims about women and non-European cultures, as well as his conception of individuals as, in some sense, accidents of the state. However, my move is justified by Hegel's having presupposed in ethical life the recognitive understanding elaborated in the *Phenomenology*. I claim that the final shape of recognized and reconciled conscience that Hegel calls 'actual conscience' in the *Phenomenology* (*PhS* ¶662; *PhG* 486) is the shape of 'true conscience' whose appearance marks the dialectical emergence of ethical life in the *PR*, and whose existence secures its fulfillment (*PR* §137R). Without the ethical disposition of 'truly' conscientious, mutually recognizing individuals there is no ethical life.[1]

I devote the greater part of this chapter (and the next) to Hegel's account of civil society, the primary domain of public social interaction in ethical life. In the section 'Particularity in the Free Market,' I highlight the significance and ambiguities of particularity as it relates to freedom, which are illuminated by Hegel's speculative analysis of the free market system, the 'system of needs' (§189). Hegel writes that in the free market, the moment of particularity, individual difference, is given the right to 'develop and express itself in all directions' so that individuals can pursue their interests and welfare (§184). Thus the free market is necessary for self-actualization. However, the excesses of wealth and poverty generated by the market system, which Hegel attributes to individuals' atomistic and abstract self-understanding, lead to such a degree of social instability that freedom is substantially undermined.

Therefore, citizens must win the *right* to express their particularity; they must be *recognized* as agents of true conscience. In the concluding section I briefly explain this claim, which I elaborate more fully in Chapter 7.

## Recognition in the *Philosophy of Right*

Some of Hegel's explicit mention of recognition in the *PR* appears to contradict my claim that for him it involves acknowledging difference; for he frequently uses the term with reference to universal personhood. One such reference appears in 'Abstract Right': 'Contract presupposes that the contracting parties *recognize* each other as persons and owners of property; and since it is a relationship of objective spirit, the moment of recognition is

already contained and presupposed within it' (§71R). Here Hegel emphasizes that right presupposes intersubjective recognition. But the sense of
recognition at work here is evidently not the 'acknowledgement of the legitimacy of conscientious, albeit particular and different, styles of agency'
that I derived from the *Phenomenology* account and argue is presupposed in
ethical life. Rather, Hegel has only said here that right presupposes recognition, and in this case the right of property presupposes the recognition
of personhood, that is, universality.[2]

Furthermore, Hegel carries this sense of recognition as the acknowledgment of personhood into his account of ethical life. His opening discussion of the administration of justice includes this claim about how we come
to recognize right:

> It is part . . . of *thinking* as consciousness of the individual [*des Einzelnen*]
> in the form of universality, that I am apprehended as a *universal* person,
> in which [respect] *all* are identical. *A human being counts as such because
> he is a human being*, not because he is a Jew, Catholic, Protestant, German,
> Italian, etc. (§209R)

This passage clearly extols universal personhood, and not particularity,
as the basis of recognizing right. However, it is crucial to distinguish that
here, as earlier, Hegel is addressing the recognition of *legal* right. Insofar
as right, or law, is *thought*, 'one must adapt the form of universality to the
objects,' in this case, to individuals (§209A). Hence, Hegel intends these
passages to support his argument that in *law* we recognize individuals in
their universality as equal persons.

Still, because most of Hegel's explicit uses of the term 'recognition' in
the *PR* appear in discussions of legal right, it is not obvious that he ever has
in mind the idea of recognition as acknowledgment of the legitimacy of
conscientious particularity. Nevertheless, I find two kinds of support for my
claim that he does. First, Hegel claims that in ethical life individuals win
their 'right of particularity' (§154). If particularity is a right, then it must
be recognized, since, for Hegel, right presupposes recognition. Hegel must
therefore envision particularity as recognized in ethical life. Second, ethical life comes on the scene in the *PR* only with the dialectical emergence of
true conscience as a shape of moral subjectivity. I maintain that true conscience, which wills the good itself, is the *PR* counterpart of the mutually
recognizing and reconciled actual conscience of the *Phenomenology*, which
knows that 'the universal is the element of its existence' (*PhS* ¶662; *PhG* 486).
If ethical life presupposes true conscience, it therefore presupposes the

recognitive understanding of actual conscience and, accordingly, recognition of the conscientious agency of particular individuals.

I devote the remainder of this section to showing how Hegel's account of true conscience reveals him to presuppose mutual recognition in ethical life. I highlight two features of the account: (1) the complementarity of Hegel's discussions of actual conscience and true conscience in the *Phenomenology* and *PR*,[3] and (2) textual suggestions in the 'Morality' chapter of true conscience's recognitive understanding.

## Hegel's complementary accounts of actual and true conscience

In the *Phenomenology* and the *PR*, Hegel presents two different accounts of conscience, even if in both cases conscience is presented as a distinctively *modern* shape of knowledge and volition and as the ultimate shape of *individual* knowing and willing. In the *Phenomenology* we confront two shapes of conscience as, at first, an acting and a judging conscience that have emerged dialectically out of Kantian moral consciousness (hence their distinctively modern character). As conscience they have progressed to *self*-certain knowing and agency, although their knowledge and volition lack objective validity until they both acknowledge the universal as the ground of their existence and authority and recognize the legitimacy of particularity. Their attainment of recognitive understanding marks the moment in which they achieve their 'completed form' as 'actual conscience' (*PhS* ¶662; *PhG* 486). Inasmuch as absolute knowing is implicit in the recognitive understanding of actual conscience, spirit transitions dialectically to the shape of knowledge called 'religion.'

Similarly, in the *PR* we are first introduced to 'formal conscience,' which emerges dialectically from Kantian morality and thus is clearly a *modern* shape of moral willing (*PR* §137). Furthermore, formal conscience is, like the acting and judging conscience of the *Phenomenology*, a problematically *self*-certain agent until such time as it takes for its content the universal good (the good in and for itself) and becomes true conscience. Unlike in the *Phenomenology*, in the *PR* we are not shown how this transition from formal to true conscience occurs through intersubjective recognition. Rather, Hegel emphasizes two senses in which the transition occurs as a logical development. On one hand, he highlights that the very *concept* (Idea) of moral conscience, as subjectivity that wills the good, presupposes that there is an *actual* subjectivity that wills the *actual* good, namely, the true conscience (§141, 141R).[4] On the other hand, he stresses that the 'vacuity' of the various shapes of merely formal conscience, their moral and spiritual impoverishment, stimulates a 'longing . . . for an objective condition' that can only be satisfied by the actuality of the universal good—the actuality of freedom in ethical life (§141A). Inasmuch as concrete ethical life is the actuality of true conscience, the sphere of morality therefore transitions dialectically to ethical life. It is worth noting, however, that while Hegel does not present various scenes of intersubjective recognition to account for the transition from formal to true conscience, he does stress that, unlike the various shapes of merely formal conscience he describes in §140, the true conscience *will* be found worthy of recognition by others, inasmuch as the determinate content of its action is not what it merely *takes* to be good but what is *actually* good (§137R).

Thus while Hegel's accounts of conscience in the two texts are in some respects similar, there are also significant differences, most notably that the *PR* account does not make explicit that the true conscience possesses the same recognitive understanding as the actual conscience of the *Phenomenology*. However, we can attribute this difference to the different method of the *PR*. In contrast to the *Phenomenology*, which traces phenomenologically the experience of consciousness, the *PR* is engaged in the speculative analysis of the concept of the free will. Thus in the *Phenomenology* we witness the dialectical progression of the *experience* of acting and judging conscience as they develop into actual conscience, whereas in the *PR* we critically analyze the logical unfolding of the *concept* of conscience from its formal shape to its actuality as true conscience. In the *Phenomenology* we get a recognition scene; in the *PR* we get a '*conceptual* transition' (§141R; my emphasis). My task, then, is to make explicit that true conscience possesses the same recognitive understanding as actual conscience.

We have seen that in the *Phenomenology* Hegel argues vigorously for the legitimacy of the concrete agency of conscience, which is in turn the basis for his inclusion of the intersubjective recognition scene. Hegel makes much of the agency of conscience in that text in order to highlight not only that morality, to be actual, necessarily entails action, but also that true knowing, which is the objective of spirit, cannot be attained through theoretical reason alone; practical reason is also implicated in the pursuit of the True. To show that true (authoritative) knowing is possible therefore requires that Hegel make the case for authoritative agency. But as we have seen, conscience can only know itself objectively as an authoritative agent when it is recognized. Hence the *Phenomenology* includes an explicit account of intersubjective recognition.

By contrast, because the objective of the *PR* is to show how the concept of free *will* is actualized, the text already presupposes an understanding of the significance of agency. The case to be made is that truly free agency is actualized through concrete social and institutional structures. Hegel might have presented here another full argument for intersubjective recognition as a crucial 'moment' of the actualization of the free will, but it is not clear how such an argument would fit into the speculative account of the unfolding of the concept—or that it would be necessary. The decisive move is from the *formal* shapes of conscience, whose content is always a strictly particular good, to the shape of *true* conscience, whose content is not only particular but also universal good. Hegel accounts for this transition logically, consistent with the method of the *PR*, by arguing that the presumptions that there *ought* to be both an actual good and an actual conscience that is good imply that there *can* be an actual good and an actually good conscience, that is, true conscience. It is not clear that he needs to introduce at this point an explicit account of intersubjective recognition.

Thus, whereas some commentators identify the difference between the *Phenomenology* and the *PR* as fundamentally that 'between a philosophy of consciousness and a philosophy of action' (Moyar 2004: 214),[5] I see the *PR* rather as taking up and elaborating speculatively the theory of agency already begun in the *Phenomenology*. In the *PR* Hegel's aim vis-à-vis conscience is to demonstrate both *that* conscientious agency is the highest mode of subjective freedom and *how* conscience is actualized through the concrete social and institutional structures it creates (i.e., beyond the parochial encounter of two individual subjects). The *PR* account of ethical life can therefore be viewed as an extension of the *Phenomenology* account of spirit, in which Hegel now reveals 'how the modern social world is determinately structured, how agents of conscience can be satisfied in their deeds' (Moyar 2004: 218).

### Textual suggestions of true conscience's recognitive understanding in the 'Morality' chapter

That said, I now highlight specific passages in the *PR* discussion of morality that strongly suggest that true conscience presupposes recognitive understanding. First, in his introductory elucidation of the development of subjective freedom, Hegel describes the content of the will in its final stage of morality:

> While I preserve my subjectivity in implementing my ends (see §110), in the course of thus objectifying them I *at the same time* supersede this subjectivity in its *immediacy*, and hence in its character as my individual

subjectivity. But the external subjectivity which is thus identical with me
is the *will* of others (see §73).—The basis of the will's existence [*Existenz*]
is now subjectivity (see §106), and the will of others is the existence
[*Existenz*] which I give to my end, and which is for me at the same time an
other.—The implementation of my end therefore has this identity of my
will and the will of others within it—it has a *positive* reference to the will
of others. (*PR* §112)

Hegel is here reiterating the point made in the *Phenomenology* that action,
the implementation and objectification of ends, is inescapably public. The
individual will makes positive reference to the will of others inasmuch as
action creates a new reality that has implications for the welfare of others
(§112A). Hegel stresses the distinctively *positive* character of this reference
to the will of others in order to distinguish this ultimate stage of morality (and the starting point of ethical life) from the relation to others in
abstract right, which 'contained only prohibitions,' such that 'an action
strictly in keeping with right consequently had a purely negative determination in respect of the will of others' (*ibid.*). Hegel adds, moreover, that in
this highest stage of morality—that is, in true conscience—'not just *one* will
is present,' but rather 'two wills with a positive reference to one another'
(*ibid.*). Thus, not only does the individual will have a positive reference to
the will of the others, that is, the universal will, but the universal will also
has a positive reference to the individual will inasmuch as the actualization
of the universal will, in the community's institutions and practices, affects
the individual's welfare. Hegel therefore stresses the '*right of the subjective
will,*' namely, that it 'can *recognize* something or *be* something only in so far
as that thing is *its own*' (§107). That is, the truly conscientious individual
must be able to recognize the universal will as legitimately securing his
welfare, that is, as expressing *his* will.

What, then, are the conditions of the community's recognition of the
individual will, what Hegel calls the 'right of objectivity' (§132R)? As a first
step toward answering that question, I highlight that in the *PR*, as in the
*Phenomenology*, Hegel emphasizes that concrete actions always bear the
stamp of the agent's particularity. After establishing the individual's right
to recognize as his own action only what is the expression of his own purpose, Hegel adds that the particular ends of the individual are the very
'soul' and motive of his action:

[T]he subject, as reflected into itself and hence as a *particular* entity in
relation to the particularity of the objective realm, has its own particular

content in its end, and this is the soul and determinant of the action. The fact that this moment of the *particularity* of the agent is contained and implemented in the action constitutes *subjective freedom* in its more concrete determination, i.e., the *right* of the *subject* to find *satisfaction* in the action. (§121)

Hegel is here building a bridge to the 'higher moral viewpoint,' which involves 'finding satisfaction in one's action, not in stopping short at the gulf between the self-consciousness of the human being and the objectivity of the deed,' as, for instance, in abstract Kantian morality (§121A; cf. *PhS* ¶¶632ff.; *PhG* 464ff.). This more advanced moral subject is certain of his right actually to pursue satisfaction through his concrete particular actions. He is certain not only of his right to recognize the universal will only insofar as it secures his welfare, but also of his right to realize that concrete good and welfare through his own actions.

With regard to the community's right of objectivity, Hegel writes:

[S]ince an action is an alteration which must exist in an actual world and thus seeks recognition in it, it must in general conform to what is *recognized as valid* in that world. Whoever wills an action in the actual world has, *in so doing*, submitted himself to its laws and recognized the right of objectivity. (*PR* §132R)[6]

Here we find that Hegel does, after all, make explicit reference to the individual agent's desire for intersubjective recognition in order to win acknowledgment of the legitimacy of his action. However, we have not yet explicitly encountered conscience, but rather the moral subject. In fact, the case for seeing *conscience* as eligible for recognition is made momentarily problematic by Hegel's claim that because conscience, *qua* self-certain subjectivity, appeals ultimately only to its own authority to determine its right and duty, 'the state cannot recognize the conscience in its distinctive form, i.e., as subjective knowledge' (§137R). But Hegel makes this claim in the process of distinguishing true conscience from merely formal conscience. It is true that the state cannot recognize formal conscience *qua* strictly subjective knowledge 'any more than science can grant any validity to subjective *opinion, assertion*, and the *appeal* to subjective opinion' (*ibid.*). *Insofar as* it is purely formal—solely the bare form of conviction—conscience is empty of a determinate content that can be recognized. Whether or not he actually wills true duty, the universal good, is an arbitrary matter, since he can express conviction with regard to any range of contents (§§137R, 137A, 139ff.).

However, matters are different where true conscience is concerned, for it does will a determinate content, namely, the good in and for itself. Accordingly, Hegel quickly adds, as a caveat to his claim about the state's inability to recognize conscience in its distinctive form, that '[w]hat is not distinct within the true conscience is nevertheless distinguishable' (§137R), namely, its commitment to universal good. It is distinguishable in true conscience because conscience as a bare *form* (as *formal* conscience) can express conviction with or without having the universal good as its content. But this capacity is not *actually* distinct in true conscience precisely because true conscience is by definition the will that unites form and content as the conviction to will the universal good.

It is because willing the universal good *just is* true conscience that true conscience is characterized by its 'ethical disposition,' that is, its 'disposition to will what is good *in and for itself*' (§137). As the disposition of an individual, true conscience is the agent's observable propensity to act in a manner consistent with the community's rational laws and principles (§137R). Accordingly, the ethical disposition, conscientiousness, is an evaluative quality recognized in ethical life. It is grounded in recognitive understanding inasmuch as it is characterized by the individual's awareness of his universality as a social member and of his authority to act as a particular agent. Agents of true conscience possess a robust understanding of themselves as existing in unity with their community and as being partly constituted by it.

It stands to reason, then, that while formal conscience *qua* subjective knowledge cannot be recognized by the community, true conscience can, insofar as it has a determinate content—the universal good—that, when actualized in action, can be 'recognized as valid in that world' (§132R). While the actualized good is what is explicitly recognized as valid, the action is always indivisibly the action of a particular agent (*PhS* ¶¶619, 637; *PhG* 455, 468). Therefore, in recognizing the validity of the actualized good, the 'truly' conscientious agents of ethical life recognize each other, manifesting their recognitive understanding. True conscience therefore presupposes intersubjective recognition.[7]

Of course, Hegel's stipulation that only true conscience can be recognized seems actually to suggest the suppression of individuality, since the individual is recognized only insofar as she wills the universal good. True conscience, that is, would seem to have to be completely loyal to and uncritical of the state in order to be recognized by it. I do not think this is the case, for Hegel stresses that the determination of the true universal good does not ultimately depend upon the fact that the state endorses it, but rather upon its rationality. He suggests that a conscientious individual convinced that a law of the state is not rational is entitled to 'question' that law, since 'what is law may differ in content from what is right in itself' (*PR* §212, 212R). This seems to suggest, in turn, that the state should recognize true conscience insofar as her conviction is indeed rational. Thus, even though the judgments and actions of true conscience attain objective validity only through recognition, it is not a foregone conclusion that only those judgments and actions that conform to the *status quo* can win recognition. Individuals may critique the established order.

My main point is that inasmuch as it is clear that ethical life presupposes true conscience, it must also presuppose recognitive understanding. In fact, because ethical life is inhabited by agents of true conscience (albeit, not exclusively so) the right of particularity is both actualized and legitimized.

## Particularity in the Free Market: The Benefits and Liabilities of Free Subjectivity[8]

I have argued that because ethical life presupposes agents of true conscience, it presupposes the attainment of recognitive understanding among its citizens.[9] Hence, citizens of true conscience in ethical life not only recognize individuals as universal persons of legal right, but they also acknowledge the legitimacy of each other's 'truly' conscientious agency. That is, they recognize each other as particular individuals committed to actualizing the good of all. Furthermore, they know that denying some citizens the right to realize the good in a manner consistent with their own interests amounts to denying them one ground for recognizing the universal good as their own good. It is to deny citizens full, concrete freedom.

My objective in this section is to establish that Hegel's language concerning the right of particularity translates into the language of public recognition. This amounts to elucidating the significance of particularity and its right in civil society; for although it is the whole structure of ethical life taken together (the institutions of family, civil society, and the state) that secures concrete freedom, it is mainly in civil society that individuals have the opportunity to actualize their particularity. Hegel argues that they must win the *right* of particularity, because particularity that is not cultivated to the standpoint of true conscience, and that seeks exclusively its own interests, leads to such extremes of wealth, poverty, and contempt for law and society, that civil society subverts itself. The right of particularity is therefore a normative notion indicating that an individual's expression of particularity can be recognized as legitimate.

## The positive significance of particularity in ethical life

Hegel's introductory analysis of the Idea of will in *PR* §§5–7 is an early indication of the significance of particularity for freedom. There he stresses that the differentiation of the universal will into determinate, particular willing is a crucial stage in the actualization of freedom. This notion stems from his logic, which posits that a pure, undifferentiated unity in fact has no being—no concrete existence—at all. Just as in the *Phenomenology* we are told that the absolute concept has first to be posited in order to exist and be known, so also in the *PR* Hegel writes that the universal will as Idea must become determinate in order to exist (§7). Thus, again, for Hegel, differentiation into particularity (actuality) is a positive moment in the development of the concept (essence or Idea), for differentiation is the condition of the Idea's existence.

From this line of thinking comes Hegel's account of the moments of the will as universality, particularity, and individuality, manifested concretely in the realm of right as, respectively, abstract right, morality, and ethical life. The first aspect of the will, universality, or 'pure indeterminacy' is the will as pure thinking: the will understood not as the will of any particular ego, shaped by an ego's drives or desires, but as willing without any specific content (§6). By contrast, the differentiated and determinate will *is* the particular will, which has for its content the needs, drives, and desires of a particular ego.

The universal will's (i.e., thought's) differentiation into particular human wills is, according to Hegel, the very existence of freedom. However, he stresses that as *individuals* humans at the same time retain their universality, for individuality is the unity of universality and particularity (§7). We possess both abstract personhood (a universal shared identity) and particular selfhood, which makes us unique. This structure of individuality is crucial, Hegel says, since 'freedom lies neither in indeterminacy nor in determinacy, but is both at once . . . [it] is to will something determinate, yet to be with oneself [*bei sich*] in this determinacy and to return once more to the universal' (§7A). Thus, one is free only to the extent that one is able to will one's particular ends as a person with needs, drives, and desires but also is able to achieve a reflective distance vis-à-vis one's willing, recognizing both that (1) what one wills in this moment is just one possibility among a veritably infinite number of possible contents that one could will

in this instance, and (2) one is a human being among human beings having particular wills of their own.[10]

At the same time, one acknowledges that one's own particular will is not
absolute but contingent. One can be free only if one expresses one's particular will in light of this awareness. I will show in Chapter 7 that this structure of individuality as the unity of particularity and universality is the
structure that makes it possible for citizens to win the right of particularity.
It is because individuals, though they pursue particular and different ends,
are nevertheless capable of advancing common ends that they are capable
of winning recognition of their particularity.

In the 'Morality' chapter, Hegel reiterates his claim that particular subjectivity is the concrete existence of the Idea of free will: 'subjectivity, in
its comprehensive particularity [i.e., as the *life* of an individual], is itself
the existence [*Dasein*] of freedom' (§128). Moreover, Hegel stresses again
that by 'particular subjectivity,' he means not just the 'abstract and formal
freedom of subjectivity' that in its indeterminacy can give itself any content (as the pure thinking of the universal will), but rather the subjectivity
that 'has a more determinate content only in its *natural subjective existence*
[*Dasein*]—its needs, inclinations, passions, opinions, fancies, etc.' (§123).
The life of the concrete, particular subject, then, is to be the manifestation
of freedom.

Accordingly, when in the introduction to 'Ethical Life' Hegel claims
that 'the right of individuals to their *particularity* is . . . contained in ethical substantiality, for particularity is the mode of outward appearance in
which the ethical exists' (§154), he means that ethical life depends upon
the concrete expression by individuals of particular needs, interests, and
concerns—that these are indeed essential to the actualization of freedom.
Of course, our particular needs, interests, and concerns are importantly
influenced by our cultural, biological, and historical conditions. Every particular subject is of a certain gender, ethnicity, physical and mental ability, and so on, that shape her particular desires, moral values, interests,
and modes of acting. The right of particularity, then, must entail the right
and freedom to give concrete expression to *these* facets of one's identity.
Furthermore, since particularity is 'the outward mode of appearance' of
ethical substance, it must be the case that these facets of identity are given
the right of *public* expression.

Particularity, or subjective freedom, is a significant moment in all three
structures of ethical life—the family, civil society, and the state. But securing the right of particularity is, to Hegel's mind, distinctively the legacy of
modern civil society. In the immediate ethical unity of the family, the particularity of members is acknowledged, but only immediately in feeling, in love.

The embracing of particularity is here distinctively unreflective. I love my mother, father, sister, and brother and embrace their particularity simply *because* I love them. I may even express this by saying that I love them no matter what they do. Thus here individuals 'count for something' simply by being family members (*HER* 233). However, in Hegel's view, just as all concepts have existence only through their being posited, so the particularity embraced immediately in the family must be posited if individuals are really to 'count for something' in the wider world. The immediate ethical unity of the family—the concept of the ethical—differentiates into moments of essence and actuality, in which the actuality of the ethical becomes material for reflection. The *logical* dissolution of the immediate, unreflective ethical unity of the family therefore constitutes the logical emergence of civil society, 'the [stage of] difference [*Differenz*] which intervenes between the family and the state' (*PR* §182A). Here, in Hegel's emphasis upon the status of civil society as the intermediate stage between the unreflective ethical unity of the family and the differentiated ethical unity of the state, we see again the continuity of the private and public spheres.

In calling civil society the 'stage of difference' Hegel is deploying his technical notion of difference as the diremption of the unity of the concept into essence and actuality. Again, in this case, the *essence* of ethical unity is the immediate, unreflected unity of universality and particularity that is the substantial unity of the family. Meanwhile, the *actuality* of ethical unity is now posited as a potential object of reflection in civil society. However, Hegel says that in civil society ethical unity is not, in the first instance, comprehended by individuals *as* a unity but, rather, only as its distinct moments of universal and particular willing. In this case they perceive, on the one hand, *particularity* as the subjectivity of the particular individual, which is accorded the freedom to pursue its interests and ends in the marketplace, or the 'state of necessity (*Staat der Not*)' (§183). On the other hand, members of civil society distinguish this domain of free agency from *universality*, the objective will of the community, which they identify as the domain of law (the administration of justice).

Civil society, then, has the following structure. The marketplace is the primary sphere in which particularity (subjective will) is actualized through individuals' agency in pursuit of their own interests. Meanwhile, the administrative justice system is concerned exclusively with the actualization of universality (objective will) that is the law; its concern is social stability, the good of all. However, because individuals' self-interested activity in the marketplace threatens freedom and social stability, Hegel highlights the role of the public authority (*Polizei*) and corporations (voluntary associations organized around professional and social interests) as ethical mediating institutions. These institutions constitute the actualization of the *unity* of particularity and universality in civil society, inasmuch as they have the interests of both individuals and the community as their concern. Hegel stresses, however, that these mediating institutions, especially the corporation, are oriented toward particularity, because they are primarily concerned, not with legal right (the domain of administrative justice), but with the welfare of their particular, local constituencies and members.

Because I am primarily concerned with public recognition of particularity, I focus mainly upon Hegel's analyses of the marketplace and corporations as oriented toward particularity: the market as the broad sphere in which individuals pursue their particular interests exclusively, and corporations as associations (comprised of persons of true conscience) pursuing more consciously interests of both particularity and universality. However, I must stress that, in one sense, the unity of universality and particularity is actualized *immediately* in corporations and that social members only come to *reflect* on this unity in the constitution of the state. In §157C, Hegel notes that the constitution of the state is the *actualized Idea* and thus is the actualized *concept* (thought) of the unity of particular and universal will—the laws and institutions of the state *as such*, which are, accordingly, the concrete manifestation of the Idea of universal freedom. Inasmuch as this unity is actualized in civil society but not conceptualized as an object of reflection, and, moreover, inasmuch as the dominant principle of civil society is particularity and not universality, Hegel calls civil society the 'external state,' signifying in one expression civil society's similarity to and difference from the constitutional state (§157). The constitutional state also regards both universal and particular interests but is oriented toward universality.

Thus, civil society emerges as a logical development of the universal will as freedom out of ethical immediacy. However, it is also the stage of the natural dissolution of the family, in which subjects begin their process of social differentiation, establishing their own identities as individuals with particular needs and interests. Now they understand themselves both as legal persons of abstract right and as moral subjects: 'as owners and disposers of private property, and as choosers of their own life-activity in the light of their contingent and subjective needs and interests' (Wood, *PR* xviii). Hegel highlights the historical significance of the emergence of a differentiated civil society as a distinctively modern phenomenon:

> [T]he creation of civil society belongs to the modern world, which for the first time allows all determinations of the Idea to attain their rights. If the state is represented as a unity of different persons, as a unity which

is merely a community [of interests], this applies only to the determination of civil society. (*PR* §182A)

Civil society is distinctively modern, because prior ages were almost exclusively agrarian societies in which family units had to remain cohesive for their survival. Only in the technologically and agriculturally advanced modern age has it become typically the case that young adults leave their families to enter the wide world and fend for themselves as independent social members. This is the first time in history that the particular will gains prominence relative to the universal will; hence, it is the first time that 'all determinations of the Idea . . . attain their rights' (*ibid.*).

### The free market's undermining of subjective freedom: the problems of pure self-interest

In keeping with civil society's intent to secure citizens' freedom to express their particularity, Hegel says that it posits as its fundamental and guiding principle, 'the principle of self-interest . . . Each is his own end' (*VPR 19* 147–148). Thus, even though civil society contains the moment of universality—explicitly in its administrative justice system, public authority, and corporations, and implicitly in the social and economic *interdependence* of its members—social members perceive the universal as being in the service of the particular. Hegel writes: '*[W]e do not yet have life within the universal for the universal.* Rather the end is the subsistence and right of the individual . . . The purpose of acquiring rights is to satisfy one's needs; the purpose of the state based on need is to secure and protect property' (*VPR 17* §89).

Accordingly, Hegel says that in the marketplace the moment of particularity is given the freedom to 'indulg[e] itself in all directions' (*PR* §185). The free market is essential, of course, as an economic model through which, at least in principle, individuals have the highest degree of freedom to apply their skills, talents, and ingenuity to the satisfaction of their needs and interests. They pursue their good and secure their livelihood in their own way. The free market is therefore necessary for the realization of concrete freedom. Furthermore, it conduces not only to the good of individuals but to that of the whole community, which also prospers as a result of free market energy, vitality, and innovation.

However, genuine freedom is not just the ability to do or forbear doing but, rather, involves rational self-determination—it 'is both at once' (§7A). Accordingly, Hegel does not see all expressions of particularity in civil society—that is, all agency—as objectively valid. This issue looms large in Hegel's account; he insists that agency motivated purely by self-interest, unmediated by a concern for the good of others, leads to a degree of social and economic instability that undermines the freedom promised by and avidly pursued within civil society. The very presupposition of individuals that they pursue their interests independently (atomistically) contradicts the truth that all are necessarily and inextricably *interdependent*:

> [T]he individual's subsistence and welfare are conditioned by the welfare and preservation of all. Individuals care only for themselves, have only themselves as their purpose, but they cannot care for themselves without at the same time caring for all and without all caring for them. In pursuing their own self-interest they at the same time work for the others. (*VPR 17* §89)

In Hegel's view a member of civil society is not just 'a self-interested, calculating *homo economicus*' (Wood, *PR* xviii); we must therefore *robustly* comprehend individuals as more than this. The recognitive understanding of individuality as constituted in part by membership in a shared community, 'a universal family' (*PR* §239), must supplant the false consciousness asserting that we are mere atoms: separate, private, and unencumbered.

Hegel's conviction of our inextricable interdependence was reinforced by his study of political economy (Adam Smith and others) and its claims that rational principles, a kind of internal necessity, underlie the collective market behavior of individuals. Accordingly, Hegel stresses that in civil society '[t]he relation of individuals to each other is *not* a relation of freedom but of necessity. They are related to each other against their knowledge and their will' (*VPR 19* 147; italics mine).[11] Whether or not I, as a member of society, am robustly aware of the fact, I depend upon others:

> This is the sphere of dependence and need . . . Since I can satisfy my needs only through the will/cooperation of others, I am thus for the others; I must be what they want, and I must conform myself to their ideas. Thus I must in general depart from my idiosyncrasies and posit myself in conformity and correspondence to them. I must give myself the form of universality, to make myself something for the others. (*VPR 19* 147–148)[12]

While I may perceive myself as being free and independent, in a market society, I cannot meet all my subsistence needs independently. My freedom is conditioned by countless others, many of whom I will never see.

Because I depend on these others, I must—and I actually do—adjust my behavior to their expectations and needs. This fact of interdependence is, Hegel says, 'accordingly the root which links self-seeking with the universal' (*PR* §201A). *Members of civil society must become robustly aware of this fact.*

Moreover, according to Hegel, individuals in civil society must abandon their erroneous conception of the universal as designed to serve self interest, their belief that 'what unites [them] is universal egoism and reciprocal exploitation' (*HER* 233). They must understand the universal as *spirit*, an ethical community united by a commitment to securing not only individuals' property rights, but also their welfare and livelihood, and that of the community. Williams states the problem well by noting that 'difference [i.e., particularity], *asserted without qualification*, means that civil society is not a genuine society with an immanent cohesion of its own but an atomistic, externally related aggregate that is *geistlos*' (234; my emphasis; see *PR* §156A).

Hegel's main point, however, is that civil society's false consciousness undermines this sphere's promise of freedom: 'Particularity . . . indulging itself in all directions as it satisfies its needs, contingent arbitrariness and subjective caprice, *destroys itself* and its substantial concept in the act of enjoyment' (*PR* §185; my emphasis). This is so for two reasons. First, rampant economic overproduction results from individuals' pursuit of a false recognition (associated with property ownership and conspicuous consumption) and their unreflective acceptance of increasingly mechanized mass labor (mirroring the social isolation and alienation presupposed by their atomistic self-conception) (§§198, 245). Second, overproduction contributes, in turn, to extreme wealth and poverty. These are especially problematic because the wealthy and the poor are exceptionally vulnerable to the 'rabble mentality' (*VPR 19* 196; cited in *PR*, p. 454), a contempt for law that undermines social stability. The wealthy may develop this disposition as a result of the power they wield in a culture that accords honor and recognition primarily to ownership. However, Hegel says that the poor who become a rabble do so in response to the wrong they suffer at the hands of civil society, which fails to secure the freedom it promises to all contributing members (*VPR 19* 194–196; cited in *PR*, pp. 453–454). In this way, civil society's false consciousness generates a cycle of 'extravagance and misery as well as of the physical and ethical corruption common to both' (*PR* §185).

How does this disintegration occur? When individuals leave their families and enter the wide world, they pursue employment in one of three general fields, or 'estates' (*Stände*): agriculture (the '*substantial* or immediate estate'), trade and industry (the 'reflecting or *formal* estate'), or civil service (the 'universal estate') (§§202–205). In modern societies most enter the estate of trade and industry, which depends largely upon mechanized manufacture and the specialized modes of labor that support it. Unlike in traditional agrarian economies, labor is no longer directed toward immediate subsistence—not even in the modern agricultural estate, which has also become mechanized—but is part of mass production, which often ends in both overproduction and the alienation of labor. Hegel comments that 'man no longer works up what he uses himself, or he no longer uses what he has worked up himself; that becomes only the *possibility* of his satisfaction instead of the actual satisfaction of his needs' (*FPS* 247; my emphasis; cf. *HER* 237).

Hegel observes, furthermore, that the mechanization and specialization of labor makes the market into a kind of mechanical 'beast' that feeds on the energies of its own young. The corresponding breakdown of traditional modes of work and, most significantly, of the ethical relationships that stem from them reinforces the belief of individuals that their condition in civil society is one in which every person is for himself. In *The First Philosophy of Spirit*, Hegel laments of this condition:

> Need and labor, elevated into this universality, form on their own account a *monstrous* system of community and mutual interdependence . . . a life of the dead body, that moves itself within itself, one which ebbs and flows in its motion blindly, like the elements, and which requires continual strict dominance and taming like a wild beast. (*FPS* 249; My emphasis)

The industrial 'beast' needs taming in part because, left to its own devices, it culminates in rampant overproduction. The division and universalization of mass labor means that work becomes 'abstract, homogeneous and easier' (*VPR 17* §121). This leads to an increase in productivity and efficiency that very easily crosses over from optimal production to overproduction, since individuals, seeking to insure their livelihood as well as to ensure it, welcome surplus. However, insofar as overproduction results in the creation of more goods than a particular market can consume, it also generates extensive unemployment and poverty (*HER* 243).

This tendency toward overproduction is further fueled by individuals' pursuit of recognition through property ownership and conspicuous consumption—their desire to confirm their status as 'self-made individuals,' another byproduct of their false consciousness. Williams states the point succinctly: 'In the external "machine" state, recognition is formal and mechanical' (238). Hegel writes, of the modern worker who does not associate recognition with community membership, that his 'isolation reduces him to the selfish aspect of his trade, and his livelihood and satisfaction lack stability. He will accordingly try to gain recognition through the external manifestations of success in his trade, and these are without limit' (*PR* §253). Here we confront again the problem of desire, that when a subject's aim is consumption, the object is revealed to be the essential moment of the relation and, hence, the true object of recognition. In the case of civil society, it is not particular subjectivity that is recognized but rather material wealth. The pressure therefore to accumulate material goods and wealth (indeed, much more than one needs merely to subsist) and to demonstrate *thereby* that one is 'somebody,' exacerbates civil society's already pronounced tendency toward overproduction.

A major consequence of an overproducing market economy is extremes of wealth and poverty. Because many welcome surplus as security for their welfare, others must bear the burden of the unemployment and poverty that accompany it. Even among those who can sustain employment, there are many whom the efficient and high-producing 'machine' thrust into poverty. The value of labor diminishes proportionally with the increase in volume of goods produced (*FPS*, 248) such that there is, first of all, a significant number of 'working poor,' who accept low-wage jobs in order to keep jobs at all. Capitalists are then in a position to increase their profits while driving down prices. This means, second, that small business owners, independent craftsmen, and farmers, although employed, also suffer losses and the risk of unemployment, since their traditional products are unable to compete with the mass-produced goods of industry (*VPR 4*: 610; Wood, *PR* xxi). Therefore, poverty and wealth in civil society can be essentially, in Schlomo Avineri's words, 'two aspects of a zero sum equation' in which 'poverty in one quarter is the price society pays for wealth in another' (1971: 148). The promise of freedom and prosperity is fulfilled for *some* members of civil society, but it is devastatingly broken for many, and begins to look very suspect for countless more.

Hegel is especially concerned with the plight of the poor, since theirs is quite obviously a condition of *unfreedom* in (at least) two respects. First, their opportunities for free agency, for the expression of their particularity, are seriously thwarted. Second, their very life itself is threatened as a consequence of this hindrance to their agency.

The threats to the agency of the poor come primarily from two sources: their lack of resources and their social marginalization and exclusion. With regard to the first, it is obvious that active participation in the market requires in the first place that one have skills, health, and decent clothing with which to enter the market. Indeed, Hegel acknowledges that market participation 'is *conditional* upon one's own immediate basic assets (i.e., capital) on the one hand, and upon one's skill on the other' (*PR* §200; *17:* §118). The poor typically lack these resources, most often not because they lack motivation, intelligence, or ingenuity. Their ability to acquire skills depends every bit as much on their access to adequate education, which is often lacking. Their health depends on their access to medical care, but with what will they procure it? Of course, money is also required for decent clothing. Accordingly, Hegel observes, the poor lack the means to satisfy their needs, which was to be the purpose of civil society:

> In this condition [the poor] are left with the needs of civil society, and yet—since civil society has at the same time taken from them the natural means of acquisition [§217] and also dissolves the bond of the family . . . [§181] they are more or less deprived of all the advantages of civil society, such as the ability to acquire skills and education . . . as well as the administration of justice, health care and often even the consolation of religion. (§241)

The result is that the poor have little or no opportunity to cultivate through their agency whatever skills and talents they may possess. Their particularity, that is, their subjectivity, and agency are thwarted since their agency has no application.

Of course, in a culture that accords recognition and honor primarily to property ownership and wealth, the poor, who obviously lack both, are denied recognition. They are excluded from society: marginalized and invisible. Nonrecognition is as effective as the lack of resources in frustrating the poor's opportunities for agency, since it, too, limits their access to places of work and, moreover, to other social venues wherein they might satisfy needs and pursue interests beyond the purely economic. However, civil society's nonrecognition of the poor has the further effect that others absolve themselves of any responsibility for restoring the right of the poor to be able, at the very least, to provide for their subsistence through their agency. The more advantaged members of society, believing that opportunities abound for gainful employment and prosperity, blame the poor for their condition: if some do not take advantage of the opportunities 'obviously' available to them, it is because they are too lazy or unintelligent. Success and prosperity are the just desert of those who diligently promote their own interests. Thus, civil society thinks it fulfills its obligation to citizens by providing them the *possibility* for satisfying needs through their agency, whether or not they are *actually* able to do so (*HER* 255–256; cf. *PR* §230 and *VPR 19* 191). Hegel writes, concerning this attitude: 'Now that states have recently entered the field of business and commerce, it has been said that [ensuring basic needs] is no affair of the state, and, even if individuals are ruined, only raises the level of the whole' (*VPR 17* §118). On the contrary, Hegel urges, '[The poor individual] is conscious of himself as an infinite, free being, and thus arises the demand that his external existence should correspond to this consciousness' (*VPR 19* 194–195; cited in *PR*, p. 453). Thus arises, that is, the emancipatory demand for recognition.

To Hegel's mind, the mere possibility of the satisfaction of needs amounts to the mere possibility of concrete freedom, especially when one considers that, *qua* possibility, it entails its opposite, namely, the possibility that one will not satisfy one's needs. In this way it is plain that this condition in civil society undermines some citizens' rights to life, the second respect in which the poor are rendered unfree. On this point Hegel observes first that

> all people have the right to live, and not only must this right be protected, not only do they have this negative right, they also have a positive right. The aim of civil society is the actualization of freedom. The fact that human beings have the right to live means that they [must] have this right positively fulfilled. The reality of freedom should be essential. The life and subsistence of individuals are accordingly a universal concern. (*VPR 17* §118)

Hegel argues here that (1) inasmuch as everyone has a right to live; (2) the right to life entails that they must be able *actually* to live, which requires the actuality of freedom; and (3) civil society's purpose is to actualize freedom; therefore (4) civil society does have a responsibility to ease the plight of the poor—to provide, at the very least, for their subsistence. While he does not oppose charity or public welfare, Hegel thinks that an individual's freedom is better secured when she is able to subsist through her own agency. To provide welfare would mean that 'the livelihood of the needy would be ensured without the mediation of work; this would be contrary to the principle of civil society and the feeling of self-sufficiency and honor among its individual members' (*PR* §245). On the other hand, simply finding jobs for the poor does not solve the problem either because of the problem of overproduction. Hegel therefore concludes 'that despite an excess of wealth, civil society is not wealthy enough . . . to prevent an excess of poverty and the formation of a rabble' (*ibid.*).

Inasmuch as this is, to Hegel's mind, 'a universal concern,' and not just the problem and responsibility of the poor, he argues that the poor are justified in invoking a 'right of distress (*Notrecht*)' (*VPR 17* §63) when their poverty indeed threatens their life:

> Life, as the totality of ends, has a right in opposition to abstract right . . . If someone whose life were in danger were not allowed to take measures to save himself, he would be destined to forfeit all his rights; and since he would be deprived of life, his entire freedom would be negated. (*PR* §127A)

Whenever poverty is so extreme that an individual's very life is in jeopardy, her right of distress for good reason trumps the right to ownership and property proclaimed by others, since life is a *totality* of ends and of greater worth than any other single end. We might interpret this claim simply as support for economic justice, but it goes deeper than that. Hegel also suggests that the right of distress challenges the atomistic self-conception that both underlies abstract right and is responsible for overproduction.

Because Hegel sees civil society as largely responsible for poverty, because of its false consciousness, he insists that the poor actually suffer wrong at the hands of civil society. 'No one can assert a right against nature,' he writes, 'but within the conditions of civil society hardship at once assumes the form of a wrong inflicted on this or that class' (§244A). He acknowledges that many among the poor are themselves aware of this. Their resulting moral indignation, if attended by moral degradation, becomes the 'rabble mentality,' an attitude of contempt for civil society and its laws that often culminates in open rebellion and criminality (*ibid.*).

We understand the poor's sense of indignation if we agree with Hegel's diagnosis of the causes of poverty: that it results not primarily from a lack of will or intelligence on their part but rather from the structure and functioning of the *laissez faire* market, which is both undergirded and reinforced by the atomistic conception of the individual. From this perspective, poverty looks less like a problem that the poor bring on themselves than a social by-product. Williams comments that 'poverty is *experienced* as due to faceless human arbitrariness and malevolence . . . Thus the wrong and injustice of poverty are not simply bad luck or bad breaks; they are *ethical* and political' (*HER* 248; my emphasis). Similarly, Hegel emphasizes the distinctively ethical character of poverty as a relationship of wills, highlighting that a significant source of the rabble disposition is moral indignation:

> The poor man is opposed not only by nature, a mere being, but also by my will. The poor man feels as if he were related to an arbitrary will, to

human contingency, and in the last analysis what makes him indignant is that he is put into this state of division through an arbitrary will . . . In this position, where the existence of freedom becomes something wholly contingent, inner indignation is necessary. Because the individual's freedom has no existence, the recognition of universal freedom disappears. From this condition arises that shamelessness that we find in the rabble. (*VPR 19* 194–195; Cited in *PR*, p. 453)

Hegel is quick to note that the rabble mentality is not a necessary consequence of poverty itself but of a certain disposition—and not all of the poor exhibit this mentality: '[p]overty in itself does not reduce people to a rabble; a rabble is created only by the disposition connected with poverty, that involves an inner rebellion against the rich, against society, the government, etc.' (*PR* §244A; cf. *PR* §195).

In fact, Hegel observes that the same shamelessness, rebellion, and contempt for law are also exhibited by the wealthy. Wealthy individuals develop the rabble mentality insofar as they think they can buy anything, including people, and that their sense of worth and their power really are indexed to their ownership of capital and property. The powerful wealthy can come to think they are above the law (*VPR 19* 194–195; *PR*, p. 454).

Both the poor and the wealthy, then, can display contempt for ethical principles and law. A criminal disposition develops on both ends of the socio-economic spectrum, posing the perpetual threat that the fabric of civil society will be unraveled from margin to center, bringing with it, as Williams insightfully observes, 'a return to the unequal, asymmetrical recognition of master and slave, domination and servitude' (*HER* 247).

## Conclusion: The Significance of the 'Right of Particularity'

I have argued that Hegel considers the expression of particularity to be essential to ethical life and freedom. Moreover, although particularity is a significant moment in all three structures of ethical life—the family, civil society, and the state—he envisions civil society as the primary domain in which particularity is assured the right to 'develop and express itself in all directions' (*PR* §184).

However, particularity must *earn* this right, because the venue of individuals' free agency—the marketplace—can also be the vehicle of social oppression and socio-economic instability. In this case, civil society promises prosperity and freedom but subverts itself. For Hegel the problem is not the bare fact of economic inequality, which is a predictable outcome of the free market (§200R). Rather, civil society *as traditionally conceived* is self-subverting because of its false consciousness, its sense that 'each individual is his own end, and all else means nothing to him' (§182A). Particularity that is not cultivated to the standpoint of true conscience—which exclusively seeks its own interests—culminates in such social and economic excesses that the promise of freedom goes unfulfilled. Hegel therefore stresses that this 'reflective standpoint of our time, this atomistic spirit, the spirit that places its honor in individual private interest and not in what is social and communal, is *harmful*' (*VPR 17* §121).

Civil society therefore requires ethical mediation: it must come to acknowledge the necessary interdependence of modern social existence, meaning that individuals must understand themselves recognitively as *spirit*. This is not to say that they must, for that reason, disregard their particularity or regard it as a purely private matter. Quite the contrary, Hegel proclaims, 'The great progress of our time is that subjectivity is recognized as an absolute moment. Subjectivity is essential. But everything depends on how subjectivity is *understood*' (*LPR*, 166; my emphasis). Indeed, he thinks that acknowledging our interdependence, our *inter*subjectivity, is what actually secures our right of particularity, since it is when civil society embraces and advances recognitive understanding, the 'ethical disposition,' that individuals find both their particularity and their universality *recognized*, and hence acknowledged as rights. How this transpires is the subject of Chapter 7.

Chapter 7

# Winning the Right of Particularity: Recognizing Difference in Ethical Life

*[D]emocratic justice does not require that all people be known and respected as who they really are. It requires, instead, that no one be reduced to any characterization of his or her identity for the sake of someone else's achievement of a sense of sovereignty or invulnerability . . . It demands that each of us bear our share of the burden and risk involved in the uncertain, open-ended, sometimes maddeningly and sometimes joyously surprising activity of living and interacting with other people.*
*(Patchen Markell)\**

In the preceding chapter, I launched my examination of Hegel's vision of ethical liberal modernity, in which particularity—*difference*—is assured the right to 'develop and express itself in all directions' (*PR* §184). A free market is essential as the venue in which such liberty is actualized; however, when atomistic self-interest predominates among social members, the market generates extremes of wealth and poverty that substantially undermines social stability and freedom. Hegel therefore stresses that citizens must become agents of true conscience who harmonize their particular interests with the universal good; the expression of particularity must be secured by recognized *right*.

According to Hegel, securing the right of particularity requires the inclusion within civil society of distinctively *ethical* mediating institutions that cultivate mutually recognizing agents of true conscience. In particular, it requires the cultivation [*Bildung*] within agents of the *recognitive ethical disposition* of true conscience. Ethical *Bildung* accompanies citizens' free choices to become members of estates, or social classes, through which they develop habits of honor associated not with heredity, as in premodern societies, but with 'true' conscientiousness, an evaluative quality celebrated in *ethical* modernity.

Agents of true conscience exercise their right of particularity within corporations, voluntary associations modeled upon the medieval guild and thus organized around professional and social interests (cartels are the

nearest equivalent, but professional associations, trade unions, civic organizations, and even townships are examples). Corporations have the distinctive role of being the chief sites of public recognition in ethical life.
In corporations, social members form solid ethical bonds, grounded in
recognitive understanding, such that agency expressing particularity is not
merely tolerated but *recognized*.

In the first two sections of this chapter, I explore Hegel's accounts of
ethical *Bildung* and of corporations as sites of recognition. In the section
titled 'Two Challenges to Hegel's Treatment of Difference in Ethical Life'
I consider two objections raised against Hegel's conception of ethical life
that bear significantly upon my effort to appropriate his recognition theory: first, that Hegel denies freedom to women by excluding them from
the public sphere and, second, that while he succeeds in demonstrating
the benefits of economic differentiation to freedom and social stability,
he fails to account for the disruptive potential of moral, cultural, and
individual differences (Stern 1989). I answer both objections by appeal
to Hegel's account of the ethical disposition grounded in recognitive
understanding.

I conclude by demonstrating that Hegel's theory of recognition satisfies
the third criterion of an adequate conception: it indicates the means by
which a whole society affirms, in solidarity, the legitimacy of cultures as
sources of identity through which social members contribute to collective
life. Accordingly, Hegel's recognition theory supplies us with useful concepts for contemporary efforts to end oppression.

## How Particularity Wins Its Right: The *Bildung* of True Conscience

### The basis of ethical *Bildung*: the requirements of concrete freedom

Another way of formulating the condition of securing the right of particularity (that individuals must become 'truly' conscientious) is to say that
social members only do so when they learn to harmonize two components
of concrete freedom: *subjective freedom*, that is, free agency, and *objective freedom*, their rational will actualized as the community's collectively endorsed
laws, customs, and institutions. Hegel insists that individuals must adopt the
perspective of universality: 'The principle of modern states has enormous
strength and depth because it allows the principle of subjectivity to attain
fulfillment in the self-sufficient extreme of personal particularity, *while at
the same time bringing it back to substantial unity* and so *preserving this unity in*

*the principle of subjectivity itself* (*PR* §260; first emphasis mine). Harmonizing one's subjective freedom with ethical substance in this way brings about the condition of genuine freedom that Hegel calls 'being with oneself in an other,' or 'be[ing] at home with [*zu Hause sein*] something other than [one]self' (*VPR 4* 102). Again, it is 'to will something determinate, yet to be with oneself [*bei sich*] in this determinacy and to return once more to the universal,' the condition of freedom exemplified by the recognitive relationship of love, or friendship (*PR* §7A). At the level of ethical life, this means freedom involves allowing the *community* to influence (to limit) one in virtue of its being a kind of significant other—integrating the community's interests with one's own. One identifies the universal good as one's own good.

At the same time, for individuals to *harmonize* subjective and objective freedom the community must secure subjective freedom. Hegel stresses that 'the universal does not attain validity or fulfillment without the interest, knowledge and volition of the particular' (§260). The individual and community, then, must recognize each other. Furthermore, individuals are only free to the extent that the community's norms and laws are truly rational and really procure the good of individuals (§268). As Allen Wood rightly observes, 'there is no freedom at all in a society whose members "identify" themselves with it only because they are victims of illusion, deception, or ideology' (*PR* xiii). Insofar as the community's norms and laws are rationality actualized, individuals can find *satisfaction* in acting rationally.

One way that Hegel formulates the idea that in ethical life individuals find satisfaction in acting rationally is by claiming that in this realm right and duty are *coextensive*: '[D]uty and right coincide in this identity of the universal and the particular will' (§155). This is in contrast to both the sphere of abstract right, in which 'I have the right and someone else has the corresponding duty,' and the perspective of morality, in which 'it is merely an *obligation* that the right of my own knowledge and volition, and of my welfare, should be united with my duties and exist objectively' (*ibid.*). The moral subject's way of formulating the relation of right and duty, as distinct moments that merely *ought* to be united, makes especially clear that to say that right and duty *coincide* in ethical life means that I can say, 'I have a right *actually to do* my duty.' I have a *right to do* what I ought to do. Stated this way, it is evident that Hegel emphasizes the individual's *right of agency* as much as her obligation to be dutiful. Since agency always bears the mark of particularity, winning the right of agency in ethical life means winning the right of particularity. This is one important sense in which in ethical life '[t]he individual . . . finds his *liberation* in duty' (§149).

Recall that in the *Phenomenology* Hegel claims that it is conscientious individuals who know both that duty is always something actual and that they determine in any given instance what their duty is (*PhS* ¶635; *PhG* 467). For Hegel, duty is determined not merely by an abstract formula, but importantly by the concrete functions of practical social life: 'For the universal aspect of good . . . cannot be fulfilled as an abstraction; it must first acquire the further determination of particularity' (*PR* §134A). One's duties are determined partly by one's social roles as parent, spouse, employee, employer, citizen, magistrate, and so on. When these roles are clearly defined by the community, conscientious individuals can indeed *know* what their duty is. Individuals who actually commit to fulfilling duty so defined, uniting their particular interest with the good of all, are agents of *true* conscience.

Hegel therefore claims that to experience concrete freedom the individual's goal in ethical life must be to become an agent of true conscience—a true *individual* who manifests his nature as the unity of universality and particularity in his possession of recognitive understanding. The individual achieves this quite 'naturally' through his free choices of a career and estate; for the ethical *Bildung* of estate membership educates the individual to the standpoint of true conscience.

### The role of education in the cultivation of true conscience[1]

In ethical life, students receive a formal civic and ethical education, *Pädagogik*, that emphasizes the value of social membership and the concrete duties of social life. In this way they are inspired to embrace conscientious individuality and citizenship. Hegel does not give an extensive account of *Pädagogik*, but what he does say is significant: he describes it as 'the art of making human beings ethical: it considers them as natural beings and shows them how they can be reborn, and how their original nature can be transformed into a second, spiritual nature so that this spirituality becomes *habitual* to them' (*PR* §151A). Thus, just as right is coextensive with duty in ethical life, so virtue becomes, through *Pädagogik*, 'simply *identical* with the actuality of individuals,' such that they become habitually ethical: 'the ethical [*das Sittliche*], as their general mode of behaviour, appears as *custom* [*Sitte*]; and the *habit* of the ethical appears as a *second nature*' (§151). A conscientious will replaces 'the original and purely natural will' and becomes 'the pervading soul, significance, and actuality of individual existence' (*ibid.*). The individual's 'natural' tendency to pursue self-interest exclusively is replaced by a will to harmonize his particular interest with the good of all. Only in this way, Hegel writes, 'does the substance of spirit begin to exist as spirit' (*ibid.*).

In contrast to *Pädagogik*, *Bildung* is *practical* education and acculturation into a way of life. However, like *Pädagogik*, ethical *Bildung* brings it about that the individual is transformed from a purely self-interested person into an ethically disposed one. Here, too, it is the process of cultivating 'the universality of thought' that 'purifies' human desires of their 'crudity and barbarism,' through 'representing them, estimating them and comparing them with one another and then with the means they employ, their consequences, etc., and with the sum total of satisfaction—i.e. with *happiness*' (§20). This uniting of universal thought with particular willing, Hegel says, is the 'absolute value' of *Bildung* (*ibid.*).

Thus the aim of *Bildung* is to facilitate an organic integration of social meanings with the self-understanding of individuals. Their membership in ethical institutions cultivates their deep awareness of the social functions and practices that ground their ways of life and inform their free choices, which are implicated in the construction of their identities. As an educative process, *Bildung* involves reflection upon social practices such that individuals are positioned, in a sense, to 'choose' their institutions. Accordingly, Rupert Gordon observes, 'the connection between social identity and individual difference is defined neither by force nor caprice, but by reason and right mediated through the subjective will' (1999: 94; *PR* §152, 152R). *Bildung*, then, is the means by which individuals discover for themselves, experientially, the value to their self-actualization of identifying with the ethical substance, integrating its interests and good into their own purposes. It is how they *discover* the satisfaction of acting rationally.

However, Hegel acknowledges that against the background of the rampant self-seeking typical of civil society, 'naturally' self-interested individuals will experience *Bildung* as *difficult*: as 'the *hard work* of opposing mere subjectivity of conduct, of opposing the immediacy of desire . . . and the arbitrariness of caprice' (*PR* §187R). It is difficult because such persons originally view the universal as merely a means to their satisfaction and not as a proper end. However, Hegel says they will learn through experience that attaining their ends is conditioned by the universal good. Individuals discover that they only really achieve their ends successfully when these are consistent with the social good; when they are not, individuals meet resistance. Accordingly, Hegel describes *Bildung* as 'the process whereby their individuality [*Einzelheit*] and naturalness are raised, both by natural necessity and by their arbitrary needs, to *formal freedom* and formal *universality of knowledge and volition*, and subjectivity is *educated* in its particularity' (§187). The individual becomes robustly aware of social members' interdependence, and that when he habitually harmonizes his will with the universal good, he meets little resistance from others. Hegel therefore concludes that '*Bildung* . . . [is] *liberation* and *work* towards a higher liberation' (§187R).

## The *Bildung* of estate membership

Let us now see how estates facilitate *Bildung*, the cultivation of recognitive understanding. The estates are three general fields of endeavor that become the new basis of social class in civil society: agriculture (the '*substantial* or immediate estate'), trade and industry (the 'reflecting or *formal* estate'), and civil service (the 'universal estate') (§§202–205). As estate members, individuals gain two important benefits. First, each individual assumes a professional role with associated concrete duties—'a determinate social identity' (Wood, *PR* xix). Second, each becomes cognizant of the social significance of her role and duties and their relationship to other functions that conduce to the thriving of both her estate and civil society as a whole. Thus social members come to identify with the larger goals, interests, and objectives of the community and cease being exclusively self-interested 'atoms.' The agency of each is a determinate contribution to the good of all and 'recognized for what it is by others' (*ibid.*).

The achievement of a determinate social identity is crucial as the means by which the individual's particularity acquires social significance. Just as, for Hegel, abstract essence achieves actuality (existence) through determination, so '[t]he individual attains actuality only by entering into *existence* [*Dasein*] in general, and hence into *determinate particularity*; he must accordingly limit himself *exclusively* to one of the *particular* spheres of need' (*PR* §207). The individual, if he is really to '*be* somebody,' must choose an estate to belong to: 'being somebody [*etwas*] means that [one] has substantial being,' that is, being within ethical substance (§207A). By choosing a determinate social identity, a profession, an individual's being—his particularity, or difference—becomes socially meaningful.

The determinate social identity an individual chooses involves responsibilities into which she is educated by other estate members. This is significant: already the harmonizing of private interest with a larger social good is in evidence as the individual learns to direct her agency toward the accomplishment of specific tasks that she *understands* as beneficial to society's functioning and not only to her own livelihood. Through this

*Bildung*, then, she comprehends her universality—not as the abstract person of legal right, but more concretely as one who is tangibly part of a social whole. Thus, as Gordon points out, 'education matters not only so that farmers will know how to farm, and spice merchants how to choose and bargain for the best product,' but also for the sake of 'the cultivation of extreme parochial particularity toward a more self-conscious, socially universal standpoint' (1999: 191).

In one sense, then, the significance of estates lies in their division along functional lines. The deeper importance of this functional division is that it makes evident to the individual the rational basis for uniting his interests with those of society. Hegel envisions estates as a kind of organism whose functioning, like market activity, is an inherently rational process representing the coordination of needs in the *Notstaat*: 'reason which is immanent in the system of human needs and their movement articulates this system into an organic whole composed of different elements' (*PR* §200R). The individual's entry into this system, by means of her estate, is not determined by birth, property ownership, or income, but rather by the functional nature of professions and her suitability for them. It is ultimately the product of individual *choice*. The bases of the individual's identification with and commitment to her social class and the good of civil society are located in her own reasons.

Moreover, the role and duties into which the estate member is educated have not merely an instrumental significance for her but also a manifestly ethical one. Because *Bildung* cultivates her awareness of the wide-ranging value of securing her needs as part of a coordinated social process, the individual learns (as presumably she did in childhood, if we accept Honneth's account), to harmonize her needs with those of significant and generalized others. Her estate becomes a 'second family' (§252). Hegel observes that '[w]hile the family is the primary basis of the state, the estates are the second,' since they are 'the root which links selfishness with the universal . . . which must take care to ensure that the connection is a firm and solid one' (§201A). As a member of such a 'second family,' each individual gains a solid sense of what is involved in being a *successful* member of her estate to which she is ethically bonded. She thus enjoys the '*rectitude* and the *honor of [her] estate*'—that is, *recognition*:

[E]ach individual by a process of self-determination, makes himself a member of one of the moments of civil society through his activity, diligence, and skill, and supports himself in this capacity; and through this mediation with the universal does he simultaneously provide for himself

and gain recognition in his own eyes [*Vorstellung*] and in the eyes of others. (§207)

The real beauty of this system is that while the different functions within estates are themselves ethically significant, since they determine some of an individual's concrete duties, they are also a source of an ethically signif-icant social diversity. Estates unite individuals of diverse socio-economic and geographical backgrounds, another mode of determinate particular-ity, such that *as* a social unity estates robustly have the character of spirit as identity-in-difference (Gordon 1999: 201).[2] Now in identifying with the functions of their estates, diverse estate members can also appreciate the significance of others' many *different* contributions to it. The university president, in identifying strongly with both the mission and purpose of the universal estate and the value of determinate contributions to it, can appreciate the significance not only of his own position, but also of many others. He can also appreciate the importance of other public service insti-tutions to the universal estate. Furthermore, he can acknowledge the sig-nificance of the other estates supporting civil society's functioning. Thus he discovers a rational basis for acknowledging the legitimacy of the many different contributions of civil society's diverse members.[3]

Ethical *Bildung* via estate membership clearly provides, then, a basis for relationships of mutual recognition among all contributors to civil society. Hegel writes that '[i]n this way, it is . . . recognized that [the individual] belongs to a whole which is itself a member of society in general, and that he has an interest in, and endeavors to promote the less selfish end of this whole' (*PR* §253). At the same time, they themselves are recognized as agents who pursue their particular ends and interests in *different* ways, and whose different styles of agency can be acknowledged as legitimate and worthwhile contributions to the greater good. Again, because the individ-ual identifies with his determinate role and performs it conscientiously, his 'particularity is difference that is understood and respected as difference in circumstances of social meaning. This is difference which is recognized' (Gordon 1999: 194).

I maintain, then, that when Hegel says an individual possesses the *honor* of an estate (*PR* §207), he means that the individual has won the right of partic-ularity; he has won public recognition of the legitimacy of his particularity expressed through conscientious agency. The individual pursues his inter-ests (actualizes his identity) but does so ethically, acknowledging his partic-ularity and harmonizing his efforts with the community's rational interests and standards. He is *recognized* in his particularity insofar as this is true.

In this way it is clear how the public recognition of difference results from recognitive understanding. Hegel writes that

> [h]onor is now a reflex of education [*Bildung*], that I am recognized and that in the particular relations of individuals to each other this recognition is expressed. In this I treat the individual in all his particularity not as a mere particular, but as a universal. This is the peculiarly modern element of honor . . . In abstract right the individual is only an abstract person; in civil society on the contrary the individual is somebody who belongs to a particular association. (*VPR 19* 205)

Now when I recognize an individual I treat him as a *concrete* universal: as a determinate social member committed to the collective good. Thus I do not fix *only* upon his particularity, nor *only* upon his legal status, but rather conceive of his particularity in relation to, or in the context of, his universality as a contributing social member. Particularity is united with universality in the individual's 'truly' conscientious agency. In this context, Hegel writes, 'the member . . . has no need to *demonstrate* his competence . . . the fact that he is *somebody*' (*PR* §253). He has won the *right* of particularity.

## Exercising the Right of Particularity: Corporations as Sites of Public Recognition

Hegel assigns a distinctive role to corporations as chief sites of the recognition of particularity, since he believes that 'the ethical must exist not only in the form of universality of the state but also essentially in the form of particularity' (*VPR 4* 628). The corporation is ethical substance that, like the state, unites particularity and universality. However, unlike the state, which is oriented toward universality, such that the ethical substance has the *actual* form of law and right, the corporation is oriented toward particularity and is ethical substance that has the *actual* form of security for welfare and the good. The state accordingly recognizes universal, legal persons, whereas the corporation recognizes particular agents of true conscience.

### How corporations recognize particularity

The corporation is the chief site of public recognition because it is the primary locus of activity in which individuals are able to experience their agency as objectively valid. Unlike in the family, in which the individual is loved 'no matter what he does,' in the corporation he is recognized *for* what he does, namely contribute conscientiously to the common good. Moreover, in contrast to the state, which recognizes him as an abstract person, that is, without regard to his ethnicity, sex, and so on, the corporation understands that while his collective identity characteristics are not the sole determinants of his agency, they may play a significant role in shaping his interests and ends, which *are* the 'soul and determinant' of his actions (*PR* §121).

Again, corporations are voluntary associations organized around professional and social interests. Members of such organizations, as Hegel conceives them, are agents of true conscience who are disposed toward recognizing each other. In particular, they recognize each other's ethical disposition. For them, attributes such as title, status, income, and even level of competence are no longer the primary bases of recognition, in keeping with Hegel's claim that the corporation member need not 'demonstrate his competence . . . by any further external evidence' than his choice of an estate (§253). Instead, because corporation members regard each other as cultivated agents of true conscience, they acknowledge each other's competence—the legitimacy of their different styles of conscientious agency. In this way, they *secure* for each other their right of particularity.

Hegel specifically associates the corporations with the estate of trade and industry, since this turns out to be the estate that *by nature* requires ethical mediation. The agricultural and universal estates naturally integrate ethical substantiality as their chief concern and interest: the agricultural estate insofar as its members are still integrally connected to family life, and the universal estate insofar as its concern and interest are the universal ends of civil society, the general welfare (§§203–205). The estate of trade and industry, by contrast, is primarily concerned with the satisfaction of individual needs and requires ethical mediation to make individuals robustly aware of the social and economic interdependency that makes satisfaction possible. Corporations are the specific institutions within the estate of trade and industry through which ethical substance becomes an explicit concern for members.

The corporation primarily undertakes the following kinds of functions in its role as a 'second family' to its members: it (1) looks after the interests of members, in terms of both their individual welfare and their professional or social concerns; (2) recruits members on the basis not only of their skill, but also their rectitude, and in appropriate numbers as indicated by the needs of civil society as a whole; (3) protects members against the detrimental effects of 'particular contingencies' (such as unemployment) that undermine individuals' efforts to be conscientious contributors to the good; and (4) provides education that equips others to become members (§252). These functions acquire even more significance when we consider that corporations are, moreover, *legally* recognized (§253R).[4] If members win recognition within corporations, the legitimacy of their different styles of agency gains full public acknowledgment.

Because an individual's estate and corporation membership are not ultimately determined by birth, but rather by free choice, the corporation (like the estates) may be quite heterogeneous. As Gordon observes, 'corporations collect together individuals with different "given" attributes—country-folk and town-folk, Schwabians and Württembergers—in the name of a new, non-naturalized social identity, an identity that is beyond their given, purely individual, parochial attachments and interests, in the name of a common good' (1999: 201). Of course, in the corporation a collective interest is at stake, so there must be shared standards for deciding what kinds of action conduce to the satisfaction of these interests and hence are eligible for acknowledgment as objectively valid. But with so much diversity in corporate membership who determines these standards? Unfortunately, Hegel does not tell us explicitly, but inasmuch as corporations are *ethical* institutions inhabited by rationally self-determining agents of true conscience, he must envision corporate standards as decided democratically. This would surely be the case among such agents, who grasp that members can only recognize as legitimate standards that are rational, meaning they can identify with them as their own and as conducive to their welfare. Hegel stresses *both* that '[t]he right to recognize nothing that I do not perceive as rational is the highest right of the subject,' *and* that '[t]he *right of the subjective will* is that whatever it is to recognize as valid should be *perceived* by it *as good*' (§132). Accordingly, the condition of members' endorsement of corporate standards is that the members can acknowledge them as rational, good, and *their own*.

Ethical corporations, then, surely have democratically determined, rational collective standards by which to establish the objective validity of different styles of agency and particular cases of action. These standards stipulate criteria for acting in ways that conduce to the interest and good of all. This being the primary if not the sole basis of legitimacy, corporate members find they have a great deal of latitude for actualizing the good in many different, innovative, and meaningful ways; for their particular styles of agency are not only meaningful to them by virtue of contributing to their own good and that of others, but also inasmuch as they are expressions of their very being, their particular interests, needs, and desires. Because these different styles of agency are '*truly*' conscientious, they can for that reason alone be acknowledged as legitimate and recognized publicly.

Thus, for example, if I find it useful and meaningful to teach the history of Western philosophy critically by incorporating texts that reflect the perspectives of different cultures and groups, then even if my colleagues do not themselves *value* this method or the perspectives represented, they can still acknowledge my practice as legitimate insofar as they know me to be a person of true conscience committed to advancing the good of our students, university, and profession. They will only resist my method if they have *good reasons* to think that either I am not a 'truly' conscientious faculty member or, although I am on the whole 'truly' conscientious, this particular action conflicts with our institutional and professional goals. In such cases, they will present their reasons to me so that either they can convince me that my action conflicts with our standards, or I can convince them that it does not and is therefore legitimate. That is, we will undertake something like Taylor's language of perspicuous contrast. This will not always be an easy negotiation. In fact, sometimes it may result in the collective standards themselves being renegotiated. In any event, it will not be enough that the others simply do not appreciate my method. In fact, they can actually *dislike* my practice but acknowledge its legitimacy. In being thus recognized, I am rendered concretely free to express my particularity in public.

### The benefits of corporate recognition

In Hegel's corporation, members replace the false recognition tied to property ownership and conspicuous consumption with the true honor and recognition associated with the ethical disposition. They know their concrete duties and exercise their right to perform them through agency that expresses their particularity.

We can also appreciate the significance of corporate recognition when we consider the consequences suffered by individuals who fail to secure it: they are left in a condition of alienation and freedom-thwarting marginalization. We have already considered some of the implications of marginalization for the poor, but Hegel suggests that the wealthy, too, can suffer from marginalization, from the failure to win the support and genuine recognition of others. Of course, many among the wealthy will be skeptical of this claim, or not care to win others' recognition or support. As Williams observes, they may see 'nothing to be gained from such membership, but only losses and unprofitable compromises' (*HER* 255). Hegel suggests, however, that in gaining the support of others through corporation membership, the wealthy individual actually wins valuable security for his pursuit of his private interests, since the corporation looks out for his interests, and he his not left on his own to safeguard them.

Perhaps more importantly, Hegel writes that wealth, 'in fulfilling the duty it owes the association, loses the ability to provoke . . . envy in others,' and that, on the contrary, 'rectitude . . . receives the true recognition and honor which are due it' (*PR* §253). Williams elaborates this point eloquently:

> The corporation presents the affluent individual with an ethical task, something for him and his wealth to do, that is more than self-seeking and self-glorification through conspicuous consumption. Now he works for a universal-ethical end, the good of the cooperative. This in turn brings the welfare of others into view and reveals their unemployment and poverty to be intolerable wrongs and not simply unfortunate but inevitable byproducts of the allegedly neutral market system. (*HER* 257)

The wealthy corporation member, who develops and acts in accordance with the recognitive ethical disposition, exchanges his false recognition for genuine recognition and experiences the rectitude of true conscience: he knows his duty and does it. Most significantly, it is a duty that he himself acknowledges as rational and good, not only for others but also for himself. It secures *his* right of particularity and concrete freedom just as it does for others, and he knows this.

Ultimately, then, the poor, the wealthy, and everyone in between benefit from corporate membership. The poor, like everyone else, receive security for their livelihood without being humiliated in the process, insofar as the associations to which they have at one time contributed continue to support their good and interest. The wealthy, by contributing conscientiously to the good, both avoid the envy of others and earn *genuine* recognition, honor, and support from their fellows. All win public recognition of their legitimacy and, accordingly, concrete freedom.

## Two Challenges to Hegel's Treatment of Difference in Ethical Life

Two objections raised against Hegel's portrait of ethical life bear significantly upon my interest in appropriating his recognition theory. The first is the well-known criticism that Hegel denies freedom to women by excluding them from the public sphere on the basis of an essentialized conception of women's nature. The second, advanced by Robert Stern (1989), concerns Hegel's treatment of difference more broadly. Stern contends that while Hegel succeeds in showing the benefits of economic differentiation to freedom and social stability, he fails to acknowledge that moral, cultural, and individual differences can be extremely disruptive socially. I answer both charges by appeal to Hegel's account of recognitive understanding.

## Hegel's controversial treatment of gender

In *PR* §166 Hegel advances a series of provocative claims concerning the 'rational' social and political implications of the '*intellectual* and *ethical* significance' (*PR* §165) of sexual difference. The male sex ('the *one*'[5]), he writes, is 'spirituality which divides itself up into personal self-sufficiency with being *for itself* and the knowledge and volition of *free universality*, i.e., into the self-consciousness of conceptual thought and the volition of the objective and ultimate end' (§166). Male consciousness, that is, distinguishes knowledge and volition as the distinct activities of theoretical and practical reason. By contrast, the female sex ('the *other*') 'maintains itself in unity as knowledge and volition of the substantial in the form of concrete *individuality* [*Einzelheit*] and *feeling* [*Empfindung*].' That is, female consciousness does not 'divide itself up' but rather knows and wills the ethical from a single mode of understanding expressed as subjective feeling, the feeling of *this* individual.

The implication of these differences in consciousness, Hegel argues, is that man's propensity for reflection (his 'differentiating' thought) determines him to *work* his way toward ethical understanding, which he does through self-reflection and engagement with the external world. The result is the actualization of the state, which becomes the primary domain of man's ethical life: '[m]an . . . has his actual substantial life in the state, in learning [*Wissenschaft*], etc., and otherwise in work and struggle with the external world and himself, so that it is only through his division that he fights his way to self-sufficient unity with himself' (§166). At the same time, family life, where man 'has a peaceful intuition of this unity, and an emotive [*empfindend*] and subjective ethical life,' *inspires* him to actualize ethical unity. Meanwhile, woman's more intuitive consciousness determines her to have 'her substantial vocation [*Bestimmung*] in the family, and her ethical disposition consists in this [family] *piety*' (ibid.). Man actualizes his consciousness as ethical unity through *Bildung* and labor in the public sphere, whereas woman expresses hers within the family, at home. Accordingly, Hegel adds, 'In its external relations, the former is powerful and active, the latter passive and subjective' (*ibid.*).

Hegel associates masculine and feminine consciousness, respectively, with human and divine law. The former pertains to the *actual*, constructed, explicitly ethical life of the state, whereas the latter is the *essence* of ethical life, implicitly rational, but intuited and felt rather than reflected upon. Hegel illustrates by citing the example of Sophocles's *Antigone*, 'one of the most sublime presentations of piety,' which is

> declared to be primarily the law of woman . . . the law of emotive [*empfindend*] and subjective substantiality, of inwardness which has not yet been fully actualized, as the law of the ancient gods and of the chthonic realm [*des Unterirdischen*] as an eternal law of which no one knows whence it came, and in opposition to the public law, the law of the state. (§166R)

These essentializing claims have rightly been contested. Hegel seems to commit a logical error in attributing an ethical significance to biological difference, since it is not immediately evident how, as he asserts, '[t]he *natural* determinacy of the two sexes acquires an *intellectual* and *ethical* significance by virtue of its rationality' (§165). Gordon observes that Hegel's assertion is 'the analogue of ascribing the highest form of rationality to the tossing of a coin,' since 'pure chance develops as the foundation for social and ethical positioning' (1999: 124–125). Indeed, it would seem that, in this view, it is not reason after all, but rather the random biological determination of an individual as male or female that ultimately determines his or her social role, a notion that flies in the face of Hegel's claim that individuals must *transcend* [*aufheben*] nature and adopt the standpoint of the rational free will.

However, three things must be said in Hegel's defense. First, there is reason to think he is primarily making a descriptive rather than normative claim, consistent with his conviction that '[t]o comprehend *what is* is the task of philosophy, for what *is* is reason' (*PR*, p. 21).[6] Accordingly, Hegel may be making the purely descriptive claim *that* humanity has ascribed an intellectual and ethical significance to sexual difference insofar as humanity has deemed it rational to do so. This reading is supported by Hegel's subsequent claim that '[t]his significance is determined by the difference into which the ethical substantiality . . . divides itself up in order that its vitality may thereby achieve a concrete unity' (§165). Hegel might be suggesting here that human communities (ethical substantiality) have ordered themselves in a manner *they* deem most conducive to successful ethical life. This has culminated in a sexual division of labor that is 'rational' insofar as it is the product of collective thinking generally accepted and established as the norm. Of course, Hegel seems to affirm the rationality of this convention since his speculative analysis of family life does not expose any inherent contradictions.

My second observation is that if Hegel sees the social significance of sex differences as conventional, he would agree with his critics. That is, it is not necessarily the case that '[f]or Hegel, a woman's sex defines her gender' (Clarke 1996: 170, n.2) Rather, Hegel might acknowledge with Gordon that 'we have a "system" in our culture that determines specific roles, behaviors, and characteristics which are appropriate to each gender (masculine and feminine) and which then develops those characteristics to [sic] individuals with particular sexes' (Gordon 1999: 124). Hegel simply conceives of this system as community rationality, such that when he claims that sex acquires a rational intellectual and ethical significance, he means that humans engage in gender construction. Gordon and other critics may therefore have made precisely Hegel's point in *PR* §165.

However, again, this does not entail that Hegel is *critical* of these constructions and, unfortunately, it seems clear that he is not. Comments in *PR* §166A suggest that Hegel endorses the rationality of the sexual division of labor and in a way that is more problematic. 'Women may well be educated,' he writes, 'but they are not made for the higher sciences, for philosophy and certain artistic productions which require a universal element. Women may have insights [*Einfalle*], taste, and delicacy, but they do not possess the ideal.' Here it becomes less clear whether Hegel is (1) making an ontological claim, (2) merely 'reporting' the conventional position, or (3) commenting upon the *effects* of social conventions. His claim that women are 'not made' for these pursuits seems to suggest option (1). If so, he plainly voices an incorrect assessment of women's cognitive abilities. However, it is not obvious that Hegel is making an ontological claim.

Finally, although we may fault Hegel for failing to subject the conventional view of women to a more rigorous critique, he does, to his mind, ascribe an important ethical role to women. Women cultivate the ethical sensibility within the home that ultimately inspires men to order their more divided energies into a public ethical life. Women, that is, already 'get' ethical life intuitively; they create an atmosphere and relationship of love at home that is the template and impetus for cultivation of the recognitive ethical disposition in public. This points again to the continuity of private and public forms of recognition.

Hegel therefore praises the intuitively ethical disposition of women—as do some contemporary feminists, especially many of the gynocentric stripe.[7] Accordingly, when he says, 'The difference between man and woman is the difference between animal and plant' (§166R), we do not have to read this essentializing claim as necessarily disparaging of women. Rather, because Hegel adds that woman is 'a more peaceful [process of] unfolding' (*ibid.*), we may see him as contrasting men's restless activity and struggle toward the ethical against women's quiet and confident possession of it already as an inner principle. This is likely the basis of both his lavish praise of Antigone as 'the most magnificent figure ever to have appeared on earth' (*W*18:509), and of his repeated insistence that in modernity marriage is ideally an *ethical* relationship grounded in mutual recognition (e.g., *PR* §162). Nevertheless, it remains an essentializing claim.

Whenever we confront essentialism, whether it be sexist, racist, or otherwise, we must ask to what extent the views advanced can be jettisoned without substantially altering the theory. In the present case, the question is to what extent Hegel's account of the sexual division of labor is essential to the theory of ethical life. Inasmuch as Hegel assigns these social roles on the basis of cognitive abilities, and these capabilities are *not* determined by sex, Hegel's portrait of ethical life is salvageable. All that is required is what we more or less have already done culturally: acknowledge that both sexes manifest intuitive ethical understanding and the capacity for reflective ethical and intellectual pursuits. Individuals display these qualities in varying degrees, but that is the significant point: today, on the whole, the manifestation of these qualities reflects *individual* differences more than sex differences. Some individuals—men and women—are more intuitive than reflective, more socially passive than active, and vice versa.[8] Others may display both characteristics of each set: a person may be equally intuitive and reflective.

The ethical disposition, which focuses upon securing the good of all, helps us perceive the rationality of a nongender-specific conception of the cultivation of ethical life within the family, civil society, and state. From that perspective, securing the good of all entails creating structures through which individuals can actualize their capabilities. Some individuals, both male and female, actualize their capabilities best through cultivating home life, while others, both female and male, succeed primarily through more public pursuits. Still others require both kinds of activity. A contemporary ethical disposition committed to the good of the community will encourage individuals to choose roles they themselves see as best suiting them.

## Hegel's 'incomplete' account of the impact of difference on social life

I turn, then, to a second criticism of Hegel's treatment of difference in the *PR*. In 'Unity and Difference in Hegel's Political Philosophy,' Robert Stern acknowledges Hegel's logical thesis that differentiation is essential both to concrete existence itself, as its necessary condition, and to spirit's dialectical progression to higher unities. However, he argues that although Hegel succeeds in demonstrating, in his account of civil society, that social differentiation can lead to greater social unity, the account betrays a 'narrow understanding' of the full range of modern pluralism, and this 'leads Hegel to be over-optimistic regarding the possible integration of difference into unity within the state' (1989: 76). Stern accuses Hegel of focusing on economic differentiation at the expense of recognizing the crucial empirical fact that moral, political, ethnic, and sexual differences can lead to substantial social disruption and disunity. 'Hegel was wrong,' Stern argues, 'in thinking that the only kind of differentiation that occurs between individuals is one which brings them together as parts of an interlocking economic system' (87). Stern's quarrel ultimately concerns Hegel's suggestion that individuals, in asserting their particularity, can *always* be re-integrated through reflection into a higher social unity. He argues, to the contrary, that 'differentiation amongst individuals can and does take the form of a religious, political, sexual or racial *separatism*,' and 'individuals who "particularize" themselves in these ways cannot be "brought back to unity" using the mechanism of economic interdependence' (*ibid*.; my emphasis). In other words, some other re-integrative process is required to overcome the subversion of freedom these forms of social differentiation cause, but Hegel fails to give an account of one.

Stern's objection is important, since it suggests that Hegel has committed another failure of recognition. Either he presumes a culturally and morally, as well as sexually, homogeneous civil society (white, secular liberal, and male) that excludes difference, or he fails to acknowledge the particular subjectivity of members who might wish, for instance, to organize social institutions not only on the basis of labor functions, but also along the lines of other particular interests, some of them separatist and potentially disruptive to social unity—as, for instance, if they espoused 'separate but equal' policies on the basis of ethnicity, sex, sexual orientation, and so on. I think Hegel's moral–epistemological argument for recognitive understanding, presupposed in the *PR*, sufficiently answers the question about civil society's ability to accommodate specifically moral differences. However, Stern's concern about Hegel's 'oversight' is still pressing in light of Hegel's racism, which raises the question of whether his disparaging claims about non-European peoples undermine both the notion of particularity as really encompassing collective identity differences and his credibility as theorist of freedom (see *PH* and *PWH*). For Hegel's racism strongly suggests not only that he does envision a culturally homogeneous civil society, but also that he might not see certain kinds of social separatism as contrary to freedom. Let us explore, then, Hegel's racism.

Hegel not only deems non-European peoples—Africans, Asians, and American Indians—to be inferior to Europeans, but he asserts a *philosophical* basis for this: they are less human than Europeans because they lack, in varying degrees, *self-consciousness*, awareness of themselves as spirit. Thus, for example, he describes the 'chief characteristics' of American Indians as that of a 'mild and passionless disposition, want of spirit, and a crouching submissiveness' (*PH* 81). Meanwhile, he observes of the 'peculiarly African character' that it

> is difficult to comprehend, for the very reason that in reference to it, we must quite give up the principle which naturally accompanies all *our* ideas—the category of Universality. In Negro life the characteristic point is the fact that consciousness has not yet attained to the realization of any substantial objective existence—as for example, God, or Law—in which the interest of man's volition is involved and in which he realizes his own being. (*PH* 93)

Most significantly for our purposes, Hegel clearly maintains that these peoples, by virtue of their natures—indeed, their *closeness* to *nature*—are incompatible with Europeans and therefore cannot be integrated with them. He cites the disposition of American Indians as the reason they 'could not amalgamate, but were driven back' (*PH* 81). As for Africans, he writes, 'there is nothing harmonious with humanity to be found in this type of character' (*ibid.*).

These claims, coupled with the fact that on this basis Hegel excludes non-Europeans from historical consideration, clearly suggest that these peoples could have no place in his conception of ethical life. What, then, could he possibly have to say to *us* who seek a way of ending forms of oppression that have their philosophical roots in theories such as his? It does no good simply to excuse Hegel as an unfortunate child of his time, for we remain stuck, nevertheless, with Stern's challenge: we still need an answer to the question of how ethnic heterogeneity affects civil society's ability to secure social stability and freedom.

Before turning to my own answer to this question, I consider briefly Joseph McCarney's interesting defense of Hegel in 'Hegel's Racism? A Response to Bernasconi' (2003: 1–4). McCarney sees Hegel as ultimately blaming geography, rather than any essential quality in non-Europeans, for their failure to attain the level of spirit. In the *Lectures on the Philosophy of World History*, Hegel attributes these differences mainly to differences in climate (*PWH* 154ff.). In 'frigid' and 'torrid' zones, people find it more difficult to thrive than in temperate ones, and this presents an obstacle to their transcendence of nature into the realm of spirit. Thus, McCarney comments, 'these forces are too powerful a nature for human beings in general—for white Europeans no less than for black Africans' (1). In other words, Hegel *really* thinks Europeans were just lucky enough to find themselves in the right part of the world to make the transition from nature to spirit. Perhaps—but an equally plausible alternative is that Hegel simply *posited* this 'geographical thesis' as 'evidence' of his beliefs about the racial inferiority of non-Europeans.

The alternative is more plausible in light of Bernasconi's finding that Hegel exaggerated and sometimes fabricated stories about Africans in his lectures on history. For example, Hegel recast and sensationalized a missionary's account of an Ashanti king's ritual burial of his mother. The original record claims the king washed her bones in rum and water; Hegel reported that they were washed in blood (Bernasconi 2003: 5 and 1998: 46). Perhaps he did so to reinforce his claims that Africans were 'altogether deficient' morally, having nothing but 'contempt for humanity,' and lacking 'respect for life' as much as for death (*PWH* 184–185)—hence lacking one important qualification for the attainment of self-consciousness (*PhS* ¶194; *PhG* 153).

Nonetheless, McCarney adduces further 'evidence' of Hegel's *anti-racism*, which, if true, would indeed undermine the suggestion that Hegel presupposes cultural homogeneity in ethical life. McCarney highlights Hegel's celebration of the ethnic diversity of the Greeks—'virtually a hymn to racial impurity' (2003: 1)—in which Hegel claims,

> It is a superficial and absurd idea that such a beautiful and truly free life can be produced by a process so incomplex as the development of a race keeping within the limits of blood-relationship and friendship . . . The only real antithesis that Spirit can have, is itself spiritual: *viz.*, its inherent heterogeneity, through which alone it acquires the power of realizing itself as Spirit. The history of Greece exhibits at its commencement this interchange and mixture of partly homesprung, partly quite foreign stocks. (*PH* 226)

McCarney makes much of Hegel's distinction of the Greeks as a *people* (*Volk*) and not merely a *nation*. For Hegel, a people is a distinctively *spiritual* community, in contrast to a nation, which is a community composed of individuals of common descent.[9] McCarney sees Hegel as praising the Greeks for having constituted themselves as a genuine *Volk*, in keeping with truly spiritual life and, significantly, through cultivating ethnic heterogeneity.

From this passage in Hegel we may derive the sense, in answer to Stern, that Hegel does consistently conceive of differentiation as a source of development and vitality in the life of spirit. For in his *PR* discussion of civil society, in a rare reference to difference beyond the economic, Hegel reinforces his conception of the positive function of difference in generating more enriched unities: this time in genetics. In his discussion of marriage and family, he stresses that incest and in-breeding are clearly contrary to nature, for they involve the reproduction of *sameness*. He writes, '[W]hat is to be united must first be separate; the power of procreation, like that of the spirit, increases with the magnitude of oppositions out of which it reconstitutes itself' (*PR* §168A). In the *PH*, referring again to the value of cultivating ethnic heterogeneity, Hegel adds that '[e]very world-historical people, except the Asiatic kingdoms—which stands [*sic*] detached from the grand historical catena—has been formed in this way' (*PH* 226).

Unfortunately, this particular endorsement of ethnic diversity by no means entails that Hegel endorses the integration of *non-Europeans* with *Europeans*. Non-European peoples have not reached the level of spirit and so would have nothing to contribute to ethical liberal modernity. Thus there is considerable textual evidence that while Hegel might have celebrated cultural heterogeneity within and among different European *Völker*, he would have balked at the notion of integrating non-Europeans and Europeans. Stern is therefore correct: in Hegel's time the presence of ethnic differences in civil society would have been another source of social instability. But Hegel does not account for this source of instability because he does not envision non-Europeans as having anything to do with ethical life.

Nonetheless, I maintain, against Stern's suggestion, that Hegel's account of ethical life can succeed in securing freedom for those who are ethnically, culturally, and morally different, because ethical life presupposes the attainment of recognitive understanding. This mode of understanding can overcome freedom-blocking forms of separatism—even Hegel's own—just as effectively as it supplants the atomistic thinking of classical modernity. Hegel clearly shows in both the *PR* and the *Phenomenology* that individuals who achieve recognitive understanding *habitually* recognize particularity when it is expressed conscientiously in the service of the collective good. This understanding supplies the formal basis for mutual exchanges of recognition that can indeed promote greater social unity across a seemingly infinite range of differences.

Of course, Hegel would not have envisioned non-European peoples as included in this range since, to his mind, they are not capable of such a life. At this more concrete level, Hegel's account of ethical life fails to secure recognition of the differences that are important to us.[10] *But Hegel was wrong.* His claims about non-Europeans, like those about women's capabilities, are demonstrably false. Therefore, to the question of whether Hegel's account of ethical life provides a *means* of moral and cultural re-integration to a higher social unity, I answer that it does at the formal level of the account, since all citizens of ethical liberal modernity are capable of attaining recognitive understanding.

Indeed, according to Hegel's own logic concerning the creative potential of difference, collective identity differences may generate vitality of the highest order, in a manner analogous to his conception of the vitality of spirit in Greek life. If indeed 'the power . . . of the spirit increases with the magnitude of oppositions out of which it reconstitutes itself' (*PR* §168A), then perhaps the *spiritual* potential represented by the magnitude of *our* differences can cultivate a unity of spirit perhaps surpassing that of the ancient Greeks. Certainly one may take issue with Hegel's suggestion that differentiation generates potential for greater unity. But, granting that claim, we are not entirely justified in concluding that in Hegel's account of ethical life social unity derives solely from economic differentiation.

## Conclusion: The Public Recognition of Difference in Civil Society

Hegel's emphasis upon securing for social members their *right* of particularity as part of the solution to the undermining of freedom in civil society makes clear that he sees social justice as requiring public recognition of difference. Inasmuch as estates and corporations are the main spheres of social interaction, Hegel targets these as the primary sites for cultivating the recognitive ethical disposition. Social justice, then, is secured through the formation of *ethical* bonds among different, 'truly' conscientious, mutually recognizing social members.

Hegel's conception of recognition ($R_f$) applied to ethical life therefore satisfies the third criterion of an adequate conception. According to

Hegel's definition:

R$_f$: *Recognition is an act expressing subjects' mutual acknowledgment of the legitimacy of their conscientious, albeit particular and different, styles of agency.*

The third criterion of an adequate conception of recognition stipulates:

CR$_3$: It indicates the means by which a society as a whole affirms, in solidarity, the dignity and distinctness of cultures—their legitimacy as sources of identity through which they contribute to collective life.

To elucidate the conformity of R$_f$ with CR$_3$, I begin with the claim in R$_f$ that recognition entails subjects' mutual acknowledgment of the legitimacy of their conscientious, yet different, styles of agency. Hegel has argued that agents of true conscience in ethical life are members of estates who, through ethical *Bildung*, comprehend the value of diverse contributions to civil society. Because they possess recognitive understanding, they know that conscientious agency entails the expression not only of commitment to duty, but also of particular purposes, interests, and beliefs that inform the ways in which duties are performed. Therefore, they acknowledge the legitimacy of the others' expressions of particularity implicated in their conscientious contributions to collective life.

In supporting each other's agency in this way, social members in ethical life effectively acknowledge the legitimacy of one another's individual identity, since agency just is the expression and actualization of *self*. But individual identity is normally informed by collective identities, that is, by *cultures* (broadly construed). Therefore, insofar as social members acknowledge each other as authoritative individuals, they acknowledge the legitimacy of the cultures that are the sources of identities. It is easy to see that, given their recognitive understanding, social members will only be disposed to deny recognition to individuals if they *demonstrably fail* to support the universal good.

Furthermore, a whole society can affirm differences in a spirit of solidarity, since celebration of the ethical disposition is part of the shared value-horizon of civil society. Whatever the diverse interests and purposes of estates and corporations, all members are committed to the universal good, hence to cultivating the recognitive understanding of agents of true conscience. Recognitive understanding consists partly of the awareness that freedom requires winning acknowledgment not only of one's own authority, but that of all other agents of true conscience—and not only those individuals with whom one is closely associated, but *all* conscientious agents contributing to the interdependent organism of civil society. This entails, in turn, that one acknowledge the legitimacy of those agents' differences, which inform their agency. Notably, it does not entail embracing or endorsing (in a strong sense) the specific content of cultures.

Thus, an ethically cultivated society, by celebrating diversity for the sake of the universal good, affirms *in solidarity* the legitimacy of the diverse cultures that contribute to that good. Social members might even conceive of diversity as a supreme liberal value, inasmuch as it enriches the options for agency through which they secure the general welfare and concrete freedom. Hegel's conception of recognition therefore satisfies $CR_3$.

In the *PR* Hegel describes the social structure of a liberal polity that publicly recognizes difference: he maintains not only that a just and ethical society is one in which individuals of true conscience grant each other the social freedom to express their particularity publicly, but also that this exchange of recognition is essential to securing concrete freedom. This is the case both because such individuals know that particularity is the very 'soul and determinant' (*PR* §121) of all agency and because their ethical disposition, grounded in recognitive understanding, mitigates the false consciousness and contingencies of existence that undermine freedom and social stability. Therefore, they do not merely tolerate difference as a matter of privacy, but acknowledge the conscientious expression of difference as the fully legitimate mode of 'normal'—that is, *ethical*—public activity and conduct.

Conclusion

# Hegel, Recognition, and Ethical Liberal Modernity

*Bella Abzug always used to say about nations and this country especially, we've had our Declaration of Independence. Now this country needs a declaration of interdependence.*

*(Gloria Steinem)**

I have endeavored to bring an element of clarity to the politics of difference by clarifying the meaning of oppression and of recognition. By the *meaning* of recognition, in particular, I mean not only its definition, but also its significance for our contemporary concern with overcoming oppression. Accordingly, I have advanced two arguments: first establishing the need for public recognition as a means of abolishing oppressive practices of *misrecognition*; and second arguing for a concept of recognition adequate to that task. I found such a concept in Hegel's idea of recognition as *an act expressing subjects' mutual acknowledgment of the legitimacy of their conscientious, albeit particular and different, styles of agency.* In this concluding discussion, I explore how applying this concept of recognition helps us overcome oppression.

Crucial to my aims in this study, I have shown that Hegel's conception of recognition satisfies three criteria of a conception adequate to the task of redressing contemporary oppression. It indicates the means by which acts of recognition can undermine or reverse social and institutional modes of oppression ($CR_1$); how acts of recognition embody a new conception of liberal neutrality as a commitment to the equal inclusion and treatment of legitimate collective identities ($CR_2$); and the means by which a whole society can affirm, in solidarity, the legitimacy of cultures as sources of identity through which social members contribute to collective life ($CR_3$).

With regard to the first criterion, Hegel's conception indicates that recognition undermines oppression, in the first instance, by affirming a social and self-understanding that is a powerful corrective against two key sources of systemic social injustice: relationships of moral subordination and atomistic self-understanding. Subjects possessed of recognitive under-standing grasp that their ability to garner acknowledgment of their legiti-macy and authority as agents is conditioned by their ability to acknowledge that of others, and not *regardless of* others' collective identities, but in part *because of* them. They know that women, men, African Americans, Anglo-Americans, gay people, straight people, rich folks, poor folks—*all* groups—have contributed in *different* ways to the collective good and *ought* to be acknowledged in their distinctness as much as for what they share in common with others. Moreover, because those others have contributed to their good in countless ways of which they may not be aware, they recog-nize every other as a moral equal, whether she is the CFO of the company who manages the accounts (so that they don't have to) or the custodian who mops the floors (so that they don't have to).

Hegel's concept of recognition makes plain that only social relationships of reciprocity conduce to genuine, concrete freedom. The mutuality condition stresses that asymmetrical relationships of moral subordination, which many pursue to win recognition and prestige (as well as to amass wealth) actually *fail* to secure recognition, just as surely as it failed the 'master' consciousness of the *Phenomenology*. In fact, as in 'Mastery and Slavery,' relationships of unequal recognition are bound to devolve into modes of oppression.

Concerning the more tangible means by which acts of recognition over-come oppression, although Hegel portrays recognition as distinctively a *speech* act and dialogical, this does not preclude institutionalized forms of recognition via legislation, institutional reforms, or other means. However, it does suggest that institutionalized forms of recognition are somehow secondary to the dialogical affirmation that is the first instance of recog-nition. This is why an excellent proposal such as Anna Galeotti's argument for toleration as symbolic recognition, while an important component of a response to emancipatory demands, is not a fully adequate solution. In *Toleration as Recognition*, Galeotti argues that the tendency of majority groups to marginalize minority identities means that securing equality requires a policy beyond toleration traditionally conceived. She defends a pluralist conception of 'toleration as recognition'—whereby the state extends 'symbolic' recognition to minority cultures via legislation signi-fying the acceptance of those identities in public on a par with majority cultures (2002: 10, 11). This recognition is *symbolic* in that it is content-independent. Galeotti acknowledges the difficulties inherent in conceiving of recognition strongly as affirmative valuation judgments of value, and so argues for a mode of recognition that, like Hegel's conception, acknowl-edges the equal *legitimacy* of different ways of life.

Galeotti cites as a paradigm example Italy's extension in 1994 of the dates of a general election, originally fixed for the date of the Jewish Passover. Such an action on the part of the state, granted in order to allow orthodox Jews to vote, is, Galeotti says, 'precisely an example of what I mean by pluralist toleration and by public recognition of differences, an appropriate gesture of public respect for the whole Jewish community in the broad sense' (1994: 183; quoted in Lukes 1997: 217). She also cites the famous 1989 *'affaire du foulard,'* in which three French girls of Muslim faith were suspended from school for wearing the required *hijab* (veil), and recent demands in the US for legal recognition of same-sex marriages. If the *hijab* were accepted into the dress code for French schools, and if the US were to recognize same-sex unions, these public gestures would symbolize our acknowledgment of the legitimacy of these ways of life, considered among the normal options in our society. Thus toleration would manifest our commitment not only to refrain from interfering with individuals' private cultural expressions, but also to support their presence in public.

Galeotti acknowledges that one difficulty of her thesis is that it is only one step toward full inclusion that does not respond fully to the demands of marginalized groups (2002: 196). We might say it does not necessarily improve social interactions in the short term since tensions will surely escalate between minority groups and the majorities of whom demands are made. A second difficulty has to do with the asymmetry implicit in the notion of toleration, which Galeotti herself argues does not do justice to the dignity of the tolerated. It is, in fact, primarily for this reason that I am not convinced that we can extend the concept of toleration to include recognition. When we say, from the perspective of toleration, that different identities are admitted as equal, implicit in this notion is that one group exercises its power to accept or deny another's equality. By contrast, the mutuality of recognition requires that interaction partners confront one another as equals. Most significantly, Hegel suggests that their recognitive understanding precedes and grounds political acts of recognition.

Because of its grounding in recognitive understanding, Hegel's concept of recognition enables us, moreover, to re-conceive neutrality as the commitment to the *equal* inclusion and *equal* treatment of different identities, a second way in which recognition overcomes oppression. I highlight in particular that subjects' recognitive awareness of the particularity of all spheres of value and actions is a powerful preventative against cultural imperialism. It is a contradiction for agents possessed of recognitive understanding to claim they are justified in imposing their *particular* ways of life upon conscientious others against their will. The impulse to interfere with another's legitimate cultural expression must be tempered by one's robust acknowledgment of the other's authority and autonomy.

It is also conceivable that recognitive understanding can ground a whole society's commitment to affirm the legitimacy of cultures as sources of identity, a third way in which recognition overcomes oppression. Hegel's concept of recognition enables us to trace a direct line from an ethically cultivated civil society's commitment to the universal good to its collective affirmation of diversity as a value conducive to that good and, hence, to concrete freedom. The commitment to promote diversity becomes part of a society's shared value-horizon, because social members understand both the legitimacy and significance of individuals' conscientious contributions to the collective good, and that those contributions are the by-products of different cultures, which are sources of identity and agency.

Furthermore, Hegel has presented a concrete vision of how a whole society cultivates recognitive understanding. Education is the key. Ethical life presupposes recognitive understanding, but Hegel makes clear that social members are socialized into it through *Bildung*. Thus he does not presuppose that everyone possesses it all at once—only that sufficiently many do to stimulate educational reform. In fact Hegel assigns most responsibility for ethical *Bildung* to trade and industry, because he thinks it is in the greatest need of ethical cultivation. The method is quite practicable. Part of our vocational and professional training begins to involve something like ethical apprenticeships: indoctrination not only into the technical skills required by our professions, but also into awareness of the significance of professions to the overall functioning of civil society, and the value of professional ethics (of an ethical disposition) to one's success and that of civil society. But this *Bildung* can be accomplished by a variety of organizations—not only by businesses, but also by trade unions and professional associations.

Ethical education, especially focused upon corporate activity, is an important corrective against exploitation, disempowerment, and marginalization. Social members at all levels of business and government recognize each other, first and foremost, as autonomous agents of true conscience. Possessed of recognitive understanding, they cooperate with each other in a spirit of reciprocity and solidarity, understanding, again, that their experience of their own legitimacy and freedom is conditioned by their recognition of the legitimacy and freedom of their fellows. Accordingly, they create democratic work environments. Furthermore, they recognize each other's right to secure their livelihood on fair terms.

Finally, Hegel's concept of recognition is also a valuable diagnostic tool. A society committed to social justice can assess the extent to which it succeeds or fails to secure equal dignity and genuine neutrality by fairly straightforward questions about its social and institutional practices. For example, do citizens largely agree that their collective identities are represented *equitably* in institutions and offices? Do organizations function democratically, such that members at all levels and of all backgrounds have some authority in determining how the work of the organization is carried out? These and similar questions are crucial for a society that is serious about ending oppression.

Hegel's suggestion of the continuity of private and public forms of recognition holds great potential for our understanding of what citizens of a liberal society most fundamentally need, desire, and expect from their interactions in the social world—that is, in addition to the liberty to secure their survival needs without undue interference from others or the state. Hegel expresses it by claiming that in ethical life we find ourselves at home in the world, which is to say, in one sense, that we find ourselves enjoying a life in the public sphere that is very like that we enjoy at home with family and other significant others: we find ourselves recognized in our distinctness, which, combined with respect for our dignity, *effectively* empowers us for self-actualization. But this requires us—if we are indeed committed to freedom, equality, and justice—to follow Hegel's advice and concern ourselves not only with the organization of the state, but also with its foundation in everyday social life. Again, we must give critical attention to the social relationships that function either to support or to undermine liberal political aims.

If my thesis is correct that liberal theory must be grounded in a social theory of recognition—and if public recognition is primarily a mode of social and self-understanding, and only secondarily instantiated in legislation and reforms—then we must acknowledge that any attempts to compel recognition legislatively will not be wholly adequate to the goal of overcoming social oppression. This is true for the same reason that Rawls's, Kymlicka's, and Galeotti's proposals are not wholly adequate: strictly political solutions tend to obscure the ways in which social attitudes can undermine them.

My argument for a concept of recognition took as its starting point the emancipatory concern with contemporary oppression. I asked: Given the commitment of liberal democracies to the principles of equality, freedom, and justice, are we obligated to ensure the positive public recognition of the identities of diverse individuals and groups? My study now ends by observing that Hegel answered this question long before it occurred to us to ask it, for his theory of recognition as acknowledgment of the legitimacy of conscientious diversity already makes evident that the question must be answered affirmatively. Combating contemporary oppression indeed requires that we not merely tolerate differences, but rather publicly recognize their legitimacy. Furthermore, Hegel's theory not only encourages us to recognize diversity, but more importantly tells us what this *means, why* we ought to do it, how we become *motivated* to do it, and *how* to carry it out.

I have argued that recognition as acknowledgment of legitimacy is the very form of recognition sought by emancipatory movements, not necessarily the desire to have the specific content of their cultures endorsed by the majority. Many have grasped that there may be limits to our ability to understand each other, hence to form judgments about that content. Furthermore, the abolition of social and institutional practices that oppress citizens whose identities are 'different' does not *require* that those differences be valued in the strong sense, but rather only that they be acknowledged as having a right to be expressed in public. From this perspective, the emancipatory demand for recognition can be understood as a demand for acknowledgment, not only of the right of all citizens to make their differences visible in public, but also of the fact that American liberal democracy is after all the very product of diversity, of the creative and conscientious agency of many different groups.

But now that we really understand the claim for recognition, we have an obligation, as we have seen, to respond to it: to enter into dialogue and exercise our response-ability to actualize ethical liberal modernity. This is just to deliver on our own claim to being a liberal democracy committed to freedom, equality, and justice.

# Notes

## Introduction

\* The epigraph to this chapter is from Vaid (1993).

[1] See, e.g., Galeotti (2002), Honneth (*RMO*), Kymlicka (*MC*) and Taylor (*PoR*).

[2] See Rawls (1999) and (*PL*); Kymlicka (*MC*).

[3] Exceptions would be Hegel and Honneth. Honneth has recently advanced a definition of recognition in *GR*.

[4] Charles Taylor and proponents of multicultural education are commonly taken to espouse this view, although I argue in Chapter 4 that neither really endorses it.

[5] See, e.g., Honneth (*SR*) and Taylor (*PoR*).

[6] Throughout this study I use the term 'self-actualization' to refer to the actions or processes through which individuals express their individual identities (their beliefs, desires, interests, purposes, etc.). Thus I mean the term primarily in Hegel's sense of the concrete expression of identity in action (its realization, or actualization). This meaning is closely connected to two well-known senses of 'self-actualization': (1) that derived from psychology of individuals' cultivation of their abilities toward their full potential; and (2) the liberal ideal of realizing one's authentic nature, most often associated with positive freedom.

[7] Translation modified; A.V. Miller renders '*Verdopplung*' as 'duplication,' but I agree with Robert R. Williams that 'doubling' captures better the structure of spirit as the unity of identity and *difference* than does the stronger term 'duplication.' The latter might lead one to think that the second subject is a copy of the first, which Williams observes, 'implies that it is derivative of a first or primal ego.' See *HER* 51 n. 10.

[8] For this way of characterizing Hegel's theory of freedom, I am indebted to Axel Honneth (2000: 23–27).

[9] This is true provided, of course, that the relationship itself is grounded in free choice and not compulsion.

[10] I do not aim, i.e., to address the whole spectrum of demands for recognition made by various kinds of groups worldwide, nor do I presume to derive a solution that will be universal in application.

[11] I. Young (*JPD*), Frye (1983), Harvey (2000), Cudd (2006), Zutlevics (2002) and Bartky (1990).

[12] The achievement of mutual recognition is the penultimate moment in the sense that absolute spirit's *appearance* is the second-to-last moment of spirit's development; the final moment is its completed *actualization* as absolute knowing.

13  The idea that 'Mastery and Slavery' does exhaust Hegel's theory of recognition is largely the legacy of the French reception of Hegel, inspired by Alexandre Kojève's famous lectures at *L'École des Hautes Études*, from 1933 to 1939.

## Chapter 1

\*  The epigraph to this chapter is from Frye (1983: 2). Reprinted with permission. A version of part of Chapter 1 was published as 'A Moral Imperative: Retaining Women/of Color in Science Education,' *Atlantis: A Women's Studies Journal*, 33 (2), spring 2009; copyright 2009 Atlantis, www. msvu.ca/atlantis. Reprinted with permission.

1  The scenarios illustrate what Young calls 'the five faces of oppression': respectively, exploitation and powerlessness, cultural imperialism, marginalization, and violence (*JPD* 9, 39). I elaborate upon these cases in Chapter 2. Hereafter I refer to powerlessness as 'disempowerment' to shift the focus from the experience of the victim of oppression to the activity of the agent of oppression.

2  This example is inspired by one cited by Zutlevics (2002: 83–84).

3  Isaiah Berlin generally associates the negative sense of freedom with the liberal tradition and the positive with perfectionist and 'communitarian' traditions (2002: 169ff.). Although I agree that the negative conception of freedom is distinctively liberal, I stress later that the positive conception also figures prominently in liberal notions of freedom.

4  Benjamin Constant, 'De la souveraineté du peuple,' quoted in Berlin (2002: 173).

5  Joel Feinberg identifies four different meanings of 'autonomy': (1) the capacity for political self-government; (2) the actual condition of being self-governing politically; (3) the ideal of self-mastery and control; and (4) the set of rights associated with and reflecting one's degree of self-sovereignty (1986: 27–51). John Christman (2003) observes that 'central to all of these uses is a conception of the person able to act, reflect, and choose on the basis of factors that are somehow her own (authentic in some sense).'

6  Rousseau is also an important source of Hegel's thought, as Hegel himself attests (*LHP* III: 401). Although the following cursory summary of Rousseau's conception of freedom will hardly do justice to his influence on Hegel's account of ethical life, I hope the connections will nevertheless be detectable in my later discussion of Hegel's *PR* in Chapters 6 and 7. For an excellent treatment of Rousseau's influence on Hegel, see Neuhouser (2000: 55–81).

7  Similarly, in the *PR*, Hegel reveals the ethical social order, 'the system of right [as] the realm of actualized freedom' (*PR* §4), to be constituted of individuals who are self-legislating members of a rational state. In Hegel's *Sittlichkeit*, as in Rousseau's ideal civil society, each citizen can acknowledge that the law expresses his own will and that of all rational social members.

8  This is, of course, a more complex issue than this example suggests. For this notion of autonomy has only so far addressed the right of individuals to be offered reasons; surely, some nonliberal doctrines will grant that right but

nevertheless deny individuals' rights to *reject* those reasons. I cannot go into this here; I can only suggest that in many cases, the thin conception of autonomy may be acceptable.

[9] Several proponents of negative liberty insist that oppressive acts *are* deliberate. See, e.g., Hayek (1960: 134).

[10] This claim seems to contradict Berlin's earlier assertion that '[c]oercion implies the deliberate interference of other human beings within the area within which I could otherwise act' (*TCL* 169). However, I take Berlin to distinguish between coercive and oppressive acts. For him, coercion involves deliberate exertions of force, which may be oppressive (they may severely constrain one's freedom) but are not necessarily so. Similarly, not all oppressive acts are coercive.

## Chapter 2

[*] The epigraph to this chapter is from *JPD* 39. Reprinted with permission.

[1] Rawls argues convincingly that self-respect is a necessary condition of autonomous agency because it is necessary for citizens' confidence in the worth of their life plans. Hence, self-respect is a primary good to be secured by principles of justice, and mutual respect is a political duty (1999: 79, 297).

## Chapter 3

[1] My intuitions on the subject dealt with in this chapter have been confirmed and enhanced by the recent work of Morag Patrick (2000) and Anna Elisabetta Galeotti (2002). I discuss Galeotti's 'toleration as recognition' thesis in my concluding chapter, after I have elaborated on the concept of recognition.

[2] The epigraph to this chapter is from Feinberg (1978: 7). Reprinted with permission.

[3] Kymlicka sees women (although they are not a numerical minority), homosexuals, the poor and the disabled as cultures of a kind. I will at times use the term 'culture' interchangeably with 'social group.'

[4] Similarly, in the *Philosophy of Right*, Hegel distinguishes three social–political roles of a community member corresponding to the three realms of ethical life. An individual is (1) a family member; (2) a '*Burgher*,' or bourgeois, in civil society; and (3) a '*citoyen*,' or citizen of the state (*PR* §190).

[5] For example, the National Academies of Science reports that even after controlling for productivity and the significance of their work, women scientists (especially women scientists of color) are paid less, promoted more slowly, given fewer leadership positions and awarded fewer honors than male scientists (Committee on Maximizing the Potential of Women in Academic Science and Engineering 2007).

[6] Charles Taylor also targets the problem of multiculturalism. He also endorses a non-procedural liberalism, 'grounded very much on judgments about what makes a good life' (*PoR* 61) that institutionalizes certain special rights and

immunities for cultural minorities (e.g., the *Québécois* in Canada) for the sake of their cultural survival against the homogenizing effects of assimilation: 'it is precisely this distinctness that has been ignored, glossed over, assimilated to a dominant or majority identity. And this assimilation is the cardinal sin against the ideal of authenticity' (38). At the same time, he insists that certain basic individual rights (such as the right to due process, freedom of speech and so on) must be secured unconditionally. The protection of such rights is crucial for warding off the threat of group identity reification, preserving each individual's right to accept, reject or reinterpret his or her cultural heritage (59).

⁷ Puerto Ricans have a distinct societal culture, as do Americans by Kymlicka's definition. African Americans, however, do not. I say more about these distinctions later.

⁸ Of course, while most societal cultures may be sources of the *capacity* for autonomy, clearly not all of them actually inspire and nurture the autonomy of social members. Some deliberately repress some or all of their members, while others (such as, arguably, the US) do so unwittingly.

# Chapter 4

* Epigraphs to this chapter are from Cole (2004) and *PoR* 26 (reprinted with permission).

¹ I refer here to Rawls's argument for the duty of mutual respect. See also Honneth *SR*, Taylor *PoR* and Young *JPD*.

² See *SR* and *PoR*.

³ Thus, as Honneth observes, 'Hegel . . . infuses the Aristotelian concept of an ethical form of life with a moral potential that no longer arises merely out of the fundamental nature of human beings but rather out of a particular relationship between them' (*SR* 17).

⁴ Honneth offers an illuminating analysis of this reference: 'As the appropriation of Schelling's term "intuition" [Anschauung] suggests, Hegel surely intends this formulation to designate a form of reciprocal relations between subjects that goes beyond merely cognitive recognition. Such patterns of recognition, even extending into the sphere of the affective (for which the category of "solidarity" would seem to be the most likely label), are apparently supposed to provide the communicative basis upon which individuals, who have been isolated from each other by legal relations, can be reunited within the context of an ethical community' (SR 24).

⁵ For instance, a defining feature of consciousness is its ability, first to be itself, as subject; then to be other to itself, in its contemplation of external objects; and finally to make itself its own object when it seeks to understand its nature as 'producer' and cognizer of its objects. Honneth writes that now 'Hegel has the unified principle in terms of which he can make sense of the structure of reality: the constant developmental law underlying all occurrences is this double movement of externalization and return, and it is in the permanent repetition of this movement that Spirit realizes itself in stages' (SR 31).

6   Hegel focuses in these texts upon spirit, and not upon nature, because within his larger system he understands spirit as having already emerged from nature. Whenever he mentions nature now, in the earlier divisions of the Realphilosophie, it is from the perspective of consciousness as it engages with nature (not that of nature producing consciousness).

7   Honneth has since changed his view and now acknowledges Hegel's concern with intersubjectivity in the *PR*. See Honneth (2000).

8   In particular, Honneth appeals to object-relations theorist Donald Winnicott's account of the process through which practical identity and feelings of love are cultivated in early 'parent–child' relationships through the 'intersubjective interplay of "mother" and child.' See (*SR* 98) and Winnicott (1965).

9   The term 'mother' designates any 'good enough' primary caregiver (*SR* 98).

10  I stress that violence does not necessarily cripple the self since much hinges on the constitution and sense of self-efficacy of victims. For an excellent discussion of this, see Brison (2002).

11  Of course, legal rights were not actually extended to all individuals, only to those who were *recognized* as 'persons.'

12  Joel Anderson rightly observes: 'This is not to say that a person without rights cannot have self-respect, only that the *fullest* form of self-respecting autonomous agency could only be realized when one is recognized as possessing the capacities of "legal persons", that is, of morally responsible agents' (*SR* xv).

13  This accords with Rawls's claim that basic rights are one of the social bases of respect (*PL* 477).

14  There is a sense in which Rawls tried to provide for this inclusion via the overlapping consensus. However, the overlapping consensus only reflects the values that all citizens share in common. The claim of minority cultures is different: they want the value-horizon of the larger society also to affirm, at the very least, the *legitimacy* of values that diverge from those of the majority.

15  This claim seems to lead to the arguable conclusion that we are not morally obligated to care for persons who are not family members or close friends, only to show them respect and, in some cases, solidarity.

16  In this way, Honneth agrees with Rawls in assigning priority to legal status and respect for moral and rational personality. He also, like Rawls, envisions esteem as garnered within one's chosen associations. A significant difference between the two is that Honneth, unlike Rawls, conceives of differences other than class as socially relevant in matters of justice.

17  Recall Hegel's thesis that recognition makes individuals cognizant of new dimensions of selfhood. Honneth cites John McDowell (1998) as a source of his own thinking about evaluative qualities. In this case, 'disposition' refers to a secondary quality, or attribute, of an object or person rather than to a practical attitude. For a helpful discussion of McDowell's 'dispositional analysis' of value, see Dancy (1993: 159–163).

18  On this point, Honneth cites Harry Frankfurt's 'identification thesis,' the claim that 'a person counts as "autonomous" in the strong sense only if she is able to identify "wholeheartedly" with her own . . . capabilities' (*GR* 510). See Frankfurt (1998: chs 7 and 12) and (1999: chs 7, 11 and 14).

19  Originally published in 1990.

[20] Taylor does not directly address the issue of esteem won through community associations, however, as Honneth and Rawls do. In noting the role of significant others, Taylor, like Honneth, cites Mead's social psychology.

[21] Like Kymlicka, Taylor endorses a non-procedural liberal approach to resolving such claims that institutionalize certain immunities for cultural minorities for the sake of their survival—but only on the condition that certain basic individual rights are secured invariantly.

[22] Some critical theorists are therefore skeptical of the concept of recognition. Some argue that conceptualizing recognition on the model of cognition, hence treating identities as already formed entities that can be known, runs the risk of essentializing them. Others see it as ultimately entailing the assimilation of otherness to sameness, hence as merely substituting one mode of domination and oppression for another. See, e.g., Markell (2003: 40) and Oliver (2001: 23ff.).

[23] See, e.g., *JPD* 106ff. and Benhabib (1992: 6).

[24] Susan Wolf expresses this concern, albeit differently, in her commentary (*PoR* 78–81).

# Chapter 5

[*] Epigraphs to this chapter are from Oliver (2001: 3) and *PR* §265A. Reprinted with permission.

[1] Notable exceptions include the recent work of Ludwig Siep (1979), Robert Pippin (2000), Dean Moyar (2002), and Evangelia Sembou (2003), who are among the few recent commentators treating Hegel's *PhG* account of mutual recognition in detail.

[2] Kelly Oliver, for instance, laments of 'the Hegelian warring struggle for recognition that dominates contemporary theory' (2001: 6). This reading is largely the legacy of Alexandre Kojève, who considered the theme of mastery and slavery central to Hegel's idea of history. He insists that the master–slave dialectic is the very key to Hegel, since he takes it to express the true nature of recognition as characterized by a fixed, unequal opposition and domination between subjects. He writes: 'History . . . is nothing but the history of the *dialectical*—i.e., *active*—relation between Mastery and Slavery,' which originates in 'a *Fight*, since each will want to subjugate the other, *all* others, by a negating, destroying *action*' (1969: 41, 44).

[3] Early attempts at mutual recognition culminate in unequal recognition but are the necessary condition of the formation of practical identity. Hegel shows the achievement of mutual recognition to be just that—an *achievement* after a series of dialectical struggles through which purportedly isolated self-conscious human *beings* develop into moral *subjects*, members of a moral community.

[4] In tracking the epistemology of the *PhG*, I follow Terry Pinkard (1994) and Robert Pippin (1989).

[5] The achievement of mutual recognition can be considered the penultimate moment of the dialectic in the sense that absolute spirit's *appearance*, the result of the achievement of mutual recognition, is the second-to-last moment of spirit's

development; the final moment is spirit's completed *actualization* as absolute knowing.

[6] Hegel, *Intelligenzblatt der Janaischen Allgemeinen Literaturzeitung*, 28 October 1807. Quoted in *SS* 1: lxvii).

[7] For example, sense-certainty, which professes to be a form of knowledge, turns out to be inarticulate, able only to utter the indexicals 'this,' 'here,' and 'now.' Thus it is not really knowledge at all (it is non-propositional).

[8] Hegel writes: '[A] new form has thereby immediately arisen, and in the negation the transition is made through which the progress through the complete series of forms comes about of itself' (*PhS* ¶79; *PhG* 74). When, e.g., Perception grasps that the apparent contradiction inherent in its conception of its object (that the *many distinct* properties it perceives is at the same time a *single unified* object) can be resolved by relinquishing its dogmatism, engaging in self-critique, and embracing the already-implied concept of the unconditioned universal, it is no longer Perception, but has transformed itself into Understanding (*PhS* ¶132; *PhG* 107).

[9] Findlay in *PhS*, p. 518.

[10] Rousseau's influence is detectable in this formulation of the problem as in the title of this section of the text: 'Independence and Dependence of Self-Consciousness: Lordship and Bondage.' Neuhouser highlights that a key function of Rousseau's concept of the general will is to show how 'human dependence admits of being reorganized in such a way that it ceases to be incompatible with freedom,' that is, with 'independence' (2000: 72–73).

[11] Thus, the encounter may make you aware of a new dimension of your selfhood.

[12] This was Sartre's claim, for instance (1956: 363ff.).

[13] See also Sembou (2003: 267).

[14] Accordingly, the trajectory of struggles in the 'Spirit' chapter mirrors Honneth's thesis (1996) that the historical decoupling of the notions of legal respect and social esteem from that of honor prompted struggles, not only for legal status, but also for recognition of particularity.

[15] These are, of course, shapes of spirit, not individuals, but for ease of exposition I anthropomorphize them.

[16] Hegel's discussion of consciousness's transition from reason to spirit, in the 'Reason' subchapters 'Reason as Lawgiver' and 'Reason as Testing Laws,' really bear this out. At the end of this transition, Hegel comments that '[e]thical disposition consists just in sticking steadfastly to what is right,' and for this consciousness something 'is right because it is what is right' (*PhS* ¶437; *PhG* 322).

[17] Hegel later writes that the 'self, *qua* a pure self-identical knowing, is the *absolute universal*, so that just this knowing, as *its own* knowing, as conviction, is *duty*' (*PhS* ¶639; *PhG* 469).

[18] Commentators frequently note the common etymological root in German of 'conscience,' *Gewissen*, and 'being certain' *gewiss*. J. N. Findlay explains that '[f]or conscience [*Gewissen*] the intrinsically right is what it is inwardly sure of [*gewiss*].' Findlay, in *PhS*, p. 573.

[19] Here the action of conscience mirrors the labor of the slave.

[20] Recall Taylor's language of perspicuous contrast, which facilitates recognition.

# Chapter 6

\* The epigraph to this chapter is from *VPR* 4: 628. The translation is Robert R. Williams' (*HER 250*). Reprinted with permission.

1  Therefore when Hegel says individuals are accidents of the ethical state, he means they are its attributes, which together constitute its *actual* substance.
2  Hegel's cross-reference to *PR* §35 confirms this. There he writes that to say that I am a *person* is to say that I 'know myself in my finitude as *infinite, universal*, and *free.*'
3  My argument here is indebted to Dean Moyar (2004).
4  The actual good is the universal good (the good of all) made concrete, and the actual subjectivity that wills it is true conscience.
5  This is Moyar's formulation, not his position.
6  Cf. *PhS* ¶640; *PhG* 470.
7  The idea that true conscience presupposes recognitive understanding is further supported by Hegel's assertion, in *PR* §4A, that willing and thinking are not two separate faculties of mind, but rather the will presupposes thought. He writes that 'the will is a particular way of thinking—thinking translating itself into existence [*Dasein*], thinking as the drive to give itself existence.' What is the thinking of true conscience? We know from Hegel's account that true conscience wills the universal good. From what Hegel has said concerning the relationship of willing to thinking, we may formulate the question as: What is the thinking that underlies the will to actualize the universal good? It is clearly reasonable to think that it is the same recognitive understanding of the actual conscience that embraces the unity of particularity and universality in the *Phenomenology*.
8  My analysis in this section is influenced by Robert R. Williams's discussion of civil society (*HER* 227ff.).
9  Although ethical life only comes on the scene with the emergence of agents of true conscience, not all citizens of ethical life are such agents. In fact, because many citizens lack true conscience, civil society generates excesses of wealth and poverty that undermine its stability, as I explain later.
10  Hence, Hegel expresses his disagreement with Kant's insistence that our highest good consists in our willing only universal good. Hegel thinks our highest good consists rather in our ability to will from the standpoint of both the universal and the particular.
11  The translation is Williams's (*HER* 233).
12  Williams' translation (*HER* 233).

# Chapter 7

\* The epigraph to this chapter is from Markell (2003: 7). Reprinted with permission.

1  My discussions in this section and the next are influenced by Rupert Gordon's (1999) excellent analysis of the role of *Bildung* in ethical life. However, our approaches differ. Gordon emphasizes the individual's decreasing identification

with her collective identity characteristics as she increasingly identifies with her free *choices* and thus conceives of herself primarily as a self-constructed *bourgeois*, albeit one with a robust social consciousness. I, by contrast, stress the process as an *integration* of natural determinacy with social rationality, such that the individual identifies strongly with both—is robustly aware of how her free choices are shaped (although not completely determined) by her facticity, as well as how she determines them rationally in accordance with the community's rational norms.

² Gordon cites the increasing diversity of German towns in Hegel's time, which, although different from our forms of social diversity, was nevertheless socially significant as it put pressure on traditional guild membership rules: 'Hegel's corporations were directly related to a new geographic and social mobility occurring in the German states during the early nineteenth century. Towns and settlements were becoming more and more diverse with immigration from rural areas to urban ones, and often these new settlers had difficulty breaking into the professions . . . Hegel's corporate doctrine represented a real challenge to the power of established guilds and thus, implicitly, an endorsement of, and recognition of, the benefits of this emergent social heterogeneity' (1999: 201).

³ Compare this result to Rawls's and Honneth's conclusions that individuals can really only earn meaningful *esteem* from members of one's more local associations.

⁴ Here Hegel writes that 'it is only through legal recognition that a community becomes a corporation.'

⁵ Hegel's use of the terms 'the one' and 'the other' in reference to men and women is one basis of Simone de Beauvoir's critique of male privilege and dominance (1989: xxi).

⁶ Here Hegel stresses that the text, 'in so far as it deals with political science, shall be nothing other than an attempt *to comprehend and portray the state as an inherently rational entity*,' and 'distance itself as far as possible from the obligation to construct a *state as it ought to be*.'

⁷ See, e.g., I. Young (1985).

⁸ These sets of characteristics do not necessarily go together; a generally reflective person may be more socially passive than he is active.

⁹ A nation, that is, is closer to nature, as its etymology suggests.

¹⁰ I am grateful to Kris Sealey for naming this distinction between formal and concrete levels of analysis.

# Conclusion

\* The epigraph to this chapter is from Steinem (2004).

# Selected Bibliography

Anderson, Joel (1996), 'Translator's introduction,' in Axel Honneth (ed.), *The Struggle for Recognition: The Moral Grammar of Social Conflicts*. Cambridge, MA: MIT Press.

Arendt, Hannah (1998), *The Human Condition*, 2nd edn. Chicago: University of Chicago Press.

Avineri, Shlomo (1971), *Hegel's Theory of the Modern State*. New York: Cambridge University Press.

Bartky, Sandra L. (1990), *Femininity and Domination: Studies in the Phenomenology of Oppression*. New York: Routledge.

Beauvoir, Simone de (1989), *The Second Sex*, trans. H. M. Parshley. New York: Vintage Books.

Benhabib, Seyla (1992), *Situating the Self*. New York: Routledge.

Berlin, Isaiah (2002), 'Two concepts of liberty,' in Henry Hardy (ed.), *Liberty*. New York: Oxford University Press.

Bernasconi, Robert (1998), 'Hegel at the court of the Ashanti,' in S. Bennett (ed.), *Hegel after Derrida*. New York: Routledge.

—(2003), 'Hegel's Racism: A Reply to McCarney,' *Radical Philosophy*, 119, 4–6.

Brison, Susan (2002), *Aftermath: Violence and the Remaking of the Self*. Princeton: Princeton University Press.

Christman, John (2003), 'Autonomy in moral and political philosophy,' in Edward N. Zalta (ed.), *The Stanford Encyclopedia of Philosophy (Fall 2003 Edition)*. Online at http://plato.stanford.edu/archives/fall2003/entries/autonomy-moral/.

Christman, John and Joel Anderson (eds) (2005), *Autonomy and the Challenges to Liberalism: New Essays*. New York: Cambridge University Press.

[Christopher, Gail C.] (2005), 'Do doctors treat all women equally?' (editorial), *Glamour Magazine*, July, 134.

Clarke, Eric O. (1996), 'Fetal attractions,' in Patricia Jagentowicz-Mills (ed.), *Feminist Interpretations of Hegel*. University Park, PA: Pennsylvania University Press.

Cole, Johnnetta (2004), 'The power of diversity,' Third Annual Women & Power Conference. New York, NY. http://www.feminist.com/resources/artspeech/genwom/powerofdivers.html.

Committee on Maximizing the Potential of Women in Academic Science and Engineering, National Academy of Sciences, National Academy of Engineering, and Institute of Medicine (2007), 'Beyond bias and barriers: fulfilling the potential of women in academic science and engineering.' Washington, D.C.: National Academy Press.

Cudd, Ann (2006), *Analyzing Oppression*. New York: Oxford University Press.

Dancy, Jonathan (1993), *Moral Reasons*. Cambridge, MA: Blackwell Publishers.

Dewey, John (1968), 'Creative democracy—the task before us,' in *The Philosopher of the Common Man*. New York: Greenwood Press.

Elam, Patricia (2005), 'Commentary: Katrina, another example of America's racial divide,' National Public Radio's 'Morning Edition,' September 22.

Eze, Emmanuel Chukwudi (1997), *Race and the Enlightenment: A Reader*. Malden, Mass.: Blackwell Publishers, Ltd.

Feinberg, Joel (1986), *Harm to Self*. New York: Oxford University Press.

Feinberg, Walter (1978), *Equality and Social Policy*. Chicago: University of Illinois Press.

Ferdinand, Pamela (2001), 'Harvard sit-in for "living wage" divides campus; many back raise for workers; some question '60s-era tactics.' *The Washington Post*. May 5.

Fichte, Johann Gottlieb (2000), *Foundations of Natural Right*, ed. Frederick Neuhouser, trans. Michael Baur. New York: Cambridge University Press.

Forst, Rainer (1997), 'Foundations of a theory of multicultural justice,' *Constellations*, 4 (1), 63–71.

Frankfurt, Harry (1998), *The Importance of What We Care About*. New York: Cambridge University Press.

—(1999), *Necessity, Volition, and Love*. New York: Cambridge University Press.

Fraser, Nancy (2001), 'Recognition without ethics?' *Theory, Culture & Society*, 18 (2–3), 21–42.

Frye, Marilyn (1983), *The Politics of Reality: Essays in Feminist Theory*. Freedom, CA: The Crossing Press.

Gadamer, Hans-Georg (1989), *Truth and Method* (2nd revised edn), trans. Joel Weinsheimer and Donald G. Marshall. New York: Continuum.

Galeotti, Anna Elisabetta (1994), *La tolleranza. Una proposta pluralista*. Naples: Liguori.

—(2002), *Toleration as Recognition*. New York: Cambridge University Press.

Gordon, Rupert H. (1999), *Hegel and the Politics of Difference: The Paradox of Identity and Freedom*. Doctoral Dissertation, Yale University.

Green, T. H. (1917), *Lectures on the Principles of Political Obligation*. Reprinted from *The Works of Thomas Hill Green*, vol. II, ed. R. L. Nettleship. New York: Longmans, Green, and Company.

Habermas, Jürgen (1996), 'Labor and interaction: remarks on Hegel's Jena *Philosophy of Mind*,' in *Theory and Practice*, trans. J. Viertel. New York: Cambridge University Press.

—(1990), *The Philosophical Discourse of Modernity*. Cambridge, UK: Polity Press.

Harvard Progressive Students Labor Movement. 'The more things change . . . the more they stay the same: the state of low wage work on Harvard campus.' http://hcs.harvard.edu/~pslm/livingwage/portal.html.

Harvey, J. (2000), 'Social privilege and moral subordination,' *Journal of Social Philosophy*, 31 (2), 177–188.

Hayek, Friedrich A. (1960), *The Constitution of Liberty*. Chicago: University of Chicago Press.

Herbert, Bob (2001), 'Disparities at Harvard,' *The New York Times*, April 30.

Hobbes, Thomas (1968), *Leviathan*, ed. C. B. McPherson. New York: Penguin.

Honneth, Axel (1996), *The Struggle for Recognition: The Moral Grammar of Social Conflicts*, trans. Joel Anderson. Cambridge, MA: MIT Press.

Honneth, Axel (1997), 'Recognition and moral obligation,' *Social Research*, 64 (1), 16–35.

—(2000), *Suffering from Indeterminacy: An Attempt at a Reactualization of Hegel's Philosophy of Right*, trans. Jack Ben-Levi. Assen: Van Gorcum.

—(2002), 'Grounding recognition: a rejoinder to critical questions,' *Inquiry*, 45, 499–520.

—'Mutual recognition as a key for a universalist ethics.' http://www.unesco.or.kr/ethics/honneth.htm.

Horkheimer, Max and Theodor W. Adorno (2000), *Dialectic of Enlightenment*, trans. John Cumming. New York: Continuum.

Kant, Immanuel (1996), *Groundwork of the Metaphysics of Morals, in Practical Philosophy*, ed. Mary J. Gregor. New York: Cambridge University Press.

Kojève, Alexandre (1969), *Introduction to the Reading of Hegel*, ed. and trans. Allan Bloom, trans. James H. Nichols, Jr. New York: Basic Books, Inc.

Kukathas, Chandran (1997), 'Multiculturalism as fairness: Will Kymlicka's multicultural citizenship,' *The Journal of Political Philosophy*, 5 (4), 406–427.

Kymlicka, Will (1991), *Liberalism, Community and Culture*. New York: Clarendon Press.

—(1995), *Multicultural Citizenship*. New York: Oxford University Press.

Locke, John (1994), *An Essay Concerning Human Understanding*. Amherst, NY: Prometheus Books.

Lukes, Steven (1997), 'Toleration and recognition,' *Ratio Juris*, 10 (2), 213–222.

Manning, Stephen (2005), 'Bolo tie creates a bind for graduating senior,' *The Associated Press*, June.

Marable, Manning (2007), *Race, Reform and Rebellion* (3rd edn). Jackson, Miss.: The University Press of Mississippi.

Marimow, Ann E. (2005), 'Cultural tie gets in the way of graduation: Md. boy wearing bolo is denied a diploma,' *The Washington Post*, June 10.

Markell, Patchen (2003), *Bound by Recognition*. Princeton: Princeton University Press.

McCarney, Joseph (2003), 'Hegel's racism? A response to Bernasconi,' *Radical Philosophy*, 119, 1–4.

McDowell, John (1998), *Mind, Value, and Reality*. Cambridge, MA: Harvard University Press.

Mead, George Herbert (1962), *Mind, Self, and Society*, ed. Charles W. Morris. Chicago: University of Chicago Press.

Mill, John Stuart (1978), *On Liberty*, ed. Elizabeth Rapaport. Indianapolis: Hackett.

Monahan, Michael (2003), 'A theory of racial oppression and liberation,' PhD dissertation, University of Illinois at Urbana-Champaign.

Moyar, Dean (2002), 'Hegel's conscience: radical subjectivity and rational institutions,' PhD dissertation, University of Chicago.

—(2004), 'Die Verwirklichung meiner Authoritat: Hegels komplementare Modelle von Individuen und Institutionen,' in Christoph Halbig, Michael Quante, and Ludwig Siep (eds), *Hegels Erbe*. Frankfurt am Main: Surhrkamp Verlag.

Neuhouser, Frederick (2000), *Foundations of Hegel's Social Theory*. Cambridge, MA: Harvard University Press.

Oliver, Kelly (2001), *Witnessing: Beyond Recognition*. Minneapolis: University of Minnesota Press.

Parekh, Bhikhu (1997), 'Dilemmas of a multicultural theory of citizenship,' *Constellations*, 4 (1), 54–62.

Patrick, Morag (2000), 'Liberalism, rights, and recognition,' *Philosophy and Social Criticism*, 26 (5), 28–46.

Pinkard. Terry (1994), *Hegel's Phenomenology: The Sociality of Reason*. New York: Cambridge University Press.

Pippin, Robert B. (1989), *Hegel's Idealism: The Satisfactions of Self-Consciousness*. New York: Cambridge University Press.

—(2000), 'What is the question for which Hegel's theory of recognition is the answer?' *European Journal of Philosophy*, 8 (2), 155–172.

Rawls John (1996), *Political Liberalism*. New York: Columbia University Press.

—(1999), *A Theory of Justice* (revised edn). Cambridge, MA: Harvard University Press.

Rockefeller, Steven C. (1994), 'Comment,' in Amy Gutmann (ed.), *Multiculturalism: Examining the Politics of Recognition*. Princeton: Princeton University Press.

Rousseau, Jean-Jacques (1967), *The Social Contract and Discourse on the Origin of Inequality*, ed. Lester G. Crocker. New York: Simon & Schuster.

—(1987), *The Basic Political Writings*, trans. Donald A. Cress. Indianapolis: Hackett.

[Rudenstine, Neil] (2005), *Wage Slaves: Not Getting by in America*. A&E Investigative Reports, July.

Sartre, Jean-Paul (1956), *Being and Nothingness: An Essay on Ontological Phenomenology*, trans. Hazel E. Barnes. New York: Philosophical Library.

Schaap, Andrew (2004), 'Political reconciliation through a struggle for recognition?' *Social and Legal Studies*, 13 (4), 523–540.

Schuster, Anike (2006), 'Does liberalism need multiculturalism? A critique of liberal multiculturalism,' *Essays in Philosophy*, 7 (1). http://www.humboldt.edu/~essays/schuster.html.

Sembou, Evangelia (2003), 'Hegel's idea of a "struggle for recognition": the *Phenomenology of Spirit*,' *History of Political Thought*, 24 (2), 262–281.

Sewell, Rob (2000), 'Police brutality and the electric chair,' *USA Today*. 23 June.

Siep, Ludwig (1979), *Annerkennung als Prinzip der praktischen Philosophie: Untersuchungen zu Hegels Jenaer Philosophie des Geistes*. München: Verlag Karl Alber.

Steinem, Gloria (2004), 'Leaps of consciousness,' Third Annual Women & Power Conference. New York, NY. http://www.feminist.com/resources/artspeech/genwom/leaps.html.

Stern, Robert (1989), 'Unity and difference in Hegel's political philosophy,' *Ratio*, 2, 75–88.

Stewart, Jon (1995), 'The architectonic of Hegel's *Phenomenology of Spirit*,' *Philosophy and Phenomenological Research*, 55 (4), 747–776.

Taylor, Charles (1994), 'The politics of recognition,' in Amy Gutmann (ed.), *Multiculturalism: Examining the Politics of Recognition*. Princeton: Princeton University Press.

—(1995a), 'Comparison, history, truth,' in *Philosophical Arguments*. Cambridge, MA: Harvard University Press.

Taylor, Charles (1995b), 'Liberal politics and the public sphere,' in *Philosophical Arguments*. Cambridge, MA: Harvard University Press.

—(1995c), 'Understanding and ethnocentricity,' in *Philosophical Arguments*. Cambridge, MA: Harvard University Press.

—(1998), 'Dynamics of democratic exclusion,' *Journal of Democracy*, 9 (4), 143–156.

Theunissen, Michael (1982), 'Die verdrängte Intersubjectivität in Hegels Philosophie des Rechts,' in D. Henrich and R.-P. Horstmann (eds), *Hegels Philosophie des Rechts*. Stuttgart: Klett-Cotta Verlag.

Thomas, Larry L. (1999), 'Rawlsian self-respect and the black consciousness movement,' in Henry S. Richardson and Paul J. Weithman (eds), *The Philosophy of Rawls: Moral Psychology and Community*. New York: Garland Publishing, Inc.

Tjaden, Patricia and Thoennes, Nancy (2000), 'Extent, nature, and consequences of intimate partner violence: findings from the violence against women survey,' http://www.ojp.usdoj.gov/nij/pubs-sum/181867.htm.

Vaid, Urvashi (1993), 'Speech at the march on Washington,' April 25, http://gos.sbc.edu/w/vaid.html.

*The Washington Post*, 'The Amadou Diallo case' (editorial). http://www.washingtonpost.com/wp-dyn/nation/specials/aroundthenation/nypd/.

Williams, Robert R. (1997), *Hegel's Ethics of Recognition*. Berkeley: University of California Press.

Winnicott, Donald W. (1965), *The Maturational Processes and the Facilitating Environment*. New York: International Universities Press.

Wolf, Susan (1994), 'Comment,' in Amy Gutmann (ed.), *Multiculturalism: Examining the Politics of Recognition*. Princeton: Princeton University Press.

Young, Iris Marion (1985), 'Humanism, gynocentrism, and feminist politics,' *Hypatia*, 3, 173–183.

—(1990), *Justice and the Politics of Difference*. Princeton: Princeton University Press.

—(1999), 'Ruling norms and the politics of difference: a comment on Seyla Benhabib,' *Yale Journal of Criticism*, 12 (2), 415–421.

Young, R. (1986), *Personal Autonomy: Beyond Negative and Positive Freedom*. London: Croom Held.

Zutlevics, T. L. (2002), 'Towards a theory of oppression,' *Ratio*, 15, 80–102.

# Index

absolute difference 11, 102, 127
absolute knowing 104, 105, 118, 142, 193n. 12
absolute spirit 8, 103–5, 126, 127, 198n. 5
abstract right 139, 140, 145, 149, 152, 160, 165, 169, 171
action
  conscience and 118–25, 143
  finitude of 131–2
  recognition of 107–15 passim, 126–8, 135, 145–7, 173–4
agency
  conscientious 118–25 passim, 138, 141–4, 148, 171, 192
  cultures as sources of 62, 65–7, 190
  development of 10, 71, 79–80
  free 72, 151, 157, 159, 161
  identity and 2–4
  limitations of 18, 27, 32, 72, 157–8
  recognition of 7, 11, 105–8, 126–36 passim, 154, 164–70 passim, 171–5, 185–6, 187
  right of 165
Antigone 117, 131, 177, 179
atomism 5, 15, 59, 72, 116, 140, 155, 160–3 passim, 183, 188
*aufheben/Aufhebung* 107, 111
autonomy 1, 17, 20, 21, 36, 38, 59–65, 194n. 5, 197n. 18
  as evaluative quality 86–7, 97
  Kantian notion of 72
  recognition and 77–8, 80, 85, 100, 135, 190
  resilient 26, 27, 34, 35, 39, 40, 44, 45, 68, 131, 137
  thin conception 27, 195n. 8

Bartky, Sandra 9, 30, 33
beautiful soul 11, 107–8, 117–27, 130–7 passim
Berlin, Isaiah 9, 17–19, 22, 23, 30, 39
Bernasconi, Robert 182
*Bildung* 102, 163, 164–71, 173, 176, 185, 190

civil society 8, 139–62, 163–86, 190, 195n. 4
coercion 14, 17, 19, 195n. 10
concept [*Begriff*]/Idea 106, 142–53 passim
confession and forgiveness 125–6, 128, 130
conscience 11, 107–8, 116–28, 130–7 passim, 185, 199n. 18
  actual 126, 140–4
  formal 142–7
  judging 125–8
  true 140–8, 152, 162, 163–75, 185–6, 190, 200n. 7
conscientiousness 11, 101, 122–8, 133–6, 139, 140–8, 163, 164–75, 184–6, 187–92 passim
consciousness 72, 181, 196n. 5
  false 154–6, 160, 162, 186
  Hegel's early philosophy of 75–7
  in the *PhG* 5, 102–25 passim, 143, 144
conviction 108, 117, 121–5, 146–8 passim
corporation 151–3 passim, 163, 164, 171–5, 184–5
Cudd, Ann 9, 14–15, 26, 28
cultural imperialism 26, 35, 40–2, 90, 189, 194n. 1

Lightning Source UK Ltd.
Milton Keynes UK
UKOW030838220812

197902UK00002BA/14/P